D0226347

The Rainy Spell
and other
Korean Stories

REVISED AND EXPANDED EDITION

The Rainy Spell
AND OTHER
Korean Stories

TRANSLATED AND EDITED BY
Suh Ji-moon

An East Gate Book

M.E. Sharpe/UNESCO Publishing

An East Gate Book

UNESCO COLLECTION OF REPRESENTATIVE WORKS
The publication of this work was assisted by a contribution of the Government
of the Republic of Korea under UNESCO's Funds-in-Trust Programme

UNESCO ISBN 92-3-103396-4

Copyright © 1998 by Suh Ji-moon

All rights reserved. No part of this book may be reproduced in any form
without written permission from the publisher, M. E. Sharpe, Inc.,
80 Business Park Drive, Armonk, New York 10504.

Library of Congress Cataloging-in-Publication Data

Changma oe Han'guk tanp'yŏn sŏnjip. English. The rainy spell and other Korean stories
/ translated by Suh Ji-moon. Rev. and exp. ed.
p. cm.
"An East gate book."
ISBN 0-7656-0138-9 (alk. paper). ISBN 0-7656-0139-7 (pbk. : alk. paper)
1. Short stories, Korean—Translations into English.
2. Korea—Social life and customs—Fiction. I. Sŏ, Chi-mun. II. Title.
PL984.E8R35 1997
895.7′30108—dc21 97-31821
CIP

Printed in the United States of America

The paper used in this publication meets the minimum requirements of
American National Standard for Information Sciences—
Permanence of Paper for Printed Library Materials,
ANSI Z 39.48-1984.

BM (c) 10 9 8 7 6 5 4 3 2 1
BM (p) 10 9 8 7 6 5 4 3 2 1

For my mother, Mrs. Duk Hee K. Suh

Contents

Preface
ix

Halmŏm
Yi Kwang-soo
3

The Seaman's Chant
Kim Dong-in
10

The Clear Water Pavilion
Yu Chin-o
25

My Idiot Uncle
Ch'ae Man-shik
43

A Ceremony of Apostasy
Chung Bi-suk
59

The Underground Village
Kang Kyŏng-ae
77

Pierrot
Hwang Sun-wŏn
107

Eroica Symphony
Park Yong-sook
122

My Idol's Abode
Ch'oe In-hoon
140

The Rainy Spell
Yoon Heung-gil
153

A Pasque-Flower on That Bleak Day
Park Wan-so
204

That Winter of My Youth
Yi Mun-yol
213

His Father's Keeper
Ch'oe Yun
248

The Image of Mija
Shin Kyoung-suuk
271

Preface

The work which eventually resulted in this book began as far back as 1972, shortly after my return from my first study trip abroad. It was not until I began my advanced study in English literature in America that I felt an intense yearning to know what the literature of my own country was like. Once abroad, I realized with shame that I was very ignorant of my own country's literature, having always taken it, like many other things Korean, for granted. But there was something much stronger than shame or curiosity or sentimentalism in my interest in Korean literature. It was an imperative born out of the realization that only literature bears the full and true record of a nation's life.

Thus, when I returned to Korea with my master's degree in English literature, I began avidly reading Korean literature. The reading enthralled me for many reasons. One delightful characteristic that I found running through almost all works of Korean literature was artlessness. Artlessness, of course, is a doubtful virtue in literature, inasmuch as literature is an art before it is anything else. And it is true that this artlessness not infrequently results in a lack of refinement in expression and in looseness of structure. But it also produces, more remarkably, a truly refreshing sense of immediacy and candor. This was the more delightful to me as it seemed a reflection of the unsophisticated Korean character, and it had a poignant beauty all its own.

This artlessness may seem surprising, in view of the fact that most modern Korean writers, especially of the earlier era, have initiated or participated in some literary movement or other, have chosen literary careers when such activities were regarded as the surest road to poverty, and were very conscious of their literary aims and mission. But I think there may be an explanation here, too, in that for Korean writers their literary aims and mission meant mainly fulfilling the role of enlighteners, chastisers and champions of the people, and their self-definition as literary craftsmen was not very strong.

Modern Korean literature had a difficult birth amid harsh circumstances. It did not grow out of a native tradition. There was, of course, a literary tradition in pre-modern Korea, but it was not the kind of literature we know today, with professional writers and a ready reading public. For the upper-class man, literature was a gentlemanly tool and accomplishment, through which he absorbed all the philosophy and culture of his predecessors and in which he left what cultural contribution he had to make. It was also his pastime and emotional outlet, and as such was shared with a small number of high-born ladies and a slightly larger number of low-born entertaining women, the evidence of which we have in many gems of short formal verses.

For the populace, such literary and pseudo-literary media as prose fiction, mask dance dramas and puppet shows were entertainment and also served as outlets for their pent-up resentments against the ruling class, which they satirized and showed as ridiculous and contemptibly hypocritical. Some of the satire was, of course, directed at themselves —at their own servility, venality, and helplessness. Most of the popular literary output is anonymous, a fact from which many inferences can be drawn.

Koreans having suffered many abuses at the hands of fate and the social structure, the dominant mood of their verse literature was regret and longing. Some verses also show pungent wit and sarcasm, and exquisite humor as well. Prose literature always contained explicit didactic lessons; but the didactic aim was offset by earthy humor, frank eroticism and uncouth satire. It is noteworthy that, while personal literature of the ruling class predominantly struck the chord of grief, the literature of the populace, while giving vent to their many grievances, celebrated life with its abundant energy.

As noted earlier, modern Korean literature did not grow out of this native tradition. It is not far wrong to say that modern literature, at least in its formal aspect, sprang fully grown out of the heads of a few modernists early in this century.

The last years of the nineteenth century and the early years of the twentieth were a period of turbulent unrest in Korea. Having long insisted on national isolation and rejection of foreign culture, Korea was still maintaining an agricultural economy and authoritarian political system that had become corrupt to the core. The masses having been exploited for centuries by the feudal bureaucracy, Korea was sick and impoverished internally and was defenseless against the foreign powers which tried to force open her doors.

Korea was on the brink of complete subjugation to Japan when Yi Kwang-soo (1892–?) and Choi Nam-sun (1890–1957) began their youth club and published the club's magazine, the first literary monthly in Korea, in 1908. Japan had forced a protective treaty upon Korea in 1905 and was soon to colonize it completely by annexation in 1910. Yi Kwang-soo and Choi Nam-sun shared a fervent zeal for national modernization, and they had set for themselves the objective of awakening the nation to the past evils resulting from a Confucian political and social structure, and the new possibilities of a more democratic society and harmonious human relationships. And they adopted literature as their chosen tool.

Yi Kwang-soo established his position as a writer and humanitarian teacher very soon. Hard upon his heels came Kim Dong-in, who was his antithesis in literary creed and personal lifestyle. Kim Dong-in rebelled against Yi Kwang-soo's didactic aim and proclaimed an "art-for-art's-sake" literature. This is not, however, to be taken as a declaration for conscious and conscientious literary craftsmanship; it was an announcement that he would write what he liked in the way he liked, without any pragmatic aim. Kim Dong-in was a powerful writer who often wrote beautifully and hauntingly, but his arrogance and egotism prevented his attaining the self-discipline and full maturity of vision necessary for making him a great master.

After these two early giants came a great many writers, most of whom made significant contributions to the establishment and enrichment of the tradition of modern literature in Korea. Naturally reflecting the circumstances of the nation, much of the literary output of Korea in colonial times dealt with the suffering and sorrows of the Korean people, and comprises a chronicle of the nation's survival.

Thus it is only in recent times that beauty of form, both of words and of structure, began to be consciously cultivated by Korean authors. The beauty of the prose of Korean literature in the early years of its modernity, therefore, has the freshness of accidental achievement, and seems truly appropriate to the subject matter and viewpoint.

A greater and deeper delight was the life and character of the Korean people that Korean literature revealed. I had always assumed that I knew my compatriots—their tragic past as victims of invading foreign powers and the feudal social system, their long and ceaseless struggle against poverty, and their dominant attitudes of withdrawal, resignation and passivity. It was not until I began reading deeply in Korean literature that I realized the full extent of the tragic implications of being born a Korean. To be born a Korean meant to be a victim of fate's caprice. There simply was no guarantee for the basic sanctities of life or the right of survival. Of course the villains of this violation could be traced—unjust or deceived rulers, the hierarchical and sexist social structure, the invading foreign enemy or the dire poverty which was the heritage of Koreans for centuries upon centuries. In almost every case, the victimizers were powers too huge to be fought individually, and thus the victimization seemed, and was conveniently treated as, a wrong inflicted by fate. More frequently than not, Koreans reacted to the wrongs that fell to their lot with tears and sighs rather than with vengeance and revolt.

These were the Korean characteristics until modern institutions of democracy and capitalism, and the newly opened possibilities of wealth attendant on industrialization, turned many of us into aggressive pursuers of gain. All these factors were known to me more or less, and to most Koreans. What I did not suspect until I read deeply in Korean literature was that such passivity, such apparent lack of determined effort for improvement of their condition, was in fact wisdom gained through generations of experience of life in this land. I had not known until I met my fellow Koreans in literature that they *had to* become submissive and yielding *in order to survive*. It was the Koreans' way of living with their fate, without battering themselves against the huge, inhuman forces that wronged them, and without consuming themselves with indignation and resentment. I understood for the first time that lack of self-assertiveness can sometimes be a strength, and more often than not wisdom. It was truly moving to discover how my compatriots, with their simplicity and humility, have borne and made livable inhuman conditions of life, and have managed to preserve their capacity for joy and affection.

I think it was this realization, this discovery, that moved me so strongly to take up the task of introducing Korean literature abroad. I wanted to share these moving chronicles with more people, with people who have hitherto had no chance of meeting the real Koreans—the Korean people.

I did not know at the time how poorly qualified I was for such a task, both in my understanding of literature and life and in my skill with the English language. Even after painstaking revisions over many years I cannot claim to have done anything like justice to these moving stories I have dared to transcribe into what is an acquired language for me.

As I was moved to the task of translation by my love of the individual works, I did not really select the stories according to a set standard. The stories in this collection are simply my favorites. But I think my intuition guided me to some extent in choosing stories centering around typically Korean situations and sentiments, as stories that can most readily engage the interest of foreign readers. I have no intention of claiming that these works represent the finest achievements in Korean literature; there are many others that I respect equally or even more highly, but these have had the strongest appeal to me, and I hope and believe they will exert a similar appeal on foreign readers.

As a translator I have been as faithful as possible to the original, the translations representing full texts. For Korean customs and traditions, I have supplied footnotes only where factual information seemed necessary for intelligibility, and have left it to the readers' imagination to recognize and understand unwritten codes of behavior and etiquette from the moods and circumstances inherent in the stories themselves.

My greatest debt in preparing the original edition of this book I owe to the late Mr. James Wade, composer and writer, for reading the translations through, most of them twice, to correct errors of grammar and to smooth out awkward renderings. Mr. Wade contributed this service when there was no definite prospect of financial remuneration, and I am doubly grateful to him for this reason. I am pleased to acknowledge also the voluntary assistance given by Professor Daisy Yang of Korea University and Dr. Esther Arinaga, a lawyer residing in Hawaii, in polishing up the three stories added to the present expanded edition.

I am also deeply grateful to Mr. Milton Rosenthal and other officials of the UNESCO headquarters in Paris who have kindly granted this anthology the UNESCO seal of approval, and to the Korean Culture and Arts Foundation for their generous subsidy for publication.

To the original authors of the stories included here, I am grateful for their authorization for translation and publication.

Finally, this book is dedicated to my mother, who watched the whole process with loving concern.

Suh Ji-moon
April 1997, Seoul

The Rainy Spell
and other
Korean Stories

Halmŏm*

Yi Kwang-soo

Today, Yi Kwang-soo's position as the virtual founding father of modern literature in Korea is impregnable. Like many others who followed him, he was a child prodigy. Born in 1892, he was orphaned at age ten and went to Japan at twelve as a scholarship student. At fifteen he organized a Korean students' club in Japan and published the club's magazine Youth, *the first literary monthly in Korea, for which he wrote poems and criticism. He wrote his first short story, "Heartlessness," at the age of eighteen. This was later expanded into a novel and marks the first real modern fiction in Korean literature.*

Yi Kwang-soo had to struggle throughout his life with severe illnesses, and suffered imprisonment for his patriotic activities. Notwithstanding, he produced a great quantity of poetry, fiction and critical essays, most of them bearing on the theme of the need for democratic human rights, reform of the feudal social and familial systems, spread of education, and marriage based on love. He also organized a campaign for use of simpler, less mannered and more colloquial language in writing. He was abducted to North Korea in 1950 by the invading Communists, and there has been no news of him since.

Although his works are criticized for excessive didacticism and ide-

---

*Halmŏm is a familiar or condescending appellation for a woman old enough to be a grandmother. Old women who worked as domestic helpers were usually called "Halmŏm," but it could also be an affectionate term when used by old husbands for their wives.

alized characterization, his importance not only as a literary pioneer and humanist teacher but as one of the great masters of fiction remains unchallenged. "Halmŏm," written in 1940, although a slight piece, is a good example of his easy style and unaffected humanism.

⌁

"Young missus, what's that sound?" asked the old woman servant who had been polishing brassware in the front yard for Chusŏk,* when they heard the keening of hired funeral palanquin bearers passing their house.

"That's a funeral procession," answered the young mistress, without looking up. She was sewing on the floor in the living room, deftly moving her needle.

"Is that a dead man being carried away to the grave?" Halmŏm asked in her heavy accent.

"Yes."

Halmŏm moved her toothless mouth for a good while and then asked carefully, "Young missus, can I go out to take a look?"

The young mistress said, "Yes, of course," and kept on sewing. The old woman carefully put on the rubber shoes she had bought the day before for 85 cents and ran toward the middle gate like a child. The lugubrious keening of the coffin bearers continued to float by.

After Halmŏm's footsteps died away, the young mistress turned and called her husband, who was reading in the inner room.

"Yes?" the young man answered without looking up from the book.

"Halmŏm's just like a child," the young mistress laughed and said, "She went to look at a funeral passing," and laughed again. The young man did not laugh but came out to the living room with a cigar and a match and an ashtray.

"She's got a lively curiosity, like anybody from the country," he said, striking a match and lighting the cigar. The young mistress ignored the generalization and went on.

---

*Chusŏk is the biggest holiday for Koreans next to the New Year. It is the Korean equivalent of Thanksgiving, and people celebrate the new harvest by visiting relatives' houses and ancestors' graves. Being the 15th of August by the lunar calendar, it usually falls in late September or early October, and marks therefore the beginning of cool, though not cold, days. [Translator]

"Oh, listen to me. She went out to look at a funeral the day before yesterday and she said she lost her way in front of the police station. How could she have lost the way here from the police station?"

The young man sat down on the edge of the floor and swung his legs,* and instead of agreeing with his wife, queried, "Dear, isn't she a very good woman?"

"Oh yes, she is. The old woman's got a heart of gold. She's rather stupid, like many country people, but she's hard-working and she never cheats us. I don't feel like scolding her even when she breaks things. But she says she'll go home before Chusŏk. She says she'd die of cold if she stayed in Seoul after Chusŏk, so she'll go back to her home and stay in her warm room and mend her grandchildren's rags. She says she won't stay here even if we let her sleep in the inner room and give her thick covers. She says she has to go home before Chusŏk. She won't stay with us even if we raise her salary. She says she doesn't need money. Darling, why is she like that? If she stayed here she'd be well fed and she'd make money, too."

The young mistress, as if worried about the old woman servant and her unreasonable obstinacy, stuck the needle in the collar of her blouse and turned to face her husband. The young man also looked interested and asked, "Is she going away?"

"Yes. From the first she said she'd go back by Chusŏk, and now she talks about going home every day. Yesterday she said she'd like to buy silver hair-slides for her daughter and daughter-in-law, so I took her to the night market. When she was told a silver one costs one won and eighty cents, she said if she bought two silver ones she wouldn't have the train fare home, and thought for a long time and said she couldn't buy them, and hurried out of the market. Isn't that funny? Maybe she thought silver hair-slides cost ten or twenty cents apiece."

She sat thinking for a while and then said in an impressed tone, "Isn't it nice of her, to work so hard to earn money and then think of buying presents for her daughter and daughter-in-law?"

---

*In a Korean house, rooms are built on an elevated plane above the ground, and one must step up from the yard to the rooms and step down to the yard from the rooms. The edge of the living-room floor is therefore frequently used as seats for momentary visitors or for brief rests between work in the yard, or for any casual relaxation. There are usually a few stone steps on which shoes are left, as Koreans do not wear shoes in the rooms. [Translator]

"What does her son do?"

"Her son seems to be a real bad sort. He hates working, and he sells off anything in the house. So she says she didn't tell her son she was coming to Seoul when she left, but that she kept looking back for miles to see if her son was coming to ask her to go back. She said she was going to go back if the son came after her and insisted on her going back home. But he didn't show even the tip of his nose, so she cried. What a worthless son he must be!"

"Then she doesn't have a house of her own?"

"She has a small house of her own. Her husband left money for her to buy one when he died. Well, maybe that son of hers has sold it by now."

"Her husband bought her one?" the young man asked.

"Yes. The old woman was widowed at thirty-five, and she didn't have any means of livelihood with her children, so she remarried. The second husband had sons and some property, too, and before he died he told his son to buy the old woman a house, so she has a small house of her own," the young mistress said, turning over her sewing. "She calls that husband's family the big house. I guess she was his 'small house.'* She says she goes to stay at the big house often even now. She says her husband's son is always inviting her to come to live with him and his family."

The older mistress of the house called "Halmŏm! Halmŏm!" from the back yard.

The young mistress laughed and shouted, "She's gone sightseeing."

"Sightseeing? What sight?" the older woman, who was still out of sight, shouted back.

"She's gone to see a funeral procession," the young mistress answered, raising her voice again. The older mistress was slightly deaf.

At last she came out through the kitchen door with unsteady steps, saying, "Oh, she might lose her way again. Why is she so fond of looking at coffins? Has she been out long?" She stepped up into the living room.

---

*To be the "small house" of a man means to be his mistress, or extra wife. Such a relationship was usually permanent, and men entered into such relations as much for the purpose of procuring heirs or for other reasons of convenience as for amorous reasons. Women usually entered into such arrangements to secure means of support. [Translator]

The young mistress said, "Oh no she won't, mother,* not again."

Right then the old servant woman came in with slow steps.

The older mistress laughed and asked, "You didn't lose your way this time?"

"No. I was afraid of that, so I didn't follow it but looked at it standing right in front of this house," the old woman said, blinking her soft dim eyes. Everybody laughed aloud. Halmŏm, not knowing what it was about, followed suit. The older mistress lit her pipe at the brazier and asked,

"Well, was it an interesting sight?"

"What?" the old woman asked back, not understanding.

"Was the coffin palanquin colorful and nice to look at?"

"Oh no. There were only a few people following the coffin, and only the hired bearers were keening. It must have been a lonely man," the old woman answered and began scrubbing the bowls again.

"Then it couldn't have been nice to look at. Only sumptuous coffins with a lot of bereaved kinsfolk are good to look at," the older mistress said and glanced at the old woman. The old woman did not understand "sumptuous" and "bereaved" but said,

"Well, what's the difference? They'll all rot after they get buried," and scrubbed hard.

"But people don't look at it that way." The older mistress relighted her long pipe and went on, "They say death is as important as birth. So people prefer to be buried well. You and me, neither of us has long to live. Don't you think so? How old are you?"

The old woman said, "Sixty-five," without emotion, and scrubbed harder, as if she was out of temper.

"Sixty-five . . ." The older mistress exhaled smoke with a sigh and said, "Then, wouldn't you like to be carried to the grave in a big colorful coffin?"

"Why, of course I would." She was now beginning to clean the chamber pot, and said, "I'd like to be buried well, but I haven't got any

---

*It is hard to tell from the contents of this story whether the mother here is the young wife's mother-in-law or own mother. It is unusual for the wife's mother to live with a married couple, and if such were the case, it would have been mentioned; on the other hand, the informality of the relationship here suggests it. The translator has assumed that it is a regular household, with an unusually fond mother-in-law and daughter-in-law. [Translator]

money. The likes of me are lucky if we get buried in a proper coffin. These days I'd be happy if only my son would mind me a little."

Everybody laughed. Halmŏm laughed, too. The young mistress said comfortingly, "It doesn't matter how you get buried, as long as you go to a good place afterwards."

"I've done nothing good, so how can I go to a good place?" said Halmŏm, scooping cold water from the water jar and drinking it.

The older mistress was silent for a while and then, putting aside her pipe, recited, "Ohm Jirijiri Baura Badara Hohmbata," and fingered her prayer beads. The young mistress gazed at the toothless mouth of her mother-in-law and then signaled to her husband in the inner room to look at his mother. The young man looked at his mother's mouth. The old servant, with one hand in the chamber pot, also gazed at the older woman's mouth. A fly made as if to alight on Halmŏm's eyelash but changed its mind and flew away. The young mistress, unable to suppress her laughter, giggled. Halmŏm laughed and the young man also laughed. The older mistress, opening her eyes wide as if startled out of a reverie, also laughed.

The young mistress squeezed her sides and mimicked, "Oh, mother, hahaha! Ohm Badara Hombatang."

The woman servant turned and said eagerly, "Missus, this Ohm Badara, would I go to a good place if I learned to say that?"

The old mistress turned to look at her and replied, "Who knows if there's anywhere for souls to go? They say chanting the scripture will do good for the soul, so . . ."

"Then can I learn, too? Oh, the likes of me have no memory. Ohm Badara Hambakdang." The old woman tried with her hardened tongue.

The young mistress corrected her, "No. Ohm Baura Badara Hohmbata. Now try."

The old woman tried, "Ohm Baura Hohmbatak." She had omitted "Badara."

This time the older mistress taught her, "Ohm Baura Badara Hohmbatang."

"Oh, I can't do it. I keep forgetting." She gave up and scrubbed the chamber pot hard.

"Halmŏm, don't go back to your home but stay with us. Then I'll teach you the scripture verses. Yes? Do stay," the older mistress earnestly pleaded with her.

"How can I, in the cold? I heard it's killing cold in winter in Seoul."
She gave her usual excuse.

The young mistress joined in, "Look, Halmŏm, we'll give you
clothes and covers. Don't go, Halmŏm. Will you stay, please?"

Halmŏm could not give a cold answer to such earnest pleas, so she
hesitated for a while and said, "Well, I'll go back *after* Chusŏk, then."
Before her dull eyes loomed her son and daughter and the countryside
in which she had lived and toiled for nearly seventy years. Then
Halmŏm said again as if she had made a big decision, "Yes. I'll go
after Chusŏk, then."

Everyone became solemn. Nobody spoke. Seeing that the shade
spread now over more than half the yard, Halmŏm went into the
kitchen. The old woman who had borne many children and labored
hard all through the near-seventy years of her life fed logs into the
stove without any sign of complaint on her face.

The Seaman's Chant

Kim Dong-in

Kim Dong-in was born in 1900 in Pyongyang into a family of great wealth. He studied in Japan from 1914, and engaged in literary activities from 1919 with other Korean students there who shared his vision of literature and with whom he formed a coterie and published a magazine called Creation. *From the first, he had set before himself a distinctively artistic objective for his literature as opposed to Yi Kwang-soo's humanitarian and didactic aims.*

One of the many precocious literary geniuses of the early years of modern literature in Korea ("The Seaman's Chant" [1920] was written at twenty years of age), his overconfidence in himself led to a lack of discipline, both in his art and in his private life. His novels convey the force of his confidence in his vision, but his vision of humanity was not a fully mature one. It was unfortunate for him that he came so early in the modern period of Korean literature, and thus lacked a frame of achievement against which to measure himself. He neglected critical evaluation of himself as artist and thinker, and his works exhibit many flaws as a result of this neglect. However, his boldness in claiming for literature a territory all its own, independent of social and moral considerations (an audacious claim indeed in the climate of the day), which is borne out by his own practice, greatly aided experimentation in, and diversification of, Korean literature. "The Seaman's Chant" is an unashamed melodrama redeemed by its haunting remorse that exerts a strong appeal on our primal sympathy.

That day it was heavenly weather.

It was heavenly weather, but not the kind in which there is hardly a speck of cloud and the sky seems unapproachably high, as if it were looking down on men with contemptuous haughtiness. It was the kind of heavenly weather when the sky looks upon us through the pink blossoms of low clouds, like an earnest sympathizer of men, offering us friendship. It was a loving sky. I was relaxing on the greening grass at the foot of Peony Hill, gazing on the Taedong River which incessantly poured its blue waters into the Yellow Sea.

It was the third of March, the day boating parties began on the Taedong. On the river flowing far below, banqueting boats were gliding and bobbing, breaking the water into a thousand gem-like glitters, and from the boats came poignant spring-intoxicated melodies, stirring the fragrant, velvety spring air. And the strains of Korean musical instruments, drifting up with the songs of the female entertainers— now slowly, now drawlingly, now volubly, now softly, now plaintively—sounded as if they would not leave you alone until they had blended everything into the sentiment of spring, nor cease before they have built a bridge of melody between the dark waters of the Taedong River, the green grass growing on its banks, and even the warm blood in the human heart pounding to the thrill of spring.

It made music, incomparably beautiful music, when the soft, light wind brushed past the dark Korean pine trees and the sprouting grass.

Ah, the beauty of the green spring that intoxicates men! That spring could not fail to make a doubly strong impression on me, as I had lived in Tokyo since the age of fifteen and had been denied the relish of this kind of spring for many years.

In the town of Pyongyang, one could perceive the arrival of spring from the new plants that sprouted through the chapped earth and the young shoots on the willow trees. It was not fully spring in Pyongyang yet, but over this area around Peony Hill and in the Changrim plain that one could see across the Taedong River (a plain as fertile as the land of Canaan), spring had poured its affectionate caresses profusely.

One could picture in the mind without actually seeing them the green fields adorned with the bluish-green ripening wheat and barley, and the figures of the farmers looking upon their fields with contented smiles.

The clouds kept floating overhead. The shadow of the clouds on the wheat field rushed far away now, and in their place spread green, as green as the green of the newly-created world. When there was a wind to stir it, the full-grown winter wheat bent low and straightened up in ranks like a wave, flashing now dark green, now light green. And hawks, floating high up in the sky as if in praise of the leisureliness of that spring, added to the happiness and beauty.

> I will rise, to the warm affection of spring,
> I will rise, to the affection of the warm spring.

I recited aloud the familiar lyric a couple of times and lit a cigarette. The smoke from the cigarette soared to the sky in wreaths.

Spring had come to the sky also. The sky was low. It looked as if, should you climb to the top of Peony Hill, you could touch it. The pinkish clouds, which seemed to be higher than the sky, were flying here and there, mingling and parting.

I cannot help thinking it is Utopia whenever I see the beautiful scenery in spring and hear the murmur of its fullness. What is our end in striving like this hour after hour? Isn't it for construction of a Utopia?

Whenever I think of Utopia, I cannot help but be reminded of that manliest of men, the one who enjoyed the greatness of manhood to the utmost, Shih Huang Ti of China.*

No matter how many thousands of historians abuse him, Shih Huang Ti, who sent off three hundred virgin boys abroad in search of the elixir of eternal life, and who built his palace of pleasure in all the perfection of luxury and beauty; and who enjoyed banqueting every day with thousands of his subjects, and who thus strove to construct a Utopia on this earth, was the truest of the true arbiters of pleasure, and the greatest man since the beginning of history. The history of man-

---

*Shih Huang Ti of China is of course the notorious Chinese tyrant of the third century B.C., whose cruelty and sensuous extravagance remain unsurpassed. He built the Great Wall of China and reputedly had thirty thousand concubines and committed other incredible deeds. The fact that he is here mentioned in glowing terms is proof enough of Kim Dong-in's amoral aestheticism and adolescent worship of power (he was twenty when he wrote this story). [Translator]

kind can boast of having produced a great man, since it produced a man of such sheer courage, even if the world were to end now.

"A great man was he indeed," I said to myself and raised my head.

Just at that moment I heard a strange, sad sound coming from the direction of Kija's tomb,* stirring the spring air. I was listening to it even before I realized it. It was a seaman's chant, the Baettaragi of Yŏng-yu.** The singer was undoubtedly an expert, for the strain was divine—far above the artistry of the average male professional singer or female entertainer.

> I pray, I pray to you, spirit
> Of the hills and the rivers, of the wind and the land,
> Of the sun and the moon, the stars and planets,
> And to God in Heaven above,
> To spare our lives, fragile as a reed,
> To grant us a span more of this life.
> Oh, sad is this existence, this life on earth.

When the chanting had progressed thus far, voices of female entertainers singing to the accompaniment of the hourglass drum† came up from the river below and the Baettaragi could be heard no more.

A couple of years ago I had spent a summer in Yŏng-yu. Whoever has spent a season in Yŏng-yu, the birthplace of the song called Baettaragi, cannot but feel the unassuageable sorrow of this melody.

Whoever has once looked upon the vast Yellow Sea from atop the nameless mountain of Yŏng-yu in the evening would be unable to forget the sight of the sun sinking below its waters. Looking at the sun, that great mass of flame, dancing on the surface of the overbrimming sea, threatening to sink into it or to soar above it the next moment, and

---

*Kija is the legendary refugee from China who reputedly founded Kija Chosŏn in prehistoric Korea. It is generally held today that Kija Chosŏn is a fiction created by the Chinese to justify their partial colonization of Korea in the second century B.C. The tomb, therefore, is also regarded as a sham. [Translator]

**Yŏng-yu is a town in the Pyŏngan Namdo Province, now in north Korea. [Translator]

†The drum is shaped like an hourglass and its two ends are covered with skins of different thickness. It is struck with the palm or a stick, and is a very popular instrument for beating time. It can be slung from the shoulders of dancers, and the hourglass drum dance shows the female body line to advantage. [Translator]

hearing a plaintive strain coming intermittently from an invisible boat, I used to shed many tears of nameless sorrow, emotionally impressionable as I was. At moments like that, you do not feel like dismissing as fantastic the story of the magistrate's wife who left behind her wealth and dignity to go and live an aimless life on the waters with a seaman.

Even after my return from Yŏng-yu, the melody of the Baettaragi was engraved deep in my memory, never to be forgotten, and I have never ceased longing to go back to Yŏng-yu once again to hear the chant and to gaze on the entrancing sunset once more.

The singing of the female entertainers and the sound of the hourglass drum ceased, and only the mournful melody of the seaman's chant was heard drifting along the wind. Sometimes, because of the gusts of adverse wind, the chant ceased to be heard, but with the aid of my memory I could reconstruct the lyrics clearly in my mind.

> My beloved, meeting me walking on the riverbank,
> Didn't know if it was life or a dream;
> She ran up to me, seized me with her thin fingers,
> And said between sobs: "Have you dropped
>   from Heaven,
> "Sprung out of the earth, blown here on the wind,
> "Or been carried by the clouds?"
> When thus we were bathed in tears, holding fast to
>   one another,
> All our folks and friends gathered to . . .

Hearing this much, I could not stay still any more. Springing to my feet, I put on the hat I had hung on a pine bough and went up to the top of Peony Hill to make out the direction of the song. The chant could be heard more clearly from the top of the hill. The singer sang the refrain of the chant:

> Even if you had to go begging for food,
> Oh, never, never go to sea again.
> Oh, sad is this lot, this life on earth.

I stood still, desperately yearning to make out the direction of the sound. "Where? Kija's tomb? The Moonlight Pavilion?" But I could not stay still very long. I was going to find him out at any cost, so I started off, determined to search everywhere.

The deep pine forest around Kija's tomb spread before me. "Where?" I asked myself again.

At that moment he began the Baettaragi anew. The sound came from my left. Heartened, I searched among the pine trees for a good while feeling for the direction of the sound, and at last found him lounging alone in a sunny place near the tomb that had a good view of the sky. His looks were as I had imagined: angular face, nose, mouth, eyes, limbs. . . . The deeply grooved wrinkles on his forehead and his dark eyebrows bespoke his tortuous past, and also the simplicity of his nature.

He sat up and ceased singing when he saw a man in gentlemanly attire looking at him.

"Please go on," I said, and sat down beside him.

"Oh . . ." He barely answered and, raising his eyes, looked up at the clear sky. They were nice eyes. The greatness and vastness of the sea were well reflected in them. He was a seaman, I guessed at once.

"Are you a native of Yŏng-yu?"

"Well, I was born there, but it's been nearly twenty years since I saw it last."

"Why have you neglected to visit your home town for so long?"

"Well, it's a man's fate. Things never go as one wants them to." So saying, he heaved a sigh. "There's no going against our destiny." His voice held a note of unmitigable bitterness and regret.

"Oh, do you think so?" I could only look at him in interrogative silence.

After a considerable pause I spoke to him again. "Let me hear your past history, if it's not a strictly guarded secret."

"What secret could a lowly man like me have that's worth guarding?"

"Well then, please let me hear it."

He looked up at the sky again. After a pause he said, "Very well," lighted a cigarette as I did, and began his story.

"It was on the eleventh of August, nineteen years back . . ." And he told me a story which went thus:

The town he lived in was a small village facing the sea, a few miles from Yŏng-yu. In the village of some thirty households he was a man of some consequence.

He had lost both his parents before he was fifteen, and the only remaining members of his family consisted of himself, his wife, and his younger brother and sister-in-law who lived next door to him. The two brothers were among the better-off villagers, and the most skilled in fishing. They had some learning as well, and excelled most in the chanting of Baettaragi. In other words, they were the most eminent people in the village.

The August Full Moon Day is a big holiday there as elsewhere. On the eleventh of August, he set off toward town to do some shopping for the Full Moon Day feast, and also to buy a mirror for his wife, which she had been yearning for for a long time.

"Buy one bigger than Mrs. Kim's. You won't forget, will you?" his wife asked him again and again, following him as far as the entrance of the road to town to see him off.

"I won't," he promised, and left his village for the town, the red sun showering rays upon him from the front.

He had doted on his wife (though such an admission always makes a man look silly, he said). His wife had been a delicate and pretty woman, such as is not frequently met with in such country villages. "I don't think you can find many like her, even if you go to the pleasure resorts of Pyongyang," he said.

So they were a devoted couple, something which was rare and regarded as ridiculous in villages like that. Aged people often told him not to lose his head over his own wife.

Although they loved each other, or perhaps because they did, he was very jealous about his wife. Not that she was unfaithful or lewd, but she was of a gay temperament, made friends easily with other people, and was affectionate to anybody.

In his village, young men used to gather in his house on holidays or celebration days, on the pretext that his house was the cleanest and most spacious.

All the young men called his wife "sister," and his wife called them "brother" and chatted and laughed with them, and her gay mouth at those times always wore an affectionate smile. At such times he would just keep glaring at her with evil eyes from a corner, and after the young men left he would jump on her without a word and kick and beat her like mad, taking away from her all that he had given her as presents before. Whenever there was a quarrel in his house his brother and brother's wife next door would come to appease them, and then he would always beat his brother and sister-in-law, too.

There was a reason for his behaving in such a way toward his brother. His brother was a well-built man with a dignity unusual for a country youth, and was of fair complexion, although always buffeted by the sea wind. That might have been sufficient reason in itself for him to be jealous, but he just couldn't contain his fury because his wife was especially kind to his brother.

About half a year prior to his departure from Yŏng-yu—that is, about half a year before his trip to the town market to buy a mirror —he had celebrated his birthday. His wife had made many delicious dishes for him. One of his habits was to save his favorite foods for later. His wife couldn't be ignorant of his habit, but when his brother came around lunchtime she started to give his brother the food he was saving for later. He raised his eyebrows to signify that she should not give it to the brother, but his wife, whether she had noticed or not, went ahead and gave the dishes to his brother. He was very upset. He was going to make her pay for it, and he was looking for the merest excuse. His wife, coming away after setting the food table before her brother-in-law, stepped on his foot by accident.

"You bitch!" He raised his foot high and kicked his wife with all his might. The woman fell across the table, and then painfully arose again.

"You bitch!" How dare you step on your man!"

"Did it get broken or something?" the wife, blushing, wailed in a tearful voice.

"You bitch! How dare you cross words with your man?" He stood up and grasped her by the hair.

"Brother, why do you treat her so harshly?" His younger brother stood up and held his arm.

"You shut up, you son of a bitch!" He pushed his brother away and showered kicks and blows on his wife.

"You dirty bitch! You get out of here or I'll kill you."

"Kill me if you want! I won't leave this house even if you kill me."

"You won't leave this house?"

"Never! This is my house!"

At that moment, he felt stabbed in the heart by his wife's protest that she would never leave his house. He did not feel like beating her any more. He stood there giving her a vicious look for some time and then ran outside, shouting, "You God-damned bitch, then *I* will leave."

Without bothering to answer his brother, who came running after him and asked, "Where are you going, brother?" he went to a roadside tavern in the neighboring village and sat down before a liquor table with a hostess.

Completely drunk, he went home that evening with a bundle of cakes for his wife.

Thus there was peace for some time. But the peace could not last forever. It was broken again because of his brother.

His brother, who used to go to town frequently, began to be absent from his home, staying in the town for days at a stretch from around the end of May. About the same time, the rumor that he had a mistress in town spread in the village. Hearing this rumor, the elder brother's wife hated her brother-in-law's trips to town more than insects, and when he returned after a few days' stay in town, she would go at once to the brother's house to upbraid him. She even quarreled with her sister-in-law for not preventing him from going to town.

Around the beginning of July, the brother returned from town after about ten days' stay there. His wife, as usual, quarreled with her brother-in-law and his wife, and even came to him reviling him for not preventing his brother going down the path of evil. Having long been resentful of his wife's attitude, he began shouting at her at once.

"What business is that of yours? I don't want to hear it."

"You fool! You can't even keep your own younger brother from going to evil places!" his wife shouted back in anger.

"What did you say, you bitch?" He stood up.

"Fool!"

Before she could finish the word, she was pitched down on the floor with a scream.

"You bitch! Who taught you to talk like that to your man?"

"Then who taught you to beat your wife like this? Fool!" she wailed in a tearful voice.

"You low-down bitch, you! You get out of my house! Get out of my house this minute!" he yelled, while beating her with all his strength without pause. And he opened the door and threw her out.

"I won't go!" she screamed, and ran out, weeping.

"The God-damned bitch!" He muttered an oath and flopped down on the floor.

His wife did not return after the sun had set and darkness covered the village. Although he had thrown her out, he was waiting for her to return. In that darkness, without bothering to light the lamp, he waited for his wife to return, shaking with fury. But he could hear his wife's merry laughter from his brother's house next door all night. He spent the night sitting riveted on the floor, and at dawn he took the knife from the kitchen and flung open the gate, determined to kill both his wife and his brother.

Had his wife not been standing there outside the gate peering into the house with a worried face, he really would have killed them both. But the moment he saw her face, he felt love filling his heart. He flung away the knife, seized her by the hair and dragged her in, yelling, "You bitch!" Throwing her down on the floor, he bit her cheeks and fondled her in a frenzy.

There would be no end to it if he were to tell all the incidents of this kind, but in brief such had been the relationship between him, his wife and his brother.

To make a long story short, he had found a good mirror that day in the town market. Compared with mirrors of today, the thing enlarged or distorted a nose or a mouth, but a mirror at that time and in such a village was something as precious as a jewel. After he had bought the mirror and did all the other shopping, he headed for his house without even taking his usual refreshment at the roadside tavern, walking in the direction of the overbrimming sea, crimson-colored with the evening sun, happy in the expectation of his wife's joy at the valuable present.

But he encountered a dumbfounding scene when he stepped into his house.

Spread in the middle of the room was a table laden with cakes, and his brother, whose hood was loosened and hanging down behind his neck, and the fastening of whose jacket was almost untied, was standing in a corner. His wife's hair was undone and the waist of her skirt had slid down to the hips. His wife and brother, on seeing him, did not stir a step, as if they didn't know what to do.

The three just stood there like that for a while, lost. Then his brother at last managed to speak: "Where has that rat disappeared?"

"Oh, a rat! A magnificent rat you were catching!" He threw down his bundle, and even before he finished speaking, grasped his brother by the collar.

"Brother! There *was* a rat!"

"A rat! You low-life! What son of a bitch catches that kind of a rat with his sister-in-law?" He gave his brother a few hard slaps on the cheek and threw him out the door, pushing him from behind. Then he swooped down on his wife, who was standing trembling with fear.

"You bitch! What bitch on earth catches that kind of a rat with a brother-in-law?" He kicked his wife to the floor and showered blows upon her, not caring where they fell.

"It was a rat, really. Oh, you're killing me!"

"You say a rat, too, you bitch? Serves you right to die!" All four of his limbs fell on his wife indiscriminately.

"You're killing me! Really, I was just going to give your brother some cakes when . . ."

"Shut up! What excuse can you have, you bitch who slept with a brother-in-law?"

"No! No! I mean it. A big rat jumped out . . ."

"Still babbling about a rat?"

"We were trying to catch it!"

"You dirty bitch! Serves you right to die! Why don't you drown your dirty body in the water and go to hell!"

He beat his wife till he had no strength left, and then threw her out by pushing her from behind as he had his brother, shouting, "Go feed the fish!"

Although he had beaten her to his heart's content, his wrath was far from appeased. He went to a corner of the room, stood leaning against the wall like a man out of his wits, and kept gazing at the cakes on the table.

The village faced west toward the sea, so night came there later than in other places, but it became dark about eight o'clock. To light a lamp, he moved away from the wall and went around looking for a match. The matches were not in the usual place. He was feeling about here and there, and pushed his hand inside a heap of old clothes when there came a squeaking sound and something ran out from the heap and rapidly scurried away to the other side of the room.

"It really *was* a rat!" He muttered faintly, and dropped down there, all his strength drained out of him. The scene that took place in the room during his absence went through his head like a scene in a play: The brother came. His wife, who was always kind to her brother-in-law, prepared a cake table for him. Then out jumped a rat from no-where. The two ran about, trying to catch the rat. The rat, which had teased them for a good while, suddenly disappeared into a corner. The two searched about, trying to find the rat. It was at that moment that he stepped in.

"The bitch. She'll come back all right. Where would she go, anyway?" He calmed himself with difficulty and lay down.

But his wife did not return, even when the night was spent and it was broad daylight again. By and by he got worried, so he set out in search of her.

She was not at his brother's house either. No one in the whole village had had a glimpse of her. Then at last about noon they found his wife on the seashore a few miles away from the village. But his wife was not the pretty, vivacious woman she used to be, but a dead woman swollen to twice her size with foam at her mouth, at the mouth that used to smile so prettily.

His mind was a complete blank while he was carrying his wife home on his back.

They buried her the next day without much ceremony. On the face of his brother who trod behind him on the way home from the grave there was a look of reproach, as if he wanted to say, "What have you done, brother?"

His brother disappeared from their small village the day after the funeral. A couple of days went by without people taking much notice of his absence, but five or six days passed and his brother still did not return. When he made inquiries, he learned that someone who fitted the description of his brother was seen several days before walking wearily toward the east, with a small cloth sack on his back and with the red rays of the evening sun lighting his back. Ten days, then twenty days went by, but his brother never again made an appearance, and his sister-in-law, left alone, sighed away her life.

He could not stand to see her thus. He was to blame for all the miseries. At last he became a seaman, and boarded a ship to be at least always near the sea that killed his wife, and to inquire about his brother wherever he went. Everywhere he made inquiries about his brother, giving out his name and a description, but he could obtain no information whatever .

Ten years went by like that, on land and on the waters. Then one autumn, nine years ago, his ship was wrecked by a storm while sailing through a thick fog on the sea off Yŏn-an, and some of his fellow seamen were drowned, but he floated on the water almost unconscious.

It was night when he regained consciousness. He found himself on land again, somehow. And, illumined by the flames of the log fire burning beside him, he saw the face of his brother, who was tending him.

Strangely enough he was not even surprised, and said slowly: "Why, brother! How have you come here?"

His brother was silent, then answered at length: "Brother, it is all up to Fate."

He was about to fall asleep again from the warmth of the fire, but he woke up startled and exclaimed: "How pale you've become, brother, in these ten years!"

"I have indeed, but you have changed too, brother."

Hearing these words half asleep and half waking, he fell into a fast sleep again. Then after a few hours of delicious sleep, he woke up to find that the red fire was still burning but that his brother was not to be seen. When he managed to question people about him, he was told that his brother had been sitting there looking into his face for a long time and had disappeared into the darkness without a word, walking tiredly, with the red flames illuminating his back.

However diligently he inquired after his brother the next day, he could not unearth the slightest information about him, so he set off on another journey by water on another ship. When the ship reached Haeju, he thought he saw someone who looked like his brother in a shop while he was in the town market making a purchase, so he ran over at once, but the man had already disappeared. His ship did not anchor in Haeju, so he had to continue his journey on the sea, leaving his heart in Haeju.

Then for three years after that he caught not a glimpse of his brother, though his journey took him far and wide.

After a lapse of three years, or six years ago, while his ship was sailing fast by Kanghwado Island, he heard the strains of Baettaragi floating toward the sea from the vicinity of a steep hill near the shore. It was a Baettaragi he well knew was his brother's, the lyrics and melody of it being modified by his brother in a way no one but his brother knew how to chant.

The ship did not stop at Kanghwado, so he had to sail past the island, but as it was anchoring for about ten days in nearby Inchon, he disembarked at once and went to Kanghwado. He made inquiries all over the island, and at last got information from a small streetside tavern that one who bore his brother's name and who looked like his brother had stayed there for some time, but had left for Inchon a few days earlier. He sped back at once to Inchon and looked for him, but could not find him even in that small town.

Thereafter six years passed, but he was unable to meet his brother again, and did not even know whether he was still alive or not.

When he finished his story, his eyes shone with tears in the evening glow of the sun.

I asked after a pause: "What became of your sister-in-law?"

"I don't know. I haven't gone back to Yŏng-yu for twenty years now."

"Where will you be going from here?"

"That I don't know either. What destination could there be for one like me? I'll just be going where the wind will carry me."

Then once more he sang a strain of Baettaragi for me.

Oh, the immitigable regret in that strain! The sorrowful longing for the sea!

After he finished the song, he stood up and walked absently in the direction of the Moonlight Pavilion, with the scarlet evening sun pouring its rays on his back. Not knowing how to detain him, I just sat there, gazing at his back.

That night after I returned home I could not fall asleep, so vividly did the melody of his chant and the tale of his fateful life ring in my ears. The next day I rose up early, and without eating breakfast ran toward Kija's tomb and looked for him. The grass on which he had been sitting, flattened, bespoke of his having been there, but he was not to be found anywhere in the vicinity.

But—but the strain of the Baettaragi seemed to be ringing from somewhere, as if it would not leave off until it had made all the pine trees there vibrate to its melody.

"It's from Peony Hill! He's on Peony Hill!" So exclaiming, I ran up to the top of Peony Hill at one stride. There was not a soul on the hill. I went to the tower but he was not there either.

"It's from the Moonlight Pavilion!" I said, and went to the Moonlight Pavilion. From the pavilion to the tower on top of Peony Hill, the needles of all the pine trees—grown densely, as if not to let even a drop of water seep through, as if their roots stretched to the very heart of Hell—were singing the tremulous strain of the Baettaragi, but he was nowhere in sight. The tens of millions of needles of the pine trees that stretched skyward from Kija's tomb, and the countless blades of grass that spread thickly underneath the pines, all were singing a doleful strain of Baettaragi, but he could not be seen anywhere near the small Peony Hill.

When I inquired at the riverside, I heard that his ship had left that morning.

Thereafter, although summer, autumn, and indeed a full year has gone by, and it is now spring again, he who had passed through this city of Pyongyang and left behind that fateful tale and the sorrowful Baettaragi did not make an appearance again around this small Peony Hill.

Spring has come again to Peony Hill and Kija's tomb, and the grass he sat on last year has all grown straight again, and is about to bloom in purple blossoms; but he who made the confession of his undying regret with the doleful strains of Baettaragi was not to be seen again on this small hill near this small tomb. Only the leaves, all the small leaves, whisper the strain he has left behind, as if in commemoration, as if in consolation.

The Clear Water Pavilion

Yu Chin-o

Yu Chin-o, who passed away in 1986 at age eighty, is better remembered today as a scholar of law and educator than as an author. An outstanding student throughout his school life, Yu, like many other early giants of modern Korean literature, began writing in his teens. He organized a students' literary club in his student days and started a club magazine.

Having become a law student in 1926, he organized a student club which, with the addition of radical members the following year, turned leftist. From 1927 he began writing in earnest. At first his stories had a proletarian leaning, dealing as they did with the harsh lot of working-class people, but from 1935 there was less ideological content in his works.

"The Clear Water Pavilion" (1940) has the fresh naiveté appropriate to a recollection of childhood. In his adult stories he shows great sensitivity to the nuance and tone of everyday occurrences, to subtle hints of words and gesture, psychological penetration, and an understanding of the feminine psychology uncommon for a man of his times. However, literature was not his major occupation at any time, and he stopped writing after Korea's liberation when the country demanded his services as a scholar of law. He drafted the constitution of the new republic, and for many years was a professor of law and a university president. After his retirement he went into politics briefly, became president of the New Democratic Party, and even ran for the presidency on the opposition ticket in 1967.

1

"As soon as the sun sets, nostalgia soaks me through like salt water," sang Mr. C., a poet friend of mine. It is true that the longing for home is a feeling poignant and sweet, beautiful and unsettling, joyful and sad, residing within us but undefinable; and yet when we are tired in mind and body from disappointment or frustration, it creeps into our hearts like salt water, to dye in pink shades the memories of the past, and makes us fret with yearning for the small pine hill behind our boyhood country house and those childhood friends who used to study in the village school with us and carry out raids together on neighborhood chickens on winter days. It is a sentiment that has such strange power.

But nostalgia is not something that always unsettles the mind; if we have room in our hearts for it, it can gently soothe our coarsened emotions and collect into a single thread our torn and tangled thoughts. Let us imagine that there is a man who spent his youth hundreds of miles from home because of his great ambition. After decades of rough rain and storm, when the grooves on his forehead have deepened and the gray strands in his hair grow daily more numerous, one moonlit night he finds it hard to fall asleep because of the longing in his heart for home, and tosses and turns in bed. We might be tempted to judge that the thing called nostalgia is like a messenger of grief that eats up our hearts, but we might also say that nostalgia is like the gentle caress of our mothers, soothing our desperation into vast tranquility when we have at last realized, after failing to attain the goals of our youth (or perhaps even after having attained them), that what we imagine to be the great ambition of youth consists only of a temporary false dream of the days when we look at life through pink-tinted veils, and is not something profound, lofty and solid that can give lasting repose to mind and body. Alike to those who have achieved the goals of their youth and to those who have failed, nostalgia may be the nest to which we finally return.

The ancient poet of the "Homecoming Verses" chanted that "birds seek their nests when tired by flight"; and Goethe, who is said to have enjoyed a "permanent youth," sang when no older than thirty-one, "On every peak there is repose." We could say that they have absorbed the sad and profound meaning of nostalgia with uncommon intuition and sensitivity.

In this respect, happy are those who spent their childhoods in a beautiful countryside, because they have a warm maternal bosom to nestle against whenever the mind is wearied. But those who were born and have grown up in the city, and who change their abode every few years, or even several times a year, are unhappy indeed because they have no home to long for even when they yearn to have a home to miss. One might argue that such a person can always live for the future, but a person's mind cannot stretch rigidly upward like steel all the time; so that after every strain there follows of necessity a slackening of nerves, and every relaxation may be a prelude to greater exertion.

Anyway all of us, whoever we may be, harbor nostalgia. This goes without saying for those of us who have a home in the country to long for, but those of us who do not have a country home also become sad or happy because of our constant longing for something. The object of nostalgia for those of us without a country home may be scenery of mountains and streams that we saw one night in boyhood in a dream, or a girl in our imagination whom we have never met even in dreams. Well, a theologian might maintain that the nostalgia we speak of is nothing but our longing for the bosom of our heavenly father; that men have been fated to suffer nostalgia from the moment they were expelled from the Garden of Eden after tasting the forbidden fruit. Whatever objection there may be to this religious theory, it is an irrefutable fact that men are so made that they can discover the meaning of life only when they feel longing for something.

For myself, born and raised in Seoul, unfortunately there is no beautiful countryside that I can yearn for with aching heart. The house in which I am said to have been born and where I lived until the age of three has been demolished without a trace, and now cold-faced modern houses occupy the whole district. But I, too, have a kind of a memory of home I can hark back to when my mind is wearied. A part of the memory is that of my house in Kyedong, where I lived from six to fourteen, and the other is the memory of Ch'angrangjŏng Pavilion, which I am going to record here.

2

Ch'angrangjŏng is the name of the pavilion on the brink of Sogang, the Western Han River, that once served as the residence of a prime minister. His Excellency Kim Jong-ho, a relative of mine—a third cousin of my great-grandfather and consequently a tenth-degree kinsman to me —had served the government during the Taewŏngun regency era in a post as high as minister of internal administration. Ch'angrangjŏng is the pavilion he purchased to spend his gloomy remaining years after Taewŏngun lost power and he resigned his post because the affairs of the country went contrary to his wish for maintaining national isolation. The name Ch'angrangjŏng was given to it by His Excellency himself.

My memory is not quite clear on this point, but I think it was in the spring of my eighth year. Therefore, it was about twenty-eight years ago. The season must have been early spring, because it was about the time when the shepherd's purse sent up its shoots from underground. I went there with my father and spent a few days. Strangely, what I saw and heard then became deeply engraved in my young mind, so that even after a lapse of nearly thirty years the events traverse the land of my memory and pierce my heart from time to time in the shape of an almost painfully sweet nostalgia.

Ch'angrangjŏng Pavilion stood on a huge estate of more than 3,500 pyong,* located on a small mountain thickly covered with pine trees overlooking the river, where the land abruptly fell off in a precipitous cliff after sloping slowly toward the river. When you looked at the house from a distance, from the bank of the river, a row of servants' houses stretched in a line on the hill beyond the usually dried-up brook. In the midst of them stood the gate of the great house, tall and imposing.

"Now we're almost there. The house over there—that's your Sŏgang grandfather's** mansion."

My father, holding my tired right hand with his left hand, pointed to

---

*One pyŏng is 3.24 square meters or 36 square feet. [Translator]

**Terms like "grandfather," "grandmother," "uncle," "aunt," "brother," and "sister" are very loosely applied to relatives and acquaintances and even to strangers to show respect and affection due to the person's age and station in life. Here, "grandfather" is used because the person is a relative of the boy's grandfather's generation or older. [Translator]

the big house beyond the brook, raising his cane in his right hand. The impression of that big mansion standing with the evening sun shining obliquely on it was so extraordinary that the picture of the house at the moment my father told me that was the house of my Sŏgang grandfather is still vivid before my eyes, as if it were only yesterday. Seen close by, it revealed itself as a very rundown ancient house perhaps hundreds of years old, with the pillars all leaning or fallen. The surrounding wall of stone and clay was also caved in here and there, and in some places the holes were big enough for cows to pass through. As we entered the gate after climbing the mountain, a huge, dark old ginkgo tree obstructed our path like a monster in a nightmare. I heard later that the ginkgo tree was rumored to be inhabited by an evil spirit, so that when any of the houses in the neighborhood offered sacrifices to shaman spirits, they always began by offering food and prayers to this ginkgo tree to appease the spirit dwelling in it, and that whenever unfortunate things happened in the neighborhood people trembled in fear, thinking that the wrath of the ginkgo tree spirit was roused.

Beyond the ginkgo tree there was another steep slope, and high on the slope stood the middle gate yielding to the men's quarters. Inside the middle gate was a level garden with study and guest rooms on either side, and on the high stone embankment directly facing the river stood the main study occupied by His Excellency himself. Separating the garden from the outside was a wall only a few feet high, and if one stepped on a stone and looked over the wall, there was a cliff falling from right below the wall, so that the dark blue waters of the river were seen rolling a dizzying distance below at the base of the cliff.

His Excellency was ill in bed. On the wooden-floored veranda facing southwest, the gay evening sunlight was shining brightly, but when we first stepped into His Excellency's main study it was so dark that nothing could be discerned by the eyes. My father, after walking toward the warmer part of the floor and making a full bow,* bade me bow, too. After I bowed as I was bidden and crouched down on my knees, father introduced me, saying, "This is my son, Your Excellency."

"Oh, that's a good-looking boy." His Excellency raised himself on purpose to stroke my head, and accosted me with "How old are you?"

---

*For a full Korean bow, men kneel down and bend the body forward until the forehead almost touches the floor. Women sit instead of kneeling on the floor and bend forward as deeply as is appropriate to their relationship with the recipient of the bow. [Translator]

"Seven, sir."

"Hm . . . Bright sons are our greatest hope at a time like this."

At long last my eyes began to discern things in the room. Though His Excellency was very lean because he was already eighty years old and had been long ill in bed, even to my young eyes his narrow face, fair skin and silver beard all bespoke nobility that had grown loftier with the harshness of worldly storms and waves.

While Father and His Excellency were talking about something between themselves, I looked around the room carefully. I had known only the small men's study in my house in Kyedong, so everything seemed to me novel and interesting. Both the double sliding paper doors were firmly closed against the wooden-floored veranda, and over them a dark purple curtain was drawn; covering the length and height of the opposite wall was a big folding screen which featured a painting of mountain spirits amusing themselves among clouds above the waves. On the square table in a corner and atop the pair of stationery chests engraved in floral patterns standing near the pillow of His Excellency lay scattered big ancient books in great piles. The brush holder with a dragon carving standing on the ink slab box, the marble seal engraved with a tiger pattern, the calligraphy pieces of renowned ancient scholars hanging on the walls, the long duster made of white horsehair. . . . Oh, I feel as if I am beholding distinctly even now all these mysterious and elaborate decorations in that room.

3

In a little while the door opened and a topknotted* young man who looked around twenty came in.

"Stand up and make a bow to your elder cousin," Father told me.

I got up again and made a bow as bidden. That was Kim Chong-gŭn, the young master of that house, great-grandson to His Excellency

---

*In the Yi Dynasty, for a man to wear his hair in a topknot was the symbol of married status and adulthood, and therefore a matter of pride. In this story, however, which is set in the early years of modernization, Chong-gŭn's wearing a topknot indicates that he is under the rule of conservative family elders, and he might not have been too happy to wear the topknot, because the more advanced youths of the day wore their hair cut short, in the Western style. We see at the end of the story that Chong-gŭn promptly gets rid of his topknot upon becoming the head of the house. [Translator]

and thirteenth degree kinsman to me. His Excellency had lost his son and grandson early, so that he cherished this young great-grandson as his heir who would carry on the family line.

My father and His Excellency began to talk at length again, with Chong-gŭn seated beside them. I could not make out what they were talking about, but on looking back, as school was often mentioned in their conversation, it was probably a discussion over whether to send Chong-gŭn to school—His Excellency was consulting my father's opinion on that. His Excellency had of course a great many people to seek advice from on any other matter, but as far as modernization was concerned, my father was the only one in the whole clan who knew anything about it. My father had been a Korean government scholarship student in Japan, and was employed before the annexation in such offices as the finance ministry and the cabinet organization bureau. He continued to work in the government after the annexation of Korea by Japan.

I infer that the talk between my father and His Excellency that day concerned whether or not to let Chong-gŭn have a modern education, from my father's repeated regretful remarks afterwards that His Excellency was too stubborn to send Chong-gŭn to school. In my opinion, His Excellency, since he had been one of those most violently insistent upon keeping away the barbarians from the West, must have finally decided to keep Chong-gŭn away from school, adhering to his convictions to the last, though he felt the need to have his precious only descendant receive a modern education because he saw the world changing contrary to his wishes. But he went so far as to consult my father.

Because the grown-ups' talk lasted too long and made me feel impatient, I got up noiselessly and, opening the double sliding doors, came out on the elevated wooden-floored enclosed terrace. The doors of the terrace were shut on all sides, too, but it was intensely bright with the rays of the evening sun filtered through the paper panels of the doors. There was not much decoration there, but the high piles of books and the signboard with the characters "Ch'ang Rang Jŏng" excited my curiosity. I remember that after studying the signboard for a considerable while, I could make out the characters as meaning Clear Water Pavilion, and that it made me feel very proud. The signboard was written by His Excellency himself, so in a corner there was his sobriquet "Do-am" signed with brush.

After looking long at the signboard, I went to the edge of the floor and gave a push at the door that looked down on the river. To my surprise, the door slid open without a squeak and the unexpected sublime view from Ch'angrangjŏng Pavilion spread out before my eyes. Oh, the magnificent view which rushed into my eyes soundlessly in that one instant! That, too, is vivid before my mind's eye! The dark blue waves rolling right beneath my eyes; the wide, wide sands spreading beyond the waters that filled my view; mountain after mountain stretching from the edge of the sand far, far away to where the sky ended, undulating in peaks and valleys, just like the waves of the ocean—I stood there entranced at the grand scene, unconscious of the passing of time.

After a long while I recollected myself, perceiving gay, translucent colors thrown over the solemn view. The sunset glow had begun to spread. That was the first time I realized that although the evening glow is something that must start spreading slowly, it looks to the beholder as if it has suddenly begun. Even though it was March, thick folds of clouds of all sizes and shapes screened the sky. Some had trailing horizontal tails like smoke, some looked like blossoms of cotton wool whose edges shone silver; some rose up mountain-high and fell back like waterfalls while I was watching, giving the illusion of great beasts at war; some were immobile, shielding the sky high up at the zenith like diaphanous floral-pattern veils. All the various clouds were dyed in yellow, red, pink, purple or orange tints, so that together with the blue of the sky peeping through intermittently, they formed a wondrous sight, like a translucent, rainbow-colored magic glass. The resplendent sky was in turn reflected upside down in the water, and thus sky and earth together made an entrancing vision, as if the whole universe were a huge, radiant flowerbed. Not only was it an unforgettable sight to a seven-year-old boy, but a sight that would have been indelible to anybody.

But soon, a more impressive and unforgettable event to my young mind than even the beautiful sunset took place.

With my mind wholly absorbed in the ecstasy of the evening glow, I was unconscious of anyone coming or going in the garden under my feet below the elevated floor, but when I happened to glance down at the ground in front of me, I saw a girl of about twelve looking up and smiling at me. I did not know how long she had been there. Wearing a bright yellow blouse and a red, red skirt, and standing with the gem-like glow of the evening behind her, she was looking up at me, smiling.

I instantly experienced such a strong liking toward that girl that it made me feel as if my body was being gently squeezed. So I smiled at her before I knew, and the girl beckoned me to come to her.

4

I nodded several times and went into the main study to go past it out into the yard. But Father scolded me for having been away so long, and told me to stay beside him because we were going to the inner quarters to pay our respects to the lady of the mansion. I yearned to go out to the girl, but had no choice except to squat down on my knees beside my father.

The inner quarters stood on an even more elevated plane than the men's quarters, and were of sturdier construction. With a large, grand living room in the center, there was the innermost room on the west, the daughters' room to the east, a wooden-floored room adjoining the innermost room, another room adjoining the daughters' room, with a back room next to that, and across the inner garden were two rooms for female relatives or guests. This may sound like an imposing mansion, but since it was very gloomy from age and lack of care, and the rafters were rotten, making the curved edges of the roof droop, it looked like a deserted temple, the kind that appears in ancient tales. The roof line was ragged with dried grass from the year before which grew from the mud plaster that kept the tiles in place.

As soon as we stepped inside the inner gate, a smell of food invaded our nostrils and we could see people bustling all over the living room and the kitchen. Some were scurrying back and forth with cake steamers, some were frying seafood and vegetables, some slicing loop cakes, splitting platycodon, sorting mung bean sprouts, or marinating meat in sauce. The huge, gloomy house was all in a bustle. I was thinking to myself that this must be the scale of daily living at lords' mansions when Father said to me,

"Tomorrow's the birthday of the grandmother of this house. I have to go back home after dinner, so you sleep here with Chong-gŭn and stay for a few days. Tomorrow your mother will come."

My father, announcing himself with false coughs, went into the innermost room in which Her Ladyship was lying in bed. Some of the young ladies in the living room hid themselves at the sight of a man, but in the innermost room there were a lot of aged ladies who greeted

my father as they might a child. Her Ladyship was lying on the warmest part of the floor and did not move at all except to turn her yellowed
face a little, even when my father and I made deep bows. After bowing
to Her Ladyship, my father and I had a hard time making bows in turn
to all the ladies in that room, who were either some kind of cousins or
great aunts to me.

After a round of bowing I was collecting my breath, looking at the
intricate geometrical pattern of the ceiling—that was called *sorabanja*
—when a murmur rose again in the room, the door slid open, and a
young lady as beautiful as the full moon—to my eyes at that time she
was really fair as the moon—came in with lowered eyes. The lady
made a respectful bow to my father. My father diffidently half-raised
himself and received her bow. Looking at the beautiful lady in shapely
indigo blue skirt and bright yellow blouse, I suddenly remembered the
girl I had seen a little while ago. She must be this lady's sister or niece,
I thought.

"Bow to your sister."

Somebody told me to bow again. The lady was Chong-gŭn's bride.

When dinner was over my father left me there alone and went back
home as he had told me. As I had never slept anywhere other than in
my own house before, I wanted very much to go back home with
Father, but it occurred even to my young mind that if I stayed there I
would be able the next day to meet the girl I saw that afternoon. So I
consented without much protest and went to sleep, my heart throbbing
with expectations like one about to set out on a great adventure.

From very early the next day guests began to gather. Most of the
guests were women, and most of them were of the family clan, so that
there were many aunts and great aunts I knew.

In the meanwhile, my waited-for mother came and greeted me with
a glad expression, and asked me whether I had slept well, whether I
had washed my face, whether I didn't miss home too much, and what I
had eaten. At that moment I forgot all about the girl and resolved never
to leave my mother's side, so glad was I to see her.

When I went into the inner quarters with my mother, I found that in
a short space of time a great many young women in yellow blouses
and trailing indigo skirts had gathered, enough to fill the huge living
room. They were making a hundred times more bustle than the day
before. The young women had forgotten their modesty, and were shouting
to each other to hand over something or to put something in a corner

out of the way. Like a flock of sparrows freed for the first time after long confinement in wooden chests, they whispered, giggled, and poked each other in the ribs, while some of them swiftly put into their mouths some of the food they were making to chew and swallow surreptitiously.

The whole space of the innermost room was filled with party guests as well, so that there was nowhere I could take a seat in any comfort. Besides, none among them kept her mouth closed even for a moment. It is the same any time, now or in the old days—when women gather, they chatter and make noise. I felt I could hardly keep my senses in place, so as soon as I managed to eat a late breakfast, I escaped directly from the crowd to go to the back yard of the inner quarters.

5

To the rear of the inner quarters was another courtyard, and joined to the yard was the hillside park or garden belonging to the house. This rustic hillside garden was enclosed with a baked tile wall, and planted densely with peach, apricot, plum, cherry and other fruit trees, and also with willows, spindle, forsythia and other flowering shrubs. On the slope stood a shrine, the arabesque paintings on its eaves all discolored. I observed the shrine for a long time and started up the small pathway through the fruit trees, thinking to get to the top of the hill. It was then that someone called me with a "Hey, you," from behind. On looking back, I saw the girl in the yellow blouse and red, red skirt of the day before hurrying toward me.

I was indeed very glad, but did not move from where I was, saying only, "What is it?"

The girl, after climbing up to where I stood, said, "Shall we go up and play over there?" pointing to the top of the hill, and looked into my face.

"Yes."

When I consented, she took my hand and started up the hill.

"What's your name?" she asked, looking into my face again.

"Kim Si-kŭn."

"Where do you live?"

"In Kyedong."

"Where's Kyedong?"

"It's very far from here."

While talking, I felt something like soft happiness, for some undefinable reason. I felt like walking to the end of the earth holding hands like that with the girl. Then I thought I would like to know the girl's name, too.

"What's *your* name?"

"My name?" She smiled, perhaps thinking that my question was unlike a child's, and answered, "I'm called Ŭlsun."

I felt I wanted to know more about the girl.

"Are you the younger sister of the new bride of this house?"

"No. The bride is my little lady."

I could not understand what she meant, so I asked again, "Your little lady?"

"Yes, she is a bride now, but . . ."

I still couldn't see what she meant but didn't ask further. Later on I found out that Ŭlsun was a maid Chong-gǔn's bride had brought from her own home when she married.

In the meantime we reached the top of the hill, at the base of the baked tile wall. Beneath the wall was a level lawn.

"Let's play here." So saying, Ŭlsun seated me on the lawn and sat down herself beside me. Looking down, I saw the inner and outer quarters of the house lying prostrate, the tiled roofs looking as stately as the backs of huge whales, and beyond them the sweeping view of the river—the water, the white sand, the vast landscape that I had looked upon the day before with such great ecstasy. I felt shy at Ŭlsun's fumbling with my hand, so I said: "Why is the river so blue?" pointing to the river.

"It's blue because it's a river," she said, and moving still closer to me, looked directly into my face.

"How old are you?" she asked.

"Seven."

"Do you have an elder sister?"

"Yes."

"How old is she?"

"Fifteen."

"She must be pretty. Is she?"

I had till then never thought my elder sister pretty, but I didn't like to tell strangers my sister was homely, so I just said "Yes."

"Do you have older brothers?"

"Yes, I have one."

"How old is he?"

"Twelve."

"Is he also good-looking, like you?"

I was about to say yes but Ŭlsun suddenly squeezed my face with one hand on either cheek and shivered. That act of Ŭlsun made me somehow deliciously happy, till I felt my whole body in a tremor, but it also suddenly made me afraid. I was afraid, for some reason, that she might get at me to beat me up and pinch me.

"No. No. I don't like it."

I shook my head and tried to take Ŭlsun's hands from my cheeks, but Ŭlsun just smiled gaily and didn't let go of me.

"No. No. I really don't like it."

I shook my head more forcibly than before, and my face became tearful. Only then did Ŭlsun take away her hands and said, "Oh, poor boy. I didn't mean anything. I just like you, that's all."

Then after a little while she said, "Don't tell anybody we played here together," and looked into my face once more. I nodded my promise.

A little later Ŭlsun said, "Oh, my lady must be looking for me," as if suddenly remembering something. Then, springing to her feet and saying, "Let's play again later," she ran down the hill.

Looking at her descending figure from the back, I felt sorry. I felt regretful, too, thinking that she might have gone away because I shook my head. I also thought that if she did that again, next time I would be still. But presently I forgot all about such things and started to trot around on the hill.

6

After that, during my several days' sojourn in Ch'angrangjŏng, I became fast friends with Ŭlsun and we played together as often as we could get together in the hillside garden of the house. Sometimes we gathered shepherd's purse in baskets, and sometimes dug in the earth for bindweed root to eat. Such pleasures were novel and exciting to me, since till then I had never been away from the heart of the city. During that time a most impressive event took place which is an indispensable part of my memory of Ch'angrangjŏng.

One evening we went up the hill to collect bindweed roots again, as Ŭlsun suggested. With a wooden stick in hand, we dug up the soft earth here and there and fumbled about in the dirt with our fingers. Then the crisp bindweed root could be sorted out. If you brushed away the earth and put it into your mouth and chewed, soft juice would flow into your mouth together with the smell of the earth. The half-cent Japanese cakes or candies were nothing compared with the taste of bindweed roots. At first, from time to time I chewed on some other tough grass roots, mistaking them for bindweed roots, and spat them out in disgust, but by and by I learned to discern easily between bindweed roots and other grass roots. Ŭlsun could gather a heap of bindweed roots in no time at all, and after brushing the earth off the roots, she gave them to me to eat. She even stuffed them into my vest pockets for me to take home and eat, till the pockets were nearly bursting.

It was almost sundown. Ŭlsun was collecting bindweed roots a few feet away, and I was digging in the earth also, when the tip of my wooden stick touched something hard. At first I didn't pay much attention to it and poked the ground around. A hard object there blocked the stick again. Wondering what it might be, I dug to find that something like rotted wood came out of the earth. On digging further, a whitish gleam like that of iron appeared.

"Look, what do you think this is?" I presently called to Ŭlsun.

"What?" Ŭlsun ran to me at once. Leaning down, she dug away the dirt around it some more and looked into the hole, and then suddenly straightened up, shouting, "It's a sword, a sword!" It was indeed a sword. We had exposed the middle of a long sword buried horizontally in the earth. Ŭlsun said, "You wait a little. I'll fetch a hoe," and ran down the hill.

After a good while of strenuous digging, we bared a great sword longer than my height and so heavy I could hardly lift it. The rotted scabbard was attached to it in only a few places, and fell away while we were digging it up; but the sword itself, after we brushed the earth away from it, was whole, as if it had been made just the day before, and its blade sharp. The hilt and the grip were covered with strange engravings and the splendid pure gold decoration shone, dazzling the eyes.

"Oh!" I shouted with emotion and, mustering all the strength in my body, lifted the sword and wielded it under the darkening sky. The tip of the sword glittered in the evening sun.

"Don't! You'll hurt yourself."

I pushed away Ŭlsun, who tried to stop me, and raising the sword again, wielded it with all my might. I cannot forget till this day the magnificent sensation of that day, when I felt as if I had become a mighty general of ancient stories with a great sword.

I don't know how precious a treasure the sword was, or what became of it after that. But that it must surely have been a renowned sword could be guessed from the fact that although it had been buried perhaps scores of years in the earth and the scabbard had all rotted away, the blade itself was not rusted to any serious degree.

I can still vividly recall the deeply touched expression on His Excellency's face that night when he repeatedly opened and closed his eyes with the sword before him. His Excellency said, as if to himself, "Not such a great wonder, since this house once belonged to General Chŏng," and sat buried deep in thought. Of course there is no way of knowing who General Chŏng was, nor why he had buried such a valuable sword in the ground. But I could tell that there must be a deep secret and a hidden story behind the sword from the expression on His Excellency's face that night.

The major part of my memory of Ch'angrangjŏng is recorded above. But if this had been all, Ch'angrangjŏng would not have occupied my mind so much, nor would I have written of it in the form of a story. People are apt to feel more attachment to something gone by, something that has disappeared, than to things of the present, things before our eyes. Ch'angrangjŏng has disappeared without a trace. It evokes my nostalgia the more powerfully because it now is no more.

The chronicle of Ch'angrangjŏng after that date would in itself make a long novel, so I will not touch on it here, but only tell the main parts of it: Her Ladyship died within a year of my first visit there, and a few years after that His Excellency also passed away at almost ninety years of age. Within one year of his death his daughter-in-law, the grandmother of Chong-gŭn, also died. Not only have people passed away, but the line of His Excellency which enjoyed glory and wealth for decades also went down amid the rough climate of the changing world, like a giant tree that had withstood the wind and rain for hundreds of years silently failing to sprout new leaves one spring after a harsh winter.

7

What precipitated the downfall of the house was Chong-gŭn's dissipation. When the older people died one after another, Chong-gŭn, who

had till then studied Chinese classics at home under tutors, suddenly
cut his hair short, put on Western-style clothes and started frequenting
pleasure haunts. By the time of the second anniversary of His
Excellency's death, even the title of the house itself had gone over to
others and Ch'angrangjŏng looked just like a skull. Thus I, who had
gone to that house with Father as if visiting some longed-for country
home, could not but be astonished and grieved at such a drastic change
in it. Not a shadow remained of the many people bustling in the house;
it was caved in in several places, and the garden was overgrown with
weeds. Only about a dozen people gathered in that great house to
commemorate the death of His Excellency. On the hill where Ŭlsun
and I had played, not even a single healthy-looking fruit tree remained.
In the living room which once teemed with young ladies in indigo blue
skirts, Chong-gŭn's bride, looking sallow and shabby as a mouse, was
preparing the offering table with an old cook. I could not believe that
this was my sister-in-law who had looked as fair as the full moon.

That night, in the main study which used to be occupied by His
Excellency, seven or eight people gathered around my father to remi-
nisce about the old days in sorrowful, low voices. I was sixteen then,
so I could understand most of what the older people were talking
about. My father was relating, deep into the night, how the site of
Ch'angrangjŏng had been a battleground during the Japanese invasion
of the sixteenth century and how, when Admiral Rose of France sailed
up the Han River from Kanghwa Island leading three warships in a
reprisal for the execution of missionary priests and made the whole
court tremble in fear back in the Taewŏngun days, it was right in front
of the Ch'angrangjŏng garden that the admiral and his crew had anchored for many days. It was none other than His Excellency himself
among all the courtiers who most urgently insisted on repulsing the
Western barbarians.

I listened with emotion to my father's words, looking at the great-
grandson of His Excellency, Chong-gŭn, who squirmed now and
then, as if the ceremonial mourning robe of rough hemp bothered
him, and who was sitting with bowed head like a coward. My
father's voice flowed on like a quiet stream, and the night was deep
and all around was silence. When I raised my eyes toward the offering table in the corner, I saw the yellow flame of the tallow candle
shiver and stretch upward toward the ceiling without a breeze, and
then shrink back again.

In the course of the twenty years after that, Ch'angrangjŏng disappeared without a trace, during which time my father passed away and I have been going my own way. Chong-gŭn's family gave up living in Seoul long ago and went down to the country town of our clan. During all this while I had not forgotten Ch'angrangjŏng, but had not too painfully missed it either, but for some reason I dreamed of Ch'angrangjŏng no less than three nights in a row this spring. In my dreams I was always the seven-year-old boy, and the evening glow spread in the sky over Ch'angrangjŏng, and in the main study there was the silver beard of His Excellency and the yellow candlelight, and my father raised his stick to point out Ch'angrangjŏng to me, and on the garden hill I was playing with Ŭlsun in the evening sunlight.

After I woke up in the morning from my third dream, I could not calm my longing, so vivid was the dream of the night before. Looking back, I realized that though I had been living not far away from it I had not been to Ch'angrangjŏng even once in all the nearly twenty years since the night of the commemoration service for His Excellency. It was a Sunday, again in the month of March, so after lunch I set out from home as if to go for a walk, with a camera strapped to my shoulder.

Taking a trolley for the first time in my life and getting off at Sŏgang, I tried to find my way to Ch'angrangjŏng, reviving my memory. But strangely, I could not find my way to the house; which hill the house had stood on and which was the house itself I could not make out, even though they had been so vivid in my dreams. With difficulty I found a place which looked like the grounds where the mansion used to stand, but the hill on which the house had been standing was one bald mass of red earth, and on the site which seemed to be the old site of Ch'angrangjŏng a large, unfamiliar factory was standing, shooting up black smoke out of its sky-high chimney.

Disappointed at such a drastic change, I walked about for a good while on the heap of coal ash in front of the factory and tried to recapture memories of the past. The blue water was rolling below as in the old times, beneath the precipice in front of the yard. But from the gloomy scowling heaven only a chilly wind blew, although it was spring. The endless clicking of the machines in the factory mercilessly jolted my mind that was trying to revive old memories.

Was Ch'angrangjŏng a thing that could exist only in the fairyland of memory, in a dreamland enveloped in cloud and fog? My mind, which had been bemused in languid reverie, slowly woke up to the hard reality before me.

A loud noise of some engine streaked the sand beyond the river. Looking up, I saw an ultra-modern twin-engine passenger airplane gliding down the runway in the far distance at Yŏido Airport. While I was watching, the airplane took off and, with an atrocious explosive sound, ascended into the air slowly, then swiftly. It was an ultra-modern all-metal passenger plane that glides over rivers and mountains, over national boundaries, threatening to traverse the whole sky over many continents in one dash.

My Idiot Uncle

Ch'ae Man-shik

Born in 1902, Ch'ae Man-shik was, like the uncle of "My Idiot Uncle" (1937), an intellectual in colonial Korea, where there were few openings for decent white-collar jobs, and few opportunities for constructive work. Like many such intellectuals of the day, Ch'ae Man-shik became a writer and a sympathizer with the leftist movement. He was a charter member of the Korean Artists' Proletarian Federation (KAPF), but resigned his membership when the federation turned extremist. He worked on and off as a reporter for Korean newspapers and wrote short stories depicting the plight of intellectuals in a society where they felt themselves to be superfluous, or humorous sketches of unenlightened rural people trying to adjust shrewdly to the changing world.

From 1938 he began writing novels, which attracted notice for his keen satirical wit, power of description, fluent narrative and penetration into the complicated maladies of the rapidly changing world and the subsequent collapse of values. Although today Ch'ae Man-shik is celebrated mainly as a writer of satire, his contribution is more substantial and far-ranging. He was burdened with tuberculosis and poverty for many years of his life, and therefore his promise was not quite fulfilled when he died of the disease at the age of forty-eight in 1950.

My uncle? Oh, you mean that husband of the lady who's my father's first cousin? The one who went around preaching . . . what do they call it? . . . socialism in his youth and went to jail because of that, and is now sick in bed with tuberculosis?

Oh, don't speak of him to me. All that foolishness of his! There's simply no word fit to describe it.

Was there ever another man who ruined himself like that! His ten years of studying, his college education, all gone to waste; his youth spent with no useful outcome; his name besmirched as a jailbird; his body eaten away by that evil disease; and he just keeps lying there doing nothing in a cave-like room in that hovel, with eyes closed, day in and day out.

Needless to say, he has no property nor estate. How could he? Swing your arms right and left as freely as you like in that room, there's not a piece of furniture to hinder you. Not a thing in that dingy room but cold poverty.

It's my aunt, my nice, kind, gentle aunt who keeps him from starving, what with sewing and washing for others, peddling cosmetics, or doing whatever work she can come by.

It'd be better for everybody, for himself too, if he were to die, but he doesn't even have the decency to drop dead.

My aunt, what a pitiful woman she is! Why didn't she try to improve her lot when she still had her youth? Why go on toiling away like that? What kind of future comfort can she hope for out of that kind of life?

It's nearly twenty years since she was abandoned by her husband.

It's a pitiful sight, her going around like that trying to get work to make a living and tending his illness, after sighing and weeping away the whole twenty years of her youth, having taken back for a husband a half-dead corpse that he was.

What sins does she have to expiate that she must shoulder a burden like that? She says it's her fate, but why shouldn't one change one's fate? That's what the old-fashioned Chosŏn* women are like, ignorant and backward.

It'd be a kindness to my aunt if he'd die soon.

Kind-hearted and skilled in all kinds of household work, she could surely find a comfortable home anywhere.

Let's see. She was sixteen when she married that fool, and that was when I was three, so it's been eighteen years. That's nearly two decades, isn't it?

---

*Chosŏn is the old name for Korea. [Translator]

Well, that uncle of mine was a mere schoolboy at the time, true, but for almost ten years he roamed around Seoul and Tokyo on the pretext of studying, and then when he got old enough to know women, he just drove my aunt back to her home, asking her to give him a divorce, as if that would make him look sophisticated or something.

Why, after he came back from his studies, he just jumped into that God-damned thing, socialism, like crazy, and got himself a so-called educated woman. I saw that mistress of his three or four times, but believe me, she was no beauty, that woman. How could a woman presume to be a man's mistress with that kind of face? Well, there's an old saying that beauties get cast aside but the ugly ones don't. Anyway, my deserted aunt was at least five times as pretty as that mistress of his.

And then he got arrested and served a jail term of no less than five years. Meanwhile both my aunt's and my uncle's families had gone broke, so my aunt had no support. So she came to Seoul to try and make a living, and also to prepare to meet her husband when he got out of prison. She looked to me for help in getting on. That was the year before that uncle of mine came out of jail.

I was hardly more than a kid at the time, but I tried all I could do, and luckily I soon found her a place as a housemaid at Mr. Kurada's.

At that time I counseled my aunt over and over again that she should get married again, instead of living like that. Young as I was then, I felt sorry for her, she looked so pitiful.

And there was a good eligible man, too. There was a Mr. Minne, who sold bananas in front of the Mitsukoshi Department Store. A nice man, too, I'd say.

My master knows him well, too, and Mr. Minne asked me time and again to make a match for him with a Chosŏn woman, saying that he'd like to live with a Chosŏn girl.

He hasn't got any great wealth to speak of, but he makes a comfortable living, so wouldn't my aunt have an easy life if she lived with a man like that? But my aunt, she just rebuked me for saying shameful things, and wouldn't listen to me. There simply was no helping her.

Well, apart from that, I really did give her a lot of help. I'm not saying this to boast about my goodness. And to be frank, it isn't that I don't owe her something, too.

I lost my parents at seven. I was left destitute with no one to look after me. So my aunt, who was living at her own house after being cast aside by that husband of hers, took me in and brought me up. Until that time, her family was not badly off. My aunt was very fond of me, and her grandparents—my great-grandmother and great-grandfather—loved me dearly, having no small children in the house.

I grew up in that house until I was twelve. And I was given four years of schooling, too, even though only a primary education. If that family hadn't been ruined like that, I'd have been living with them till now, and maybe I'd be going to college.

Well, you can't say I didn't repay her for what I owe her as well as I could. Nobody can say I'm ungrateful.

Oh, well, my aunt comes to me to beg for help from time to time, saying she has run out of grain. And in truth, it's pretty bothersome. If I were to give her help every time she asked for it, I wouldn't be able to manage my own affairs. So most of the time I give a definite no.

But of course I don't neglect to send them a couple of pounds of meat at New Year, and drop in on them from time to time to make conversation. So you can't say I neglect them.

However that may be, my aunt saved her five won monthly salary for a whole year while she worked as Mr. Kurada's housemaid, and the Kuradas, they gave her a bonus of seven won for having been a good servant when she left them. All in all, she really did manage to save a good hundred won.

With that money she rented a room, bought some pots and pans, and took that precious husband of hers there after he had finished his prison term.

The day he was released, I went with my aunt to meet him. Though he had cast her aside like that, I saw tears gather in his eyes when he saw my aunt waiting there at the prison gate.

The mistress he doted on so much, not even her shadow made an appearance. Well, that's what mistresses are like, the whole lot of them. But this uncle of mine, he looked around to see if that woman had come to meet him. That's the kind of idiot he is. Except for my aunt and me, there wasn't a soul in sight, not even a puppy, to say nothing of the woman.

We were just putting him into a taxi when he vomited blood. I heard later that he began vomiting blood in prison about a month before his release. So we carried the half-dead body to my aunt's room and laid him down there. And from that day my aunt went everywhere, did everything anyone could possibly do, to get a cure for his illness. So by and by he got better, and he's almost all right by now. He's a dragon now compared to when he came out of prison. A dragon, I say.

It's an amazing thing, a woman's devotion.

It's been three whole years. For three whole years she's been working like that for him. Honest, I couldn't have done that even to bring
my dead father and mother back to life.

So if that uncle of mine has any kind of conscience or anything like
that, he'd have to make up his mind to get well as soon as possible, to
earn as much money as possible to secure his wife some comfort, and
repay her for what she's done for him and expiate the sins of his past.
Now, isn't that what he should be doing?

If he were to repay her for what she's done for him, it wouldn't be
enough even if he were to carry her around on his back all the time, so
as not to let her step on dirt again.

Anyway, he should have some resolution by now. Well, since he is
a jailbird, he won't be able to get a place in the government or in a
business, however determined he might be, but that's nobody's fault
but his own, so he has no one to blame. He should be making a living
anyway, even if by rough labor.

Say, it would be a spectacle, wouldn't it, for a university graduate to
be working as a day laborer, but what help for it can there be?

When I compare his case and mine—considering that if my great-
grandfather's family hadn't gone bankrupt like that, perhaps I'd have
finished college or university by now, and would perhaps have been
like that uncle—then I think it's fortunate that I didn't get to be a
college graduate but was placed early in the path I'm going now.

This pitiful uncle, he's gone to college and finished it too, but now
he has nothing ahead of him but to become a day laborer. But look at
me, I've had no more than four years of schooling, but I have a bright,
shining future ahead of me. My uncle's lot isn't one whit better than a
page boy's, compared to mine.

But now look at what he's doing, the fool, now that he's out of
death's jaw, instead of trying to make a living by hard labor or something like that. I can only laugh!

What devil has got into him, that he should dive into it again like a
madman? Why can't he just leave it alone? What's there to be got out
of that? Food? Fame? What except persecution and imprisonment?
Maybe that thing's just like opium. One can't leave it alone, I guess,
once one's had a taste of it.

But if you get to know something about it, there's nothing exciting or sweet or anything like that in it. It's nothing but gangsterism.

That's it, gangsterism, nothing more, nothing less.

Let me tell you what it is. My master told me all about it. In a faraway country, somewhere in the West, some lazy bums got together in a sunny place one day and tried to think of a way they could eat without working. So these bums, they said to each other: in this world there are rich men and poor men. And that's not fair at all. All men have the same features and limbs. It's utterly unfair that some are rich and some are poor, all being born alike. So it's only justice for us to take from the rich what they have and divide it equally among us poor people.

Oh, that's right! Well said! Let's all eat what the rich have.

So, that's how it became a move . . . a movement at first, started by those bums.

What is it if not a robber's game, pure and simple?

In this world, each man has his own share of luck, so that if one is born at a fortunate hour or if one is diligent he will become rich, and if one is born at an unlucky hour or is lazy, he will live poor. That's the way it is, and that's the fair providence of heaven. How dare anybody say it's unfair? What are they but gangsters, those who'd take away and eat up what other people have earned?

Not only is it gangsterism, but if the world goes on the way they want it to, the idle ones will go on idling and keep on pillaging the rich, so wouldn't the world come to be filled with robbers, the whole world? And won't the world be ruined when the rich people don't have anything left to be stolen?

If everybody stopped tilling the land, waiting for other people to grow grain so they could eat for nothing, and if everybody stopped weaving, waiting for other people to weave so they could be clothed for nothing, where in the world would grain and clothes come from? That would be the end of the world for sure!

Poor ignorant creatures, especially the lazy ones among them, not knowing that it's such an accursed thing, jump into that move . . . movement headlong, decoyed by the notion of taking away and eating up the possessions of the rich.

That's what's happening in Russia. As sure as anything, the farmers there, they wouldn't till the land to grow grain, so people are dying of hunger by tens of thousands. Didn't I tell you it's clear and simple like that? Serves them right, too.

But this pestilent fad, it spread like mad everywhere in the East and

West, and for a while it spread pretty vigorously in Japan, and all the bums in Chosŏn, they imitated that, sure enough, because it was the fashion in Japan, not knowing what it was all about. But now the movement's pretty weak, and not many bums are active in it, thanks to the strong government repression.

And that's how it should be, too. If it's a good thing, why on earth would the government forbid it, and arrest those bums and put them in jail?

If it was a good and profitable thing, the government would spur it on and would give prizes to those who do it well, too. The moving pictures, the comedy shows, the wrestling matches, the colorful ceremonies for sending dead souls to the other world, the carnivals and the exercises to radio music, they are all good and profitable things, so the government encourages them. Right?

What is a government, anyway? A government is supposed to know what's good and profitable for the people, and tell people how to do this and that and what to do and what not to do, so the people can live in peace, as well as they are able.

Take that . . . socialism, for example. What would have become of the world by now if the government had let them do as they liked? Lots and lots of people would have been ruined, and *I* would have been ruined most of all! All my plans would have been upset and me ruined, ruined!

Here's my hope and my plan. My master, he's especially fond of me and trusts me, so in ten years or so he's going to set me up in an independent trade, that's almost for sure. Then, with that as a springboard, I'll work hard at commerce for thirty years, and I plan to make a hundred thousand won by the time I'm sixty. With a hundred thousand won, that's as good as owning land yielding two thousand bags of rice a year. So I can be as proud as I choose to be.

And what with what my master told me, I've set my mind on marrying a Japanese woman. My master said he will make a match for me with a good Japanese girl. Oh, Japanese girls are swell!

I wouldn't have a Chosŏn woman, even if anybody offered me one for nothing. The old-fashioned women, they're modest but ignorant, so they can't help me make friends with Japanese people. And the new girls, they wouldn't do either, because they may not be ignorant, but they're conceited. So, old-fashioned or new, I wouldn't have anything to do with Chosŏn women.

Japanese women are the best. Every one of them is pretty, proper, tender, and even the ones that aren't ignorant are modest. How lovely they are!

Not only will I marry a Japanese woman, but I will change my name to a Japanese name, too, and live in a Japanese house, wear Japanese clothes, eat like the Japanese do, give Japanese names to my children, and send them to Japanese schools. . . .

It must be to Japanese schools that my children will go. The Chosŏn schools, they're so dirty, my children would be ruined. . . .

And I wouldn't speak this language any more either, but speak only the national language. You have to live like the Japanese do first. That's the way to earn money like the Japanese.

So I have my plan all set up for making a hundred thousand won, and I have my road clear before me, and I'm going that way with sure, giant steps. So how can I help but have the shudders to hear of these mad, murderous ruffians pushing socialism to ruin the world? Oh, it gives me the creeps to hear that word!

What would become of me if the world is turned upside down by them? All my plans and my hard work, they would all have been to no avail. Nothing could be more unfair than that.

Oh, my master, his words are all true, every one of them. Crimes like theft, robbery, swindling, those kinds of crimes take only the amount stolen or swindled one time, so they are not such dreadful crimes compared to this damned . . . socialism. This socialism just turns the whole world upside down and upsets the whole country, so they can never be forgiven, that's what my master said.

Forgive them! If it had been left to me, I'd have wrung the neck of every single one of . . . .

To be frank with you, when I think of such things, my uncle also looks almost like a ruffian. If it hadn't been for my aunt, why on earth would I bother to drop in on him now and then, when he even has that dreadful disease? I couldn't care a straw even if he were to drop dead.

Well, I wouldn't be so harsh on him if he repented his past crimes and mended his ways, but he wouldn't. Like the saying has it, like, you know, "Dye the white dog's tail a hundred times, it will turn white again," and stuff like that. . . .

That's why he's so hateful to me, and that's why, even when I do get to chatting with him when I drop in on them, I just throw in sarcastic words to hurt him or drive him in the corner by picking on what he says.

Just the other day, I gave it to him good. And look what he did. He told my aunt that I've been completely spoiled, that I was a good-for-nothing.

Boy, did that make me laugh! What kind of gall does he have anyway that he could call *me* spoiled, a worthless good-for-nothing? He, of all people!

If I was him, I wouldn't have had a word to say, even if all the dummies in Chosŏn could suddenly speak, but he seems to think that anything coming out of his mouth will be considered a revelation.

So I suppose that was an admonition? And he admonished me through my aunt, indirectly, because if he said a thing like that to my face I'd certainly teach him a thing or two, I suppose.

Oh, what presumption! That's why God gave us two nostrils instead of one, so that people can breathe, even when they hear stupefying things like that.

So he thinks I am a spoiled, good-for-nothing, washed-up man! Me, a promising youth with a bright future ahead for sure, and who's praised all around for being a bright, able, proper boy; one who got awarded for model service no less than twice, even though I didn't have as much schooling as he had, and am still a mere clerk?

Oh, yeah, that's it, of course! He thinks anything he does is right, so naturally everything I do is wrong. He'd have thought me a good, sound young man if I'd followed that accursed thing socialism and became a jailbird and a consumptive like him, instead of a spoiled, ruined man! Good heavens!

I guess the proverb about the log in one's own eye or something like that was made for people like my uncle. This is how it went that day. I just gave him a good lesson, and that made him say things like that about me to my aunt.

That day was a holiday for me, so I called on them in the morning because I had a few words to say to my aunt. Aunt was away at work sewing for a bride-to-be, and only my uncle was there, lying on the warm part of the floor as usual.

Well, he had a heap of old magazines in the Chosŏn language by his pillow (wherever did he collect all those dusty things?) and was looking through them. So to while away the time I picked one up and thumbed through it. But that was no amusing magazine, nothing interesting for reading.

Chosŏn people, they can't even make a magazine right. No pictures, no comic strips. And then they are full of all those difficult Chinese characters. How do they imagine anybody can read them?

For the likes of us, we can manage to read the Chosŏn alphabet, but it's not very easy. We can't understand things written in difficult Chosŏn alphabet mixed with Chinese characters. Those written only in the Chosŏn alphabet are novels, and believe me, they *are* hard to read. Besides, the novels Chosŏn people write are not the least bit interesting. Oh, I've kept away from those Chosŏn newspapers and magazines for a long time now.

Speaking of magazines, there's no magazine to top "King" or "Shonen Kurabu." Gee, are they swell! All the Chinese characters are annotated in Kana, so no matter where you open it, you can just start reading right on at top speed, and there isn't a thing you don't know the meaning of. And every passage in them has either a profitable moral lesson or an exciting adventure.

Oh, the novels are good, too. Those by Kang Kikuchi, especially. Are they tender, romantic, and exciting! And the glittering, jingling historicals of Eichi Yoshikawa, they make my shoulders dance, just to read them.

The novels are exciting, all of them, there are plenty of comics, lots of pictures, and are they cheap, too! For just fifteen cents you can buy a Japanese magazine no more than a month old, and after reading everything in it, you can return it too and get five cents back.

Now that's how a magazine ought to be made. But these Chosŏn people, they always boast about everything, but they can't even make a magazine right.

So that day too, I wasn't going to read any of it, but was just leafing through one of them, hoping to find a picture or a comic strip, when my eyes happened to light on my uncle's name! That was a surprise, so I lifted it closer to my eyes and glanced through it. In the title there were words like economic and social and others, which were explained in the footnotes in small letters.

That was enough for me. Economics, that's what my uncle learned in college, so he ought to know all about it. And social, he ought to know a great deal about that, too, because he followed socialism. So that's what he must have written, what's economy and what's socialism and which of them is right and things of that sort.

Oh, there was no need to read it all. Since he's a man who went all the way through college to learn economics, but got caught up in socialism instead of making money, he must have insisted that economy is wrong and socialism is right.

But I glanced through it all the same because that was the first relative of mine that got his name in a magazine, but there was simply no way to read it. I could make out most of the letters all right, except the most difficult ones, but any way I put them together, I couldn't make head or tail of what it meant.

It didn't make me feel too good, so I gave up reading and placed the article before him, to have a word or two with him.

"Uncle?"

"Yes?"

"You write here economic something and then social something. Then, which do you mean one should follow—economy, or socialism?"

"What?"

He rolled his eyes, not understanding my question. Maybe it was so long ago he wrote it that he had forgotten it, or maybe he couldn't answer it right away because I put my question in too difficult words. So I began questioning him further.

"Uncle! Economy means that one should make a lot of money, save it and become rich, doesn't it? But socialism means that one should take away the money that rich people have saved, doesn't it?"

"What on earth are you . . . "

"No, listen to me."

"Who on earth told you those definitions of economics and socialism?"

"No need to be told. Doesn't economy mean to earn as much money as possible, to spend as little of it as possible, and save the rest of it?"

"Oh, no. That's just what we mean when we say economizing. Economics and economy have far different meanings."

"How different? Economy means accumulating money. So economics must mean the science of how to become rich."

"No. Not at all. That may be management of finance, but economics isn't anything like that at all."

"Then you have gone to college in vain. What use was it for you to study economics for five years if you haven't learned how to become rich? I often wondered why, uncle, though you went to college to study economy, you still haven't made any money. Now I see that it's because you didn't learn your studies right."

"Didn't learn my studies right? Well, that may very well be. I guess you're right! You *are*."

Look at that! I had him nailed down at once. That's the kind of fool he is, even though he went to college and everything.

"Uncle?"

"Yes?"

"Then, since in college you didn't study economics to save money and become rich, but studied socialism to take money away from rich people . . . "

"Now, what are you thinking socialism is?"

"I know perfectly well what it is."

And I explained to him everything about socialism. He just lay there, looking up at my face, and then he smiled, like a fool. Then listen to what he says:

"Is that socialism? That's gangsterism."

"So you know that socialism is gangsterism, uncle?"

"When did I say socialism is gangsterism?"

"You said it just now."

"Well, I said what you described was not socialism but gangsterism."

"There! So that's what socialism is—sheer gangsterism. You say so yourself, and then you insist it isn't."

"Now, is this boy trying to pick a quarrel?"

Look at that! He just didn't know how to answer me. That's how he is with me most of the time.

"Uncle?"

"What?"

"*Do* change your mind, uncle."

"How do you mean?"

"Aren't you worried?"

"What kind of worry would a man like me have? I'm worried about *you*."

"Oh, I have my plans all set, well and good."

"How?"

"Here's how." And I explained all about my future plans.

Then listen to what he says after listening to all I told him: "My, what a pitiful boy you are!"

"Why?"

He couldn't say why.

"Now tell me. Why do you say I'm pitiful?"

He still couldn't say why.

"Why? Uncle?"

Still no response.

"Uncle?"

"What?"

"Did you say I'm pitiful?"

"No. I was just talking to myself."

"Yes?"

"For a man, whoever he may be, there is nothing so shameful as to be a flunky."

"Flunky?"

"Yes. Be he king or beggar, everyone must live within his means, in this world under this system. Nothing's more shameful than to flatter for a living, debasing one's own character, and no one's more to be pitied than those flunkies. Two bowls of rice cannot make a man's stomach fuller than one bowl of rice."

"What does that mean?"

"I mean about your wanting to marry a Japanese girl and changing your way of living completely to Japanese style, even going to the extent of changing your name."

"Why, isn't that good?"

"That's what I'm talking about. If you have decided to do that out of deep conviction, it would be different; it might even be good. But it seems to me like you have other intentions."

"What other intentions?"

"That you mean to flatter and please your master and your neighbors by doing so."

"Why, of course! I must earn the trust of my master and get along nicely with the Japanese neighbors. Isn't that what I should do?"

He had no words to contradict me with.

"How little you know about the world, uncle! Though you are older than me and had university learning, you don't know the world as well as I do, me who has struggled in it from early years. What kind of a world do you think this is we are living in now?"

"Look."

"Yes?"

"You're talking about the world?"

"Yes."

"And you say you have a guaranteed bright future ahead of you?"

"Sure."

"And you say you'll have saved a hundred thousand won by the time you're sixty?"

"Sure."

"Well, I suppose you and I mean different things when we speak of knowing the world, but keep in mind that the world is not as easy to live in as you think."

"Why?"

"A man, however hard he may strive, cannot escape the power of the force that sweeps the world, that flows invisibly but strongly—this is what we may call the current of history. One has to be governed by it, and there's no helping it at all."

"What?"

"To put it simply, however good plans one may set up, and however many opportunities one may make, things don't always go the way one wishes."

"Gosh, uncle! The other day in the magazine *King* I read about the hero of the West, Napoleon. He said that one must create opportunities oneself, and that 'impossible' is a word to be found only in the dictionary of fools. What is there in the world that wouldn't go the way it should, if one keeps on thinking, planning, making opportunities and struggling hard? If one fails once, one must stand up again with redoubled courage. Don't you know about rising up for the eighth time after the seventh fall?"

"Well, Napoleon had success when he went along with the tide of the times, but failed when he tried to go against it. Have you seen only those who rose up and succeeded after the seventh fall, but never heard that there are many who fall for good after failing at the ninth try?"

"But just wait and see! I will succeed, whatever happens with the world. That's what's wrong with you, uncle. You just despair even before you try to fight for something."

"Do you have to try climbing up to the sky to know that it's high?"

Look at that. Making a preposterous comparison because he doesn't know how to contradict me. What kind of reasoning is that? Would there be such idiots on earth as not to know the sky's high without trying to climb up to it?

I was going to let him get away with that, but it was kind of boring, sitting there in that dingy room, so I talked some more.

"Uncle?"

"Yes?"

"What are you going to do after you get completely cured?"

"What do you mean?"

"About your future?"

"My future?"

"What are you going to do?"

"What can there be for me to do, at this stage?"

"So you're going to live like that, without any plans?"

"Why do you say without plans?"

"Do you have any plan, then?"

"I may have."

"What is it?"

"Living like I have been living."

"You mean doing that thing, the . . . what you call it, again?"

"I suppose so."

"Uncle?"

No response.

"Uncle?"

"What?"

"Leave off now."

"Leave off?"

"Yes."

"Do you think I do it for a pastime?"

"Don't you?"

No response.

"Uncle?"

"What?"

"How old are you?"

"Thirty-three."

"So why don't you just leave that thing alone now and try to look after your home?"

"Look after my home for what?"

"What are you doing that thing for?"

"It's not because it's of any practical use that I follow it."

"Then you do it without any hope or goal?"

"Goal? Hope?"

"Yes."

"Well, personal goals and hopes, they're on a different level . . . .They do not matter . . ."

"My, what kind of law is that?"

"Law?"

"Law!"

"Hm . . . Law . . ."

"Uncle!"

No answer.

"Uncle?"

"What?"

"Aren't you grateful to my aunt?"

"I am."

"Aren't you sorry?"

"Sorry? Yes. I am sorry."

"So you know she is to be pitied?"

"Yes. I know."

"You know she is pitiful, but you insist on living like that?"

"Well, there are people in this world who incur pain willingly, who savor sweetness out of the bitterness of pain. I don't mean there are unusual people of that sort. I mean that when a person concentrates his heart and mind upon one thing, then one tastes sweetness in the bitterness of pain. Then pain becomes a pleasure. It is like that in the case of your aunt. She is suffering much, but she does not take it as pain. She is taking pleasure out of her hardships."

"Then you're happy about it?"

"No, I'm not."

"Then why don't you try to repay her for what she's done for you?"

"It's not that I don't know what I owe her, but . . ."

"Then when you get all right again, you must . . ."

"Oh, I've got so much to do!"

Now, just listen to that! Saying he's got so much to do, a guy who fritters away his time lying on his back! Oh, he's just impossible. He'll never be any use to anybody, any more than a clipped-off fingernail. As long as he lives he will live on other people, troubling them, doing harm to the world. A person like that ought to die as soon as possible. He ought to die, and deserves to die over and over. But he just won't do it, but keeps on squirming like that. Ah, it's just so annoying. . . .

A Ceremony of Apostasy

Chung Bi-suk

Born in 1911, Chung Bi-suk, at the beginning of his career, produced works marked by a strong romanticism. A loving contemplation of nature and a yearning for an undefiled life surrounded by clean and healthy nature were characteristic features of his early stories. They also expressed a longing for pure, romantic love and reverence for the lofty, unworldly character. "A Ceremony of Apostasy" (1937) is suffused with both his romanticism and idealism. His romanticism may have been a reflection of his dissatisfaction with, and yearning to escape the humiliating reality of, a country under the colonial yoke, and the powerlessness of intellectuals to change the situation. As did many other writers of the day, he made his living by taking reporting jobs, and made writing his avocation.

His literary career made a sharp turn in 1953 when he surprised the world with his serialized novel, The Liberated Wife, *which depicted an ennui-ridden professor's wife drifting into adultery. The novel caused moral shock in conservative Korea and gave rise to angry protests, but it was a huge commercial success, and the author from then on wrote many commercially successful newspaper serials with heavy erotic contents. It is generally conceded that his career as a literary artist was over by 1953. He stopped writing from the late sixties and lived in quiet retirement for a decade, then became active again in his old age to produce multivolume translations and fictionalizations of ancient Chinese historical chronicles and philosophical treatises, which enjoyed considerable success. He passed away in 1991.*

⌒﹏﹏✦

The steam-engine train pushed up the steep slope pantingly. From the top of the mountain the plateau spread out, eight hundred meters above sea level.

A plateau. Even the air itself felt thin. The frosty fog peculiar to mountain areas clung to the windows of the train, so that however hard you kept wiping them, you could not look out the window at the scenery.

Inside, the train was hollow as a cave. Although this train bustles with rich holiday-makers in the summer, on a late autumn day like this passengers are few, and shabby. The scanty number of passengers were mostly old men wearing rustic horsehair hats, or railway construction workers in baggy trousers and canvas shoes. Everyone was quiet, as if silenced by decree, so that only the rhythmic cacophony of the engine reverberated in the car.

Holding the railway timetable open in my hands, I sat for a long time turning over in my mind only the memory of Aera, like a man out of his wits. Then, realizing that Y station, which was my destination, was the next stop, I sprang up and opened the window.

Autumn came much earlier in that area than in Seoul, so that the evening wind blowing in through the window felt cold as ice. I buttoned up my sports jacket and looked up at the mountain that blocked my view.

Mount Sŏrak—wasn't it just last summer that we, my betrothed Aera and I, looked at Sŏrak Mountain together from this window and shared our joyful expectations of summer at the villa?

I have to seek in this chilly season the mountaintop villa where Aera and I spent a full summer of happiness, because I cannot meet Aera again except by invoking memories of the days we spent together.

Although she had never been strong, and though the mountain air must have been too harsh for her acute pneumonia, not having seen her death with my own eyes I could not believe that Aera could have died less than a fortnight after I left her in the villa. Time and again I tried to reconcile myself to her death by telling myself that death cannot be revoked, or by remembering the biblical verse that had been drummed into my ears throughout my three years in the seminary, "Except a corn of wheat fall into the ground and die, it abideth alone: but if it die, it bringeth forth much fruit." But even the sacred verse failed to have any effect on me in this instance.

In my trunk I had the crisp new diploma I had received from the seminary. It was to take the final examination for this diploma that I had left for Seoul alone, leaving Aera at the villa. And then, as soon as the exam was over, I joined the roving evangelistic team of graduating students and set out on a preaching tour to Cheju Island and other places.

Wherever I went, I delivered fervent sermons from the strength of my happiness at the prospect of meeting Aera as soon as the tour was over. And every night I confirmed my vow that we would be faithful disciples of God by dreaming dreams of her.

At the end of the two-and-a-half-month tour I stepped down at Seoul station, my heart bursting with joyful expectations. But all my hopes and dreams vanished like vapor. The first moment I heard of Aera's death from Aegyŏng's lips, I really could not feel anything. Perhaps because, during the two-and-a-half-month tour, I had used the word "death" almost every day. Did I not preach from the pulpit day and night, "Death is not something to be dreaded. There is nothing like death that can purify our lives"?

But when I came back to reality from the spiritual world of God, Aera's death caused me rending sorrow. It was a sorrow that chilled me like icy water poured over my naked body. I had wailed to numerous congregations that "Death is never to be feared." Ah, was it not a fraud? What a horrible hypocrite I was! Believing in an illusion as truth, how many seeds of unhappiness had I sown in how many people, and what a great price I was paying for that!

Time and again I tried to comfort myself with words from the Bible. But all the sacred words that used to give me so much inspiration and strength sounded now like a meaningless murmur uttered in sleep. I wanted to be buried deep in sorrow as a human being rather than to behave like a model Christian. Now I miss human beings—not men who are sons of God, but earthy, numerous, sinful men.

The story I am going to record is a mere rambling discourse concerning how I became an apostate to my faith. The good citizens of the spiritual world will call me a Judas for writing such a record, but I will dare to write.

The train stopped at Y station.

I took down my suitcase and stepped down to the platform. It was a deserted little station, and I was the only one who got off. I had been standing absently for a while, like one who did not know his way, when the station master approached me and asked for my ticket. After glancing at it carefully, he asked in a friendly tone, "Are you here for the first time?"

"Yes. Er . . . no."

I could hardly speak. Hot tears welled up in my eyes. The cordial and courtly manner of the elderly station master aroused in me undefinable feelings of trust and sorrow. I felt a longing to embrace this elderly station master and tearfully explain why I had to visit the mountain villa at such an unseasonable time. I felt as though if I asked him why Aera had to die, this old man could give me the answer.

But just then the train gave off its stentorian starting whistle, so that the old station master had to raise his hand and signal to the conductor. The train that had brought me here left the station without hesitation. After gazing at the station master's back for a long time, I dejectedly stepped into the square in front of the station.

I walked up the mountain along the narrow pathway stretching through forests of huge trees along a running brook. In full summer water ran high in the brook and you could bathe in its rapids but, as it was late autumn, stones jutted out above the shallow water in the bed of the stream.

When you go up some distance, you come to a big rock called the Buddha Rock. I can never forget the time last summer when I bathed in the rapids while Aera waited sitting on this rock. Aera, bored with waiting, was humming "Milky Way," and exclaimed on seeing me in only my briefs, "Oh, you look like a deer! A long-legged deer!" and beamed as if she had really found a deer.

"Deer? Oh, I do envy the deer who takes his fill of this sylvan freshness, until he could burst for joy."

"Well, I guess you aren't as handsome as the deer of the forest," she said, and threw the stone in her hand into the rapids, splashing water on me.

But upon this rock where once Aera was seated now only fallen leaves lay scattered, adding to the feeling of desolation. Halting my steps, I stood for a while buried in the memory of Aera, and without thinking picked up a stone and threw it into the water as Aera had done. But only the hollow sound of the splash spread in the air, and the next moment the silence was even heavier.

I resumed my heavy steps. I did not want to be freed of the searing longing that would not let me alone but made me recall Aera in every tree and every stone. Isn't it a blessing that though death can take away a person forever, it cannot deprive the living of memories?

When I reached the topmost point of the peak at the end of a mile's walk, the villa of my memory—which had been covered all over with ivy and roses but now looked deserted, the ivy leaves now red and more than half fallen—came into view.

The cosmos plants that thickly hedged the yard now looked ugly, withered by the frost of late autumn. Cosmos had been Aera's favorite flower, so that she watered them with great care throughout spring and summer, in happy anticipation of the autumn cosmos season. But Aera had passed away before the flowers bloomed. It must be lucky for those destined to die that they do not know when death will come, but what dire misfortune is that good luck to those who must go on living!

The flowers in the garden were all withered and drooping, as if they too were in mourning for Aera. After looking at the flowers for a long time, I pushed at the gate of the villa. All the doors were firmly locked and the place maintained a solemn silence.

"Aera! Aera!"

I called out the name of my beloved and knocked on the gate, because I felt as if in one corner of this firmly locked villa Aera was waiting for me. But however many times I wailed her name, no response came from Aera.

Swallowing a heavy sigh, I circled the villa once and went up the hill behind with emptiness in my heart. To visit Aera's grave. Aegyŏng had said that because Aera liked to look at the sea even more than she liked music, they buried her on this hill.

I was going up the hill peering here and there, when someone called out from a distance, "Oh, it's you, young master!" It was Sunshil, the wife of Kim, the villa keeper. Sunshil, as she walked up to me, almost smiled, but at once lowered her head modestly.

On seeing this country woman whom Aera and I used to call "Madonna" between ourselves, thoughts of Aera pierced me once again and tears welled up in me. I was at once sad and glad to meet Sunshil, who had liked Aera so much and whom Aera also had liked. Sunshil, though she was the wife of the villa keeper Kim, was an unusually intelligent woman. I felt as if there were only Sunshil and me in all the world who could mourn the death of Aera sincerely from the heart.

Sunshil and I stood facing each other for a good while without speaking. At long last I said, "Thank you so much for nursing Aera in her last hours." I recalled having heard that Sunshil had nursed Aera day and night, and felt I had to express my thanks. But Sunshil did not say anything in reply. I realized belatedly that it must be painful for Sunshil to be thanked for what she had done out of love.

When at last I began to stir, Sunshil at once guessed what I wanted and led me to the grave. Aera's grave was built on a sunny spot on the hill that overlooked the vast expanse of the East Sea. And right below the grave was the orchard, the everlasting orchard of our memory, in which Aera and I shared our first embrace last summer.

Sunshil, when she reached the freshly built grave, just lowered her head, not having the heart to tell me that it was Aera's.

In this new grave whose earth looked red in the twilight sun—could it be true that Aera was lying in this grave? The Bible had taught me that when a man dies the flesh will rot in the grave and the soul will ascend to Heaven. And I had firmly believed it; but oh, how much greater was the pain of sorrow this grave was giving me than the consolation that Aera's soul must have ascended to Heaven. With what sad reality did the tombstone, whose inscription in fresh chisel marks read "Here lies Lee Aera," touch my heart!

I fed incense into the incense burner and made three deep bows before the grave. After I bowed three times and smelt the incense, for the first time I felt with my flesh the reality of Aera's death. Not being able to suppress the torrent of grief flooding my heart, I threw myself down on the grass and wept aloud.

I realized that I had been crying only when, after a long time, Sunshil shook my shoulder and called me. And only then did I realize that I had made bows before the grave. That was my first act of apostasy before my God.

"Thou shalt have no other gods before me."

That is the first of the Ten Commandments. But how powerless were the words over me now! How could I endure the sorrow without bowing before the grave, when my heart was pierced and torn apart with longing? It may be that that bowing was a totally meaningless act. But how could I help it when the ceremony had for me a meaning of reality?

"Aera, Aera, wake up now! I've come, your Hisun has come, so wake up!" I wailed silently.

Aera's soul, why don't you answer me if you are there? Instead of feeling the reality of the soul, I felt with my whole body the reality of death before that unresponsive grave. After Sunshil had gone back to the villa to prepare supper, I kept calling and calling Aera's name in front of the grave in the spreading dusk.

When Sunshil came to the grave again in search of me I was already soaked through with the evening dew. On coming back to the villa, I found that Sunshil had cleverly prepared for my use the room that used to be Aera's. Entering this room, which had been preserved as on the day of Aera's death, I could not but mourn Aera's death again.

I lay down on the very bed where Aera had breathed her last, and waited in vain for Aera to return, and also thought about how I could follow Aera to where she was. In the vase on the piano beside the window facing west still stood the white roses, withered and dirty. With longing for whom in her heart did Aera gaze at those flowers?

Looking absently at the opposite hill which showed its distinct outline amid the spreading dusk, I lay suffused with infinite longing for Aera.

At last the cold beams of the tenth-day moon struck my window. Like one startled by something, I sprang up and ran outside. When I recovered my senses, I found myself circling Aera's grave like a wild animal.

The next moment I realized my foolishness and walked down to the orchard. When we came here last summer the leaves were thick, and on every bough hung ripe, dark-red apples, so that the whole orchard seemed to be vibrating with passion. But now the fruit had been picked and the leaves had fallen, and only the moonlight fell coldly on it, making it look as desolate as the ruins of a battleground. The moon shone brightly like this on the day when Aera and I first shared our lips under the apple trees. With what rapt feeling of mystery did we look at the globes of apples shining red in the moonlight! Though we were too happy in the present even to think about the future, hadn't we been able, in that moment of happiness, intuitively to gaze at eternity?

Although we were excited by the temptation of earthly passion, we did not pluck the forbidden fruit that night, because we felt that bliss would be ours forever very soon. But before the summer changed to autumn, our radiant hope was mercilessly shattered.

I wandered in the orchard where not even a cricket chirped. I felt as if it were the memory of Aera that I was treading under my feet at every step, so I leaned on a tree for a while and called out "Aera!" I felt as if Aera was peeping at me from behind the moon.

But surprisingly, the woman who appeared before my eyes at my urgent call for Aera was Sunshil. "Sir, you must go in and sleep now." Sunshil was beside me presently and urged me with gentle words. At that instant, Sunshil's eyes, reflecting the cold beams of the moon, shone translucent like two drops of mercury on a silver tray.

"Is Kim back from the market?"

"No. He may be planning to come back tomorrow."

After exchanging a few words I came down to the villa, preceding Sunshil. In the room the lamp was already lit, and on the piano stood a small pot of autumn chrysanthemums instead of the vase of withered white roses. The half-bloomed white chrysanthemums seemed to be welcoming me silently. I gazed at the chrysanthemums absently for a while, and realized with some surprise that Sunshil had the rather elegant hobby of growing chrysanthemums.

Past midnight I lay on my bed, but the thought that until only a couple of months ago Aera had lived in this room made it hard for me to fall asleep. After tossing and turning for a long time I fell asleep, but woke up, startled, dreaming of Aera opening the door and stepping in. I did not feel I could fall asleep again, so in ten minutes I sat up and decided to write to Aegyŏng, Aera's younger sister in Seoul.

"Aegyŏng.

"It seems my heart is too small to contain all the memory of Aera. Aera's grave says nothing to me. When I fed incense into the burner before the grave, it was only fragrant smoke that rose. I inhaled the smoke deeply, as if it were Aera's soul.

"Aegyŏng, why didn't you tell me of your sister's death earlier? If I could have seen her dead even for a moment it might have been some consolation. Just now I met your sister in my dream. When I opened my eyes with joy, holding out my arms to welcome her, she had already disappeared. It was too real to be a dream, and too fleeting to be real.

"Aegyŏng, I think this is the sixty-fourth day after your sister's death. In four days it will be the fifteenth of September by the lunar calendar, so I will commemorate her birthday with a sacrificial rite for her here. 'How awful of a Christian to offer sacrificial rites to the dead!' you might say.

"But that which to you must be shocking and ridiculous is to me a solemn wish. As the high priests of the Levites made offerings of doves and lambs to God in token of their piety, the only way I can express my love for Aera is to make offerings before her grave. I have decided to stay the whole winter in this villa, just to make offerings before her grave. You might laugh at me and think me sentimental. But I have realized for the first time that every human truth has a tinge of sentimentality."

The next morning I stepped down to the yard before the day had fully broken. It was a rather cold morning. After walking around the deserted garden, I was starting up the hill to the rear when I met Sunshil coming from the hut. When she saw me she made a friendly bow and said, "Good morning. Did you get very cold last night?"

I answered her greeting, and said, "The frost is thick," looking around the yard. The night before must have been extremely cold, for the garden was coated with a thick layer of frost, and the cosmos stalks looked sparser. "The flowers have all withered."

"Oh, I think I'd better cut down those cosmos plants."

Sunshil must have guessed my feelings, for she walked away to the hut. In a little while she appeared with a sickle, tying on her apron, and began to cut the withered cosmos stalks.

Watching the stalks being cut down one after another, I recalled once again that all of them had been planted by Aera with her own hands. Therefore, seeing them cut down pained me, as if the memory of Aera in my heart were being sheared off.

When the garden at last looked clean and spacious, I became enveloped by a nameless feeling of emptiness.

"Now it's clean, isn't it?" Sunshil straightened up, putting down the sickle.

"It's too empty."

"I think the place had better be planted with chrysanthemums next year," Sunshil said. Those casually uttered words seemed to me to presage something fateful, and I could only stand there in silence for a while, my heart heavy. Sunshil, looking at me with her deep eyes, also stood there in silence.

The dull silence had lasted for quite a while when Sunshil and I were both startled by the sound of a sudden false cough. When we looked around, coming back to our senses, we found to our surprise that Kim, the villa keeper, was standing like a wooden image within the hedge, and staring at us with eyes sharp as daggers. They were keen, poisonous eyes that cut through flesh. I intuitively felt that Kim suspected Sunshil and me, and after a brief, confused silence I said, "Ah, are you back from the market?" and moved a few steps toward him.

"Oh, the young master's come? Why, this is a surprise! I heard you were in Chejudo. When did you arrive? I went to the market yesterday and, er, a few bowls of makkoli did me up and, er, I guess I'm getting old. So, I'm sure the master and the mistress are both well in Seoul?" Kim, at once softening his expression, guffawed and bowed time and again, rubbing the back of his hand with his palm, and chattered on busily.

After exchanging a few words with Kim, I went up the hill. But I could not help feeling uncomfortable, and kept recalling Kim's poisonous eyes. Sunshil and I had been simply standing there facing each other, but perhaps it could not have failed to breed suspicions in Kim, who had stayed out all night, leaving his young wife alone in the villa.

I felt regret more on account of Sunshil than of Kim. Even though Kim had quickly laughed and started to chat, I could not believe that the suspicion once conceived could be erased that easily. I recalled reading somewhere that foolish imaginings always breed mischief, and my mind was heavy with the fear that some dreadful misfortune might overwhelm Sunshil in the future.

Three days passed. Perhaps nothing had happened in the Kim household, because Sunshil was composed as usual.

On the evening before the birthday commemoration offering to Aera, I was wandering around in the orchard. The sun had just set, and the moon had not had time to spread its beams, so that I was stepping on fallen leaves and walking among the trees in semi-darkness for a long time. Now and then a desultory wind swept past, making the boughs weep, and the earth fell to sleep by degrees.

At last the moonbeams filled the space and conjured up myriad shadows that resembled scarecrows. After a gust of wind, the whole orchard was about to sink into fathomless quiet again. Just then, a voice called from somewhere, "Young master!" The woman who was calling me from among the apple trees was Sunshil.

I was glad. I had never been so pleased to see Sunshil before. I did not know exactly why I was so glad, but I was. I knew it was unwise to meet Sunshil alone in a moonlit orchard like this, but still I was very glad.

Sunshil approached me and without a word handed me a telegram.

"Will arrive at nine. Hope to be met at the station. Aegyŏng."

Aegyŏng was coming, probably to participate in the sacrificial offering to her sister, after reading my letter to her.

"The little miss is coming, isn't she?" Sunshil asked. Sunshil could read, as she had attended elementary school up to the fifth grade.

"Yes. Because tomorrow is Aera's birthday."

"Going to stay long?"

I was silent for some time, because I did not know who she was talking about, but I answered, "Well, I think Aegyŏng will go back soon. I will pass the winter in this villa."

Sunshil did not make any further remarks.

"It must be very cold here in the winter, isn't it?"

"Not so very. But there's nothing but snow in the winter."

"Snow?"

"Yes. Everything gets covered with snow in winter—mountains, fields, houses. All you can see is snow, so that in winter you long for people."

Hearing Sunshil's words, I strengthened my resolve to stay the winter in this snow-covered villa, feeding myself on memories of Aera. I felt that it would be a good thing for Sunshil, too, who said she missed people in winter.

"I guess you can see hunters in the winter?"

"Yes. We see hunting parties from Seoul shooting now and then."

"What animals are they after?"

"Mostly roe deer."

At the word roe deer, I remembered Aera's having called me a deer, and I recited the word several times. And then, picturing the tragic and beautiful sight of the wounded deer falling in the snow bleeding red, I felt an aching in my limbs, as if I had been the stricken deer myself.

Ten minutes later we went down to the villa in haste. When it was time for me to go to the station and I started out, putting on a heavy coat, Sunshil came up to me and said, "Let me come along to meet her too."

"Oh, no. I can go alone."

I did not feel like dissuading her, but I recalled once again the furious eyes of Kim. Sunshil did not insist, but raised her head and looked at me. The moment my eyes met her pearly eyes glistening in the moonlight, I was startled, as one who saw something that must not be seen and, running down the hill like a frightened deer, I wailed, without knowing what I was doing, "Sunshil! Sunshil!"

At that moment I realized, almost with pain, that in this world there was only Sunshil to comfort me now that Aera was gone forever.

When I reached Y station it was already time for the arrival of the train. I walked back and forth alone on the platform dimly lit by street-lamps. There was no one there except me.

The train came in shortly. I ran to the door of the third-class carriage. A man in old-fashioned garb and an old woman who looked nearly sixty—only these two people got out of the train; Aegyŏng was not to be seen.

"She must have missed the train," I murmured, and was turning away when from behind me Aegyŏng called out "Hisun!" in her resolute voice, and ran toward me spiritedly, like a mare.

"Oh, Aegyŏng! Where did you get off?" I asked, running to her.

"I came in the second-class car."

"In the second-class car? Why, you had a luxury trip!"

"Yes. As if I was on a honeymoon."

"A honeymoon?"

Feeling dazed for a moment by the word "honeymoon," I looked at Aegyŏng. She was wearing a western suit over her supple, elastic body, and her curly hair blew in the wind. In fact, Aegyŏng looked as seductive as dancing Salome.

When we were past the street and had entered the mountain pathway, Aegyŏng said, "Oh, I forgot to thank you for the letter," and smiled.

I ignored the smile and asked, "Do your parents know I'm staying in the villa?"

"Of course they do! When they heard you were going to pass the winter in the villa, they were frightened. They were worried about what the mountain winter would do to your sensitive health, and told me to persuade you to leave the villa. I came as their emissary, so to speak."

Tears filled my eyes to learn that Aera's family's love for me had not changed even after Aera's death.

"But what good could the air of Seoul do for me?"

"They don't want you to come to Seoul, but to go to a hot spring or somewhere like that. And they want me to go with you and console you."

"To a hot spring? And with Aegyŏng?" I retorted and looked at Aegyŏng hard, till she shrank back from embarrassment.

I was a little displeased, and wondered whether going to a spa with Aegyŏng was her parents' idea or her own. To me, the idea of trying to allay my grief from the loss of Aera with anything other than the memory of her was profanation.

There had been an incident of sorts last summer when all three of us—Aera, Aegyŏng and I—were staying in the villa together. One bright moonlit night we were chatting on the veranda when suddenly Aegyŏng, without heeding her sister's presence, took hold of my arm, pressed it to her bosom, and said jokingly, "I like Hisun more than anybody else in the whole world!"

That was all, but from that day Aera lost her appetite for three days, and was buried in anxiety. At that time I thought Aegyŏng was simply joking so I told Aera not to be oversensitive but, on looking back, it might not have been all a joke.

All during the walk from the station to the villa, Aegyŏng did not pronounce her sister's name even once. I regretted having written to her. Upon arriving at the villa Aegyŏng, without bothering to look once into Aera's room, rushed up directly to her own room. When I suggested that she look into Aera's room, she said, "No. I like my room better. Come to my room at once. I will tell you exciting things."

I was more than a little disappointed, because I thought Aegyŏng should be more grieved by Aera's death than anybody else. Again and again I confirmed my plan to pass the winter in the villa so that I would not betray the memory of Aera.

I had a hard time falling asleep that night, with the sad fact in my mind that Aegyŏng was betraying her sister less than three months after her death. That Judas betrayed Jesus could be deemed human; it can happen that I, as a human being, should forsake Jesus. But how could Aegyŏng forget her own sister in less than three months' time? The worlds of life and death seem separated only by a thread; but are the two worlds even that far apart from each other? I could not help feeling resentful of Aegyŏng. As the night deepened, I felt more and more tense, and at last I kicked out of bed and went outside.

I breathed deeply to steady myself and walked toward Aera's grave. Does Aera know that I have come to her? Thinking that if her soul were there it would appear to me and comfort me, I threw myself down on the grass beside the grave. It was midnight, and all around was silent as death; the moon was clear and cool. The rhythmical puffs of the breeze sounded sad, or sometimes happy, or forlorn. I was thinking that it was in moments like this that sound, color and sentiments blend into one, when I seemed to hear a quarrel from afar.

Pricking up my ears, I could perceive it was a man's voice, and upon listening more carefully I recognized Kim's hoarse roar. I felt my heart sink, and at once I recalled his fiercely suspicious glance. I got up. I felt my way toward the direction of the voice, picturing in my head the sorry state of Sunshil.

As I approached the hut of the Kims, I could hear wild curses.

"You, Goddamned bitch! Why did he come, if not for you? Now, tell the truth. Confess everything, if you want to live. You bitch, I'll tear you limb by limb!"

With these savage curses I could see a shadow like that of a demon on the paper-paneled door. And the atrocious sound of palms hitting flesh could be heard. It was obvious that Kim was beating Sunshil.

But not a sound came from Sunshil.

The blows were cutting my heart like an axe. I could picture only too vividly the terrible sight of Kim beating his wife and Sunshil biting her lips, trying not to groan.

"You bitch who ought to be torn to pieces! If that dog's meat is more to your taste, get yourself out of my sight! You dirty whore." With this, another bout of curses and blows began.

"Bitch! Have you become dumb all of a sudden? Why don't you answer me? Oh, yes, what *could* you have to say? Defend yourself if you can!"

But Sunshil was still silent.

"Well, you as good as admit your guilt with that silence! Do you have to go all the way to the orchard to do that dirty thing?" There was murder in Kim's voice.

I shuddered, realizing that Kim's eyes had been following Sunshil and me all the time. We had done nothing sinful, but it was terrible nevertheless to have aroused such suspicions in other people.

I felt like jumping into that room right then and telling him that nothing like what he suspected had ever happened. But such a declaration would not convince Kim, and to have eavesdropped on a domestic quarrel would further increase suspicion, so I tried hard to suppress my urge.

It was painful to listen any further to the quarrel which I could do nothing to put an end to, so I ran to my room, but could not fall asleep. I felt I had to give up my plan of spending the winter in the villa. I realized it was best for Sunshil that I leave this villa as quickly as possible.

The night was almost spent. In Aegyŏng's room right next to mine I heard something hitting the wall. I listened, thinking that perhaps Aegyŏng had turned in her sleep, when a little later came a deep sigh. What was she sighing about? After a few moments' silence, Aegyŏng called me. I kept silent, and a little later Aegyŏng called me again, this time in a clearer voice, "Hisun! Hisun!"

I suddenly remembered Aegyŏng's seductive body, and realized that Aegyŏng was not a girl any more.

"Hisun! Hisun!" She called again, this time knocking on the wall.

"Aegyŏng! Why don't you go to sleep?" I said reprovingly, but that was an admonition to myself as well.

"Hisun! I'm scared to death! Please come to my room."

"What's there to be scared about when you have me in the very next room? Go ahead and get some more sleep. It'll be a long time before day breaks."

"Oh, I'm scared to death. Please come quickly." Aegyŏng sent off an agonized plea.

I raised myself reluctantly. I walked out to the hall and grasped the knob of Aegyŏng's door. But at that moment I instinctively felt that if I went into that room something horrible would surely happen and, telling myself that I must overcome this temptation by all means, I shuddered. I took my hand off the doorknob.

"Come in quickly!" Aegyŏng pleaded. I grasped the knob again. At that moment, the phrase in the Lord's Prayer, "lead us not into temptation," flashed through my mind like lightning, and I released the knob quickly. And I rushed outside as fast as I could.

When I came back to the villa about two hours later, the sun was already shining above the hill. I met Aegyŏng in the hall, but she was sullen, and did not even say good morning.

I came out to the well in the backyard to wash my face. Sunshil, who had been washing rice beside the well, calmly greeted me with a bow just as on any other day. She did not at all look like one who had gone through hell during the night. Only, there were some bruises on her neck. I was touched to think that there could be such beautiful patience.

At that moment Kim appeared from nowhere.

"Good morning, young master. Don't you think the weather's a bit warmer today? Oh, today is the fifteenth, so this is the day for the birthday offerings. Time flies like an arrow. Why, it's almost three months since the elder miss passed away. Oh, isn't it unbelievable?"

Kim jabbered on, without waiting for any response. How could a man who had acted that way the night before talk so glibly in the morning? I was stupefied. The phrase "with honey in the mouth and a sword in the belly" must have been coined with the likes of him in mind.

At about ten o'clock we prepared our offering table and carried it to the grave. On the table were simply a bowl of white rice, fried fish and cooked vegetables. After burning incense, I poured out wine and bowed three times before her grave. Sorrow spread in my heart like fog. Sunshil wept quietly, and Aegyŏng kept looking up at the sky. Nobody spoke. After Sunshil had made her bows, Kim prepared to bow, too, but I cut him off decisively.

It was a simple ceremony, but for the first time I felt as if I had paid part of my debt to Aera. Aegyŏng, after we came back to the villa, said, "Hisun! Now that the commemoration ceremony is over, let's leave, shall we?"

Where does she want me to go from here? Not comprehending, I answered vaguely. Had I been ignorant of the tragic scene that took place in the hut last night I would have insisted on spending the winter in the villa, but since I knew about it I could not do that either.

"What's there to make you hesitate? Now you've made the commemorative offering; let's go down by the first train tomorrow."

"I don't know."

"Why are you so indecisive, you, a man? You can't live here forever, so why not leave at once?"

"There's no difference."

"But you'll have to leave sometime."

I kept silent. By that time I had given up trusting human emotions.

All that day I roamed the hills, fields and the orchard like a mindless man. Life and death and all seemed meaningless to me. I envied the mental state of those who could trust in God as the highest reality.

I did not see anyone all the rest of the day.

Night came again. And I feared the night. I kept thinking of what had taken place in the hut the night before, and toward midnight I got up, without knowing what I was doing. Fearing that the same thing might be happening again, I noiselessly approached the hut with trembling heart. Oh, what nightmare was this? The same tempest between the husband and wife was heard again tonight. Moreover, Kim was drunk this time.

He kicked and hit his wife, threw things, fell down in the frenzy of his own fury, cried aloud like a child, and then sprang up and tortured his wife again. There was only the papered door between the dreadful scene and me.

I could not stand it. And I could not step between them and bring peace, so I had to run back to the villa again with clenched fists. Well, I would have to leave the villa as Aegyŏng had told me to as soon as it was daylight.

How could I shield Sunshil from the misfortune that engulfed her? The only thing I could do for her was to leave the villa as soon as possible. It was a very painful thing for me, but I had no choice. I must hesitate no longer but leave this villa with Aegyŏng today. Whatever rough waves might await me in the world, I had to go away with Aegyŏng in order to save Sunshil from a greater misfortune.

When day broke, I met Sunshil beside the well as I was going into the villa to wake up Aegyŏng. Sunshil was as calm as always. I was about to inquire about the night before, but I bit my tongue and swallowed the words. Then I said, "We're going to leave today."

"Yes? Why? You said you were going to spend the winter here."

Reading disappointment on her surprised face, my heart beat wildly.

"Because I think it is fate."

Sunshil just dropped her head at my answer.

It was one of those moments when mind and mind met in silence. I put my hand on Sunshil's shoulder unawares and called, "Sunshil!"

Sunshil just trembled. And she gazed at my chest silently, with blame in her eyes.

"Sunshil!" I cried out again, and grasped her hand. "You said you miss people in the winter. Wherever I go, I will never forget that. But I think meeting and parting are beyond our will."

Sunshil was still silent, her head lowered.

"Sunshil, I have realized for the first time what great happiness it is to cherish a mute love for someone. Now, goodbye."

Sunshil and I held hands for the last time. Then she raised her eyes and poured her moist glance directly into my eyes. Our eyes met. Beholding Sunshil's eyes ecstatically for a moment, I raised my arm and gently patted her on the shoulder. I did not feel any guilt in my act. On the contrary, I felt as sanctified as at the moment I was baptized before God.

So at last I left the villa, accepting as destiny my eternal hovering over the boundary between the flesh and the spirit, but no longer with sorrow in my heart.

The Underground Village

Kang Kyŏng-ae

Born in 1907, Kang Kyŏng-ae seems to have lived the lonely existence common to women intellectuals of her generation. Not much is known of her life, especially as she spent the major part of her adult years in Manchuria. There, in Kando, she worked as a reporter and head of the branch office of a Korean daily before her return to Korea in 1943 and subsequent death.

In common with many of her contemporaries, her subject was the life of poor, struggling, underprivileged people. The trend of naturalism is softened and rendered more poignant in her stories by her tenderness toward her characters and her sensitivity to their emotions, as is shown in "The Underground Village" (1935). The mother of this story is emblematic of the long-suffering Korean woman, who submits unprotestingly to her lot as a beast of burden, and whose sighs may sometimes be exhausted but whose affection never is.

The sun was burning above the western hill. Ch'ilsŏng, as usual, staggered past this village with his beggar's sack slung over his shoulder. He kept pulling down his crownless straw hat, but the sun continued to scorch his forehead, and drops of sweat rolled down. Dust rose up from the parched road like smoke and made it difficult for him to breathe.

"There he comes again!"

"Come on!"

The little urchins at play by the roadside shouted and ran toward him. Ch'ilsŏng swore to himself and took hurried steps, but the children soon overtook him and pulled at his clothes.

"Cry, lad, cry!" One of the urchins blocked Ch'ilsŏng's way and laughed. The children surrounded him in a circle.

"Hey, boy, how old are you?"

"Show us what you earned today."

One of the urchins snatched at his beggar's sack, and all the others clapped their hands. Ch'ilsŏng stood immobile and glared at the biggest of the group. He knew that if he tried to push ahead or swore at them they would pester him still more.

"Oh, he looks like a gentleman today." One bristly-haired urchin brandished before his face a stick with a bit of cowdung at the tip. The children all giggled and made as if to smear cowdung on Ch'ilsŏng with their sticks. Ch'ilsŏng could not stand it, so he ran as fast as he could.

He raised both his shaky arms high and twisted his neck convulsively as he placed one foot ahead of the other. The children mimicked his gait and followed him. They blocked him in front and behind, and jumped up to smear cowdung on his face. He scowled fiercely, and could only mutter "Goddamn!" after twitching his mouth for a long time.

The children imitated the mouth and the "Goddamn!" and roared with laughter. When cowdung touched his lips Ch'ilsŏng spat vehemently and scowled fiercely.

"Why, that's a terrible gentleman there," the children mocked, but perhaps they thought he really looked terrible, for they began to retreat. Ch'ilsŏng wiped his mouth with his sleeve and looked at the noisily retreating children. He felt furious and forlorn, like one cast aside by the world.

After the urchins had gone away, there was utter silence. Ch'ilsŏng walked on along the new highway. He tried to brush away the cowdung, but the effort only spread the bluish stain on his clothes. He stared into space, and flopped down on the slope at the foot of the mountain.

A breeze stirred the tall grasses, and insects chirped now and then. A running brook sang from somewhere, too. He scratched his head and looked ahead absently. The sun showered its oblique rays upon the forest, and the songs of the birds sounded plaintive. "Why am I such a cripple, that I am ridiculed and persecuted even by little children?" he pondered, and plucked a blade of grass beside him, which hurt his palm.

"Well, at least I'm not as miserable as Kŭnnyŏn," he thought. "Kŭnnyŏn is blind yet she lives," he mused, looking at the down-covered berries of a nearby plant. He pictured Kŭnnyŏn in his head. Her softly closed eyes! He trembled as he pictured them. He looked at his beggar's sack beside him and thought he would give Kŭnnyŏn the most delicious unbroken biscuits that he had garnered that day. "How shall I give them to her? Shall I hand them to her over the brushwood hedge tonight? To do so, Kŭnnyŏn will have to be made to come out and stand beside the brushwood hedge. Someone will have to tell her to come out. Who? No, that won't do. Then I will send Ch'il-un over with them. Oh, no, that way Kŭnnyŏn's mother and my mother will know. I will hand them over the hedge tomorrow at midday after people have gone out for weeding." His heart throbbed, and he got up.

The sun that had been pouring down heat as if to fry his skin disappeared among the mountains, and a cool breeze from somewhere stirred the grasses and cooled his body. Ch'ilsŏng fumbled with his beggar's sack and then, slinging it over his shoulder, resumed his tottering walk.

The sky spread before his eyes like a vast sea, and far off toward the horizon a red evening glow spread in waves. He pushed up his straw hat and came out of the shadows of the valley. As he moved, the smell of cowdung stung his nostrils.

When he had passed the mountain and approached the entrance to the village, his younger brother Ch'il-un ran up to him with the baby on his back.

"Oh, you're late. I've been waiting for you all day." His big eyes beaming happily, Ch'il-un went up close to his brother and, taking hold of the beggar's sack, tried to find out what he had obtained that day.

"Did you get biscuits today, too?"

"No." Ch'ilsŏng quickly shifted his sack and retreated a step. Ch'il-un moved with him.

"Give me one, will you? Just one." Ch'il-un swallowed and stretched out his soiled hand. The baby on his back also spread both her hands and looked at Ch'ilsŏng.

"Goddamn!" Ch'ilsŏng turned away quickly. Ch'il-un followed him hastily.

"Will you, please? Give me one."

"I haven't got any." Ch'ilsŏng scowled. Ch'il-un became tearful at once and looked up at his brother.

"I'll tell Mother you won't give me a biscuit. She said when she went out to the field that if I looked after the baby you'd give me sweets. I'll tell on you, I will." Ch'il-un twisted his mouth and wiped his tears with his fist.

The baby, without knowing what it was all about, also began to cry. Darkness was setting in, but Ch'il-un sobbed and ran toward the mountain where their mother was supposed to be.

"Mother! Mother!" When Ch'il-un shouted sobbingly, the baby also cried "Mama! Mama!" The echo from the mountain sounded somewhat like their mother's reply of "Coming!" Ch'ilsŏng, deeming it fortunate to be rid of Ch'il-un and Yŏng-ae, turned and began to walk.

The village was sunk in darkness and nothing could be discerned, but the old locust tree loomed tall and erect, as if it were trying to reach the stars. He walked on, resolving that he would meet Kŭnnyŏn by whatever means, and give her the biscuits without fail.

"Is it you, Ch'ilsŏng?" It was his mother's voice. He looked back. Her face could not be seen under the big bundle of brushwood, which made her neck tilt almost to the point of breaking.

"Why are you so late today?" She had looked down the road again and again to see if her son was coming until her eyes began to ache, and then had gone up the mountain from the field. She had worried that he might have fallen down somewhere or been stoned by urchins, and had thought of going to town in search of him. At his mother's question Ch'ilsŏng recalled the mortification he had received from the urchins and at once became tearful.

His mother walked up to him. She smelt of leaves. She was carrying the big sheaf of twigs on her head and also the baby on her back.

"Mother, he won't give me any sweets." Ch'il-un hung on to his mother's skirt. His mother staggered, almost fell down, but recovered her balance and stroked Ch'il-un with one hand.

"I'll kill that damned boy." Ch'ilsŏng raised his foot to kick his brother. His mother lurched in between them.

"Don't! He's had a hard time all day, looking after the baby. He's got heat rash all around his waist." Then his mother sighed deeply. Ch'ilsŏng suddenly fancied he smelt cowdung and his anger rose.

"Do you think I've been sitting in the shade all day?"

"Oh, that's not what I meant, Ch'ilsŏng!" His mother's voice choked and she could not go on. They walked in silence.

When they got home they sat down on the sheaf of twigs. His mother talked about this and that to divert Ch'ilsŏng.

"Oh, there are so many stinging insects this year. My hands are all numb from their stings." She would have liked to take a look at her hands, but restrained herself and caressed the baby. She bared one of her breasts. Ch'il-un kicked at the bundle and went on whimpering. Ch'ilsŏng could not stand to look at his mother and sister, so he got up and looked around in the dark to see if Kŭnnyŏn was somewhere around.

Entering the room, Ch'ilsŏng sat down crosslegged, pressing under his thigh the toe he had bruised on the stepping stone, and noiselessly latched the door. Then he poured out the contents of the beggar's sack. Matchsticks and rice grains scattered with a rustling sound. He winced and rapidly felt the things one by one. He thought of the money that was in the sack, so he took it out and looked down at it absently. Nothing could be discerned clearly because the room was dark, but he imagined he could see everything distinctly.

He piled up the matchboxes and the rice and the biscuits separately in a corner and thought of Kŭnnyŏn. What should he give her? He picked up the biscuits quickly and, thinking that he would give her those, put one in his mouth. It crushed with a crisp sound between his teeth, and sweetness spread in his mouth. He smacked his lips and listened again to make sure Ch'il-un was not eavesdropping.

He counted the money held tightly in his hand and, when he thought how happy Kŭnnyŏn would be if he used it to buy her fabrics for her clothes, his heart beat wildly. "Why doesn't she come to visit us at home? If she does, I'd give her money and biscuits and everything she wants." When he imagined her visiting them, he felt somehow reverential. So he wrapped the matchboxes and biscuits together and put them under the straw mat, pushing the money in under the mat too, and moved the rice near to the kitchen. Then, sitting beside the back door, he looked over at the hedge of Kŭnnyŏn's house.

Squash vines were winding round the hedge and stars were floating above it. "How can I meet her?" His hand touched his toe and it hurt. A cool breeze caressed his cheeks. His heart ached. It ached more than his bruised toe.

"Eat your supper."

Ch'ilsŏng looked up, startled. When he realized it was his mother who was standing outside the door, he felt an emptiness in a corner of his bosom.

"Did you lock the door?" His mother pulled at the door. He felt as if she were pulling at the door to ask for biscuits or for money. He thought he hated his family and everybody in the world.

"I won't eat," he shouted. His whole body shook.

"Did you eat something in the market?" His mother's voice grew weak. Every time Ch'ilsŏng got angry, his mother's voice became weak like that. After a long interval, his mother pleaded again, "Why don't you have some more?"

"I don't want to," he shouted again. His mother murmured something to herself and fell silent. Ch'ilsŏng, left alone, yearned to eat the biscuits under the straw mat. He lifted it. A sweet scent floated up and also the disgusting smell of bedbugs. He replaced the straw mat and turned around, thinking that the biscuits must go to Kŭnnyŏn tomorrow, but his hand was again fingering the mat. "I'll give them to Kŭnnyŏn." He took his hand away quickly and grabbed the doorsill.

A breeze squeezed in through the gap between the door panels and chilled his sweaty brow. He quickly took off his jacket and hugged the wind. He felt itchy all over, so he rubbed his body against the wall. It made him feel good, so he kept on doing it harder. That made him breathless, and the skin on his back tore and ached. So he got up, clinging to the wall, and went outside.

As he moved, every part of his body ached. His fingertip hurt as if pierced by a thorn, and his wrist ached and his arm felt sore and his toe stung. He ignored them all and walked on.

Among the onions planted in orderly rows beside the bush clover hedge a few white flowers shone like stars, and the smell of scallions that drifted with the wind made him feel as if a girl were sitting beside him. He stepped nearer to the hedge.

From Kŭnnyŏn's house floated the poignant smell of mugwort burning to keep away mosquitoes, and the fire itself flickered now and then. As he pricked his ears toward the conversation in Kŭnnyŏn's yard, the hedge rustled and the furry spines of squash leaves stung his cheeks. His face burned when he suddenly thought Kŭnnyŏn might be peeping at him from beyond the hedge.

After a long while he looked around. His clothes were all damp with dew, and scallion blossoms shone like pebbles under water. The mosquito fire could not be seen any more, and all around was darkness. From somewhere insects chirped. When he stepped into his room he felt stuffiness fill his chest up to his throat.

When he awoke the next morning, the backyard was full of sunshine already. As soon as he got up, Ch'ilsŏng looked around to see whether his mother and Ch'il-un were in the house still. Making sure that they were not, he sat on the doorsill and looked at the hedge of Kŭnnyŏn's house. Kŭnnyŏn's father and mother must have gone out to the field to weed, and Kŭnnyŏn must be home alone.

"Could there be some visitor? I must see her today." Thinking thus, he looked down at his arms, which hung limp inside the tattered sleeves and looked as if they were made of no bones and no flesh, but only shrivelled greenish-yellow skin. Suddenly he felt sad and, raising his head, sighed deeply. How fortunate it was that Kŭnnyŏn was blind! If she could see, she would have taken to her heels at the sight of these arms. But what if Kŭnnyŏn felt these arms and asked why they were so thin and limp? And what one could do with such weak arms? His heart tore at the thought. He kept heaving sighs and suddenly thought, "Couldn't there be a medicine for them? There must be some medicine." On the spider's web spread over the hedge of Kŭnnyŏn's house hung innumerable dewdrops. "Maybe those are medicine." He sprang up and went outside.

Praying that the dewdrops shining on the spider's web would be medicine for him, he pulled the web down carefully. His arms were weak and trembled, so that the dewdrops fell on the ground in a shower. He tried to catch them in his palms, but not a drop fell on them.

"Goddamn!"

He had a habit of swearing "Goddamn" and glaring at the sky whenever he failed at something. As he was standing thus fuming to himself he turned his head at the soft sound of rubber shoes. The furry squash leaves touched his eyelids and he became tearful. Kŭnnyŏn seen through tears! He suppressed his urge to rub his eyes and opened them wider.

Kŭnnyŏn, walking with a heavy wooden laundry basin on her head, came toward the hedge and, after putting the basin on the ground, straightened up. Her eyes were closed as if in sleep; or they seemed just slightly open. Perhaps from exertion, several red spots shone on her cheeks, and her chin seemed sharper than usual, making her look like someone who had been ill for days. Kŭnnyŏn shook the laundry piece by piece and spread it on the hedge.

Ch'ilsŏng could not breathe. As he tried to inhale noiselessly, his heart felt about to burst and the skin of his belly contracted. He bowed down once to brush away his tears and kept looking. Nothing was in his head now except every movement of Kǔnnyǒn. Kǔnnyǒn came near him with her last piece of laundry. Ch'ilsǒng wanted to stretch out and take hold of Kǔnnyǒn's hand, but he flinched back instead, and his whole body shook.

As the hedge rustled under the spreading laundry, a thousand birds' wings flapped in his chest, sirens sang in his ears, and darkness descended on his eyes. He could move and part the squash leaves to look beyond the hedge only when Kǔnnyǒn's footsteps had retreated to a distance. Kǔnnyǒn was walking toward the kitchen door with the empty wooden basin on her head. He felt an urgent desire to call out to her and make her stop, but his voice would not function. Kǔnnyǒn's bare legs showed once or twice through the torn skirt and disappeared. He stared at the kitchen door, hoping that she would come out again, but she did not reappear. He heaved a deep sigh and came away from the hedge. The sun shone hot. He wished he had given her the biscuits. He wished he had given her the money. "No, I'll save the money and buy her material for a skirt," he thought, and peeped in again. Only the hedge rustled; otherwise all was silence. The laundry washed by Kǔnnyǒn shone so bright that he averted his eyes and turned away. If he didn't buy her clothes, Kǔnnyǒn would go around showing her legs through the torn skirt forever.

"Give me sweets, will you, please?"

He looked back to see Ch'il-un coming out of the kitchen door with the baby on his back. He moved away from the hedge like one discovered in theft. Ch'il-un, thinking that his brother was coming to beat him, ran into the kitchen, but looked back and approached him again.

"Will you? Just one." He held out his hand.

The baby also tilted her head to look at her older brother, and spread out her hand. The baby's head was covered with sores which oozed all the time. The baby's thin, light-brown hair was pasted to the sores, and flies always swarmed around her head. The baby kept pulling at her hair with her tiny fingers and ate the scabs she tore from her head.

The baby held out that hand before her brother. She thrust her hand before her brother with fingers spread like a fan. Ch'ilsǒng scowled at them once and went into the room. Ch'il-un blocked the doorway and importunately begged again. "Will you? Give me just one and I'll go away." He snuffled up his snot.

"I don't want to see you!"

Ch'il-un had no shirt so he was clad only in a pair of pants. The skin of his back, parched and grilled by the sun, was peeling in flakes. The baby did not have even a pair of pants, so she was naked all the time. His eyes burned as he looked at the bare bodies of his younger brother and sister. As he turned his eyes to the wall, he pictured the pile upon pile of cloth stacked along the walls of the town store. His hand that had been raised to strike Ch'il-un fell limp.

"If you don't give me any, I won't look after the baby." Ch'il-un put down the baby and ran away. The baby began to cry, screaming. Ch'ilsŏng did not cast a glance at the baby, but turned away. Flies were swarming around the rice bowl. His mother always went out to the field after setting his rice and soup in the room under a cloth, because Ch'ilsŏng got up late. He went up to it and lifted the cloth. A drowned fly floated in the soup, and the countless flies that had been sitting on the rice flew up startled. He picked out the fly from the soup and put a spoonful of rice into his mouth. The food consisted of a little rice and many acorns. The scanty rice, when crushed between his teeth, was so soft and glutinous and sweet that it almost made him choke. But immediately the crunched acorns filled his mouth with bitter juice. He tried to swallow the acorns without chewing, but they did not go down his throat, lingering in his mouth and spreading bitterness.

When he looked a while later, the baby had already stopped crying and was crawling toward her brother. She looked at her brother and looked at the rice bowl and then looked at her brother again. Ch'ilsŏng, as a reward for having stopped crying, sorted rice grains in the bowl and gave the baby a spoonful. The baby swallowed the rice in no time and then looked up at her brother again. This time Ch'ilsŏng gave her an acorn. The baby did not put it into her mouth but kept fingering it.

He cursed loudly at the baby who could tell rice from acorn. The baby twisted her mouth and began to cry.

"Stop it!" Ch'ilsŏng kicked the baby. The baby closed her eyes tightly and lay prostrate on the floor. The flies on her head flew up once but settled down again immediately. When Ch'ilsŏng raised his foot again to kick, the baby just sniffled and stopped crying. But tears kept rolling out of her eyes. Ch'ilsŏng went on eating but turned his head at the sound of a choking cough.

The baby, who had eaten the acorn in the meantime, had vomited. The acorn thrown up with the baby's reddish saliva was not chewed at all. The reddish tint was of blood. The baby's face was flushed and muscles stood out on her neck.

Ch'ilsŏng instantly felt the acorn in his mouth taste like sand, and a bitter smell rose up. He flung away his spoon, picked up the child, and put her down on the dirt floor. When he spanked the baby's fleshless buttocks, her face turned dark but she kept sobbing silently. He kicked the rice bowl and walked across the room. He could not bear to hear the vomiting sound. He remembered the biscuits underneath the mat and, taking them all out and throwing them down in front of the baby, went out into the backyard. He circled the yard for some time and spat.

When he came into the room again, it was hot like the inside of a stove. He kept standing up and sitting down, and when he turned his head to look he found the baby asleep on the dirt floor, head pillowed on hand. On her vomit flies were crawling, and on the baby's head and inside the baby's open mouth were swarms of flies. Biscuits! Startled, he looked. Not a morsel of the biscuits remained. The baby could not have eaten them all so fast. Ch'il-un must have been home. He regretted that he had given them all to the baby, and thought he would beat up Ch'il-un when he saw him. He ran outside, kicking the baby on his way. He hated to look at the baby lying on her side with one hand under her head like a grown-up, and he hated to look at her thin limbs.

Hearing the baby's cry, he searched for Ch'il-un. Ch'il-un was playing with other children under the willow tree. He walked toward them, breathing hard. Although he walked as stealthily as he could, Ch'il-un caught sight of him and ran away. The children, chewing on Indian millet stalks, eyed Ch'ilsŏng and giggled. Some of them imitated Ch'ilsŏng's gait.

Ch'il-un could not be seen anywhere. When Ch'ilsŏng fell down because his foot caught in a vine, the children who had been following him laughed and chattered noisily. He stood up with difficulty and scowled at the children because he was afraid that they, too, might attack him in a body. The children, perhaps frightened by his scowl, took to their heels. To Ch'ilsŏng they did not look like children, but a horde of hungry monkeys after prey. He stared at their backs, thinking that all the children of this village were hateful. His forehead burned in the sun and his toe stung. The husks of Indian millet stalks that the children had peeled off hurt the soles of his feet. The children were running toward the brook. He thought Ch'il-un must be among them, and went toward the willow tree.

There were more Indian millet husks around the willow tree, and cowdung was scattered here and there, because people tied their cows to the tree. He leaned against the tree and looked. Before he knew it, his eyes had turned to Kŭnnyŏn's house. He yearned to see Kŭnnyŏn again. She'd be alone at home now. But what if somebody were there? Something stung him. Several huge ants were crawling up his legs. He brushed them off and looked again.

Far away on the hedge of Kŭnnyŏn's house were spread white garments, looking as if they would fly up like birds at the faintest sound. "No," he said to himself, "Nobody's there. Everybody's gone weeding." At the sound of footsteps he looked back. Kaettong's mother was walking toward him heavily, carrying a woman on her back.

Normally when they met she would accost him jokingly, with banter such as "Have you earned many boxes of matches? How about making a present of one to me?" But today she passed him without a word, her face tearful. Sweat poured in torrents from her forehead, her legs tottered, and she was panting like mad. Ch'ilsŏng saw that the woman being carried on her back looked like a corpse. The disheveled hair, the foamy mouth, the torn clothes. When he looked at the face inside the chaos of hair, he recognized Kŭnnyŏn's mother. He wanted to ask questions, but Kaettong's mother had already gone past the willow tree. What happened? Did she faint? Did she fight with somebody? He got up and followed them. He wanted to overtake Kaettong's mother and find out what was the matter, but his legs did not carry him as fast as he wished. He staggered even more than usual and did not advance much. He got angry, swerved wildly, and fell down. After writhing for a long time he got up and began walking slowly.

Smoke rose from Kŭnnyŏn's chimney. Oh, what had happened to Kŭnnyŏn's mother? As he went near Kŭnnyŏn's house, his feet moved toward it of their own accord, but checked himself and walked round it, hoping to overhear something.

When he stepped into the dirt yard he saw the baby defecating in the midst of a swarm of flies. As she strained hard, her anus jutted out like a finger and red blood dropped from it. The baby's eyes were dilated to the full and muscles stood out on her face like the blade of a sword. The small forehead was dripping with sweat. Ch'ilsŏng averted his face and went into the room. He wished he could step on the baby and kill it or cast it away on a distant mountain.

Putting into his mouth the acorn his foot had kicked, and scowling fiercely at the baby's groans, he came out into the backyard. He remembered Kŭnnyŏn's mother again and stepped up to the hedge.

He raised his head at the sound of a baby crying. He recognized at
once that it was not his sister but a new-born infant. He realized
Kŭnnyŏn's mother must have delivered a baby. Then his anxiety subsided a little, but he felt a bitter taste in his mouth at the thought of a
baby. He thought that babies had better be killed as soon as they were
born rather than let live like his baby sister.

Had she given birth to a girl like Kŭnnyŏn again? A blind girl? He
giggled for no reason at the thought. Before his giggle died down he
wondered to himself why it was that the women of this village produced such deformed children. Well, Kŭnnyŏn wasn't blind from birth.
And as for himself, he also became a cripple at four after suffering
paralysis following the measles. Then he recalled what his mother
always said about his illness.

At that time his mother went to the town hospital, walking miles in
knee-deep snow, carrying him on her back. After waiting in vain for an
eternity in the unheated hall in the hospital, she pushed open the door
of the consultation room, but the doctor raised his eyebrows and mo-
tioned her out, so she went into the hall again and waited another
eternity, till at last an errand boy came out with a finger-thin vial.

Whenever she recalled that day she cursed the doctor vehemently,
and cursed the world, too. Whenever his mother talked about it
Ch'ilsŏng always cut her short and told her not to say any more. He
couldn't bear to listen to it.

"Would I get better if I took medicine? Would Kŭnnyŏn be all right if
she took medicine? Oh, no. After you are crippled no medicine can cure
you. But who knows? Maybe if I could take some good medicine I might
be able to move my limbs freely like other people and go up the mountains to gather wood, and not be mocked by little urchins." He felt a
heaviness in his chest. He opened his eyes. Shall I go to a hospital and
inquire? "The doctors, they don't care about anything but money," he
repeated his mother's words and flopped down on the ground.

Silence came from Kŭnnyŏn's house and the baby's crying had
ceased. Ch'ilsŏng felt hungry. He looked at the sun and thought that
when his mother came back presently she would look at him through
her unkempt hair with anxiety and ask him why he hadn't gone out
begging today, and what would they eat tomorrow? He looked at the
bush clover trees.

"Could this bush clover tree be medicine for my disease?" he suddenly thought as he smelt the cool scent of the bush, and bit off a stalk. When he chewed on it, the smell of grass nauseated him and he felt like vomiting. But he closed his eyes tightly and chewed and swallowed without breathing. His throat felt torn, and saliva flowed and flowed. He thought the medicine would work only if he swallowed the saliva too, so he blinked his eyes and swallowed the saliva. For some reason tears flowed out of both his eyes.

He looked up at the sky and prayed that he would one day be able to gather wood instead of his mother. He had never had such a thought before; he didn't use to feel acutely sorry even when he saw his mother walking with difficulty under a big bundle of wood, but somehow he prayed such a prayer at that moment.

He stood perfectly still for a long while and then raised his arm before his eyes with a pounding heart. But the arm was still withered. He vomited suddenly and, hitting his head against the ground, began to weep.

It was after deep darkness had fallen that his mother came back, again with a load of wood.

"Are you sick?" The dim figure of his mother looked as if it would topple down any moment from the weight of fatigue. And the thick smell of grass, soaked through and through in her skirt, smelt like garlic.

"Dear, why don't you answer me?" His mother's hand as she touched him felt like a piece of log, but it had some warmth in it.

Ch'ilsŏng pushed away his mother's hand and turned away. His mother, sitting a few feet from him, studied her son and said, as if to herself, "Why doesn't he tell me if he's sick?" and got up and left the room. After some time his mother came in with rice boiled in vegetable soup and helped her son sit up. Ch'ilsŏng sat up and held the spoon with a trembling hand.

"Darling, are you sick?" Now his mother's clothes smelt of smoke, and with her breath came the smell of boiled rice. Ch'ilsŏng felt better.

"No."

His mother set her mind at ease and looked at her son eating soup.

"Kŭnnyŏn's mother had a baby today in the field. Oh, why do babies get born in poor homes?"

Ch'ilsŏng recalled the sight of Kŭnnyŏn's mother as he saw her under the willow tree, and the cry of the new-born infant rang in his ears. The miserable sight of Yŏng-ae as she tried to defecate revived before his eyes. He scowled.

"Oh, why should the likes of us conceive? Heaven's too unfeeling."

His mother sighed and went out with the empty bowl. Ch'ilsŏng, partly because it was too hot in the room and also because he wanted to know what was happening in Kŭnnyŏn's house, went outside.

From the pile of wood in a corner of the yard a strong smell of grass rose up, and the stars in the dark-blue sky shone like babies' eyes. He chased away the annoying mosquitoes and sat down on the heap of dry wood. Leaves rustled, and the warm mist rising from the wood warmed his bottom. His mother walked up to him.

"Is that you, Ch'ilsŏng? Why did you come out?" She sat down beside him and the wood rustled. Ch'ilsŏng averted his head because of the smell of sweat and baby's dung. His mother suckled the baby and sighed. It seemed as if she wanted to say something to Ch'ilsŏng, but kept fretfully caressing the baby, who looked like a sick cat.

She had weeded all day and at night had gone up to the mountain and gathered wood. Although she was dead tired, she had to look after the baby at night. Every night she felt she wouldn't be able to wake up again once she fell asleep. Ch'ilsŏng hated his mother for not looking after herself.

"Go to sleep, you chicken!" Ch'ilsŏng shouted. Yŏng-ae began to cry.

"How can she go to sleep? She's sick and she's starved all day and my milk's dried up," his mother wanted to say, but swallowed the words. Tears gathered in her eyes.

"Oh, it's all right. He wasn't talking to you. Suck your milk." She finished the words with difficulty. Tears streamed down her cheeks. She wished she could quench Yŏng-ae's thirst with her tears.

At long last his mother said, "Why would a baby get born, nearly killing its mother, if it didn't mean to live? When I looked in next door just now the baby was dead. That's better for everybody, but . . . Oh, poor things. She had writhed so in the furrow that the baby's head was all matted with earth, I heard. If it had lived it would have become nothing but a cripple. I heard that earth went into its eyes and ears, too. Oh, it did well to die," his mother murmured fretfully. Ch'ilsŏng breathed hard because of the oppression in his chest. Then he thought he would not have had to be like this if he had died as a baby.

"Oh, what's so good about living that we have to keep alive? Kŭnnyŏn's mother said she'll go weeding again tomorrow. She needs to rest at least one day, but this is no time for resting. Oh, why do babies get born to poor folks like us?"

She recalled the time she had threshed barley the very next day after she had given birth to Yŏng-ae. The sky had swirled and looked yellow, and the ears of barley became in turn big balls and tiny dots. Whenever she lifted or brought down the flail something kept sinking down from her body. Later on she felt something heavy hanging between her legs, but she could not take a look at it or do anything about it, afraid that others might notice. When at last she looked at it in the privy, a lump of flesh as big as her fist was hanging down from her insides and blood was all over her thighs. She was frightened but too ashamed to consult anybody about it, so she left it as it was. The flesh still hung between her thighs and oozed.

Because of that she was hotter in summer, and she stank. In the winter it was worse; she ached all over and felt chills as with an ague. If she walked far, the lump burned as if on fire and it also got so inflamed and swollen that she couldn't walk. Swellings erupted all over it, and as they festered and burst they pained her beyond description. But it was a pain she could not even talk about to anybody.

The mother sighed, thinking of the flesh hanging down damply even now. The dried leaves rustled. Yŏng-ae bit her mother's nipple.

"Ouch!" she cried out, but fearing that Ch'ilsŏng would swear at the baby if he knew, swallowed her next words and pressed Yŏng-ae's head to let her know it hurt. But, fearing again that she had pressed it too hard, she caressed the baby's head.

"Oh, in the midst of that bustle they had guests arrive at their house, but the guests had to leave without going in."

Ch'ilsŏng raised his head. The fragrant smell of mugwort burnt for the mosquito fire brushed past them.

"The people who'd been thinking of taking Kŭnnyŏn had come to take a look at her. Maybe you don't know about them. The man runs some sort of business in the town. I heard that he has some money. But he hasn't got a son yet. So he has taken in about a dozen women up till now, but still hasn't got a child. Oh, babies have to get born in houses like that."

His mother looked down at Yŏng-ae. Ch'ilsŏng didn't like to see his mother minding the baby even while talking. But he sat still waiting for her next words.

"So somebody talked to him about Kŭnnyŏn and the man said never. I heard it's because he felt sorry for his wife, but he came to take a look at her today. Why today, of all days? Maybe that's a sign Kŭnnyŏn will have luck. And she deserves it too. She's gentle and she can do any kind of work better than people who can see. Well, she'll get married into an heirless family and she'll bear a big healthy son. She has to live a better life."

"What would anybody want to take a blind girl like that for!" Ch'ilsŏng yelled abruptly. He was now all aflame with jealousy, and he resolved that if anybody tried to take Kŭnnyŏn away he would fight till death. That made him hot in the head and shaky in all four limbs.

"So, is she going to be married?"

His mother looked at her son and found it difficult to answer. When she reflected that Ch'ilsŏng was already old enough to yearn for girls, she felt sad and anxious about his future.

"It's not quite settled yet."

Ch'ilsŏng calmed down a little at that, but he felt sad and got up.

"Go in and sleep. And go to town tomorrow. We can't manage otherwise."

Ch'ilsŏng got angry and left his mother, to walk around aimlessly. As he walked he left behind the odor of mugwort, but the smell of grass floated on the crisp, cool air. Along the wind came the sound of grain stalks rubbing against each other; the cool, light breeze hugged him softly. His pants became wet with dew and the sound of insects undulated this way and that as if he were kicking at them with his toes.

He stood still. Before him, all was hidden under cover of the opaque darkness, and only the outline of the burnt mountain stood like a heap of clouds under the sky. Over the mountain stars shone as if in competition. When starlight lingered on his eyes, tears gushed down and he felt like crying his heart out. The mountain and the sky all looked so unfeeling to him.

"Let's go in, dear." His mother's weak voice reached him.

"Why do you follow me around all the time?" All the resentment that had been suppressed in his heart threatened to burst out at once.

"Please, let's go in. Don't walk around like this." His mother held his hand. Ch'ilsŏng tried to shake her hand off, but he lacked strength. His mother begged, half-crying. Walking back with his mother, Ch'ilsŏng decided to see Kŭnnyŏn the next day and ask her if she was going to get married, and also if she would marry him. When he had resolved thus, his heart beat fast and he seemed to behold before him a ray of hope.

"Please have pity on me and your younger brother and sister." His mother tried to soothe him by any means. Ch'ilsŏng walked home in silence.

Ch'ilsŏng got up late the next day and decided again that he would have an answer from Kŭnnyŏn that day. "What if she is already pledged in marriage?" The thought made him faint. He came out into the backyard and stood beside the hedge. All was silence inside Kŭnnyŏn's house; only the buzzing of flies around the dirty water basin could be heard. "I won't let her!" He stepped away from the hedge at once. The white stones in front of him looked yellow for some reason.

He went into the room panting. He looked at himself and thought, "I can't go to meet her like this!" There were traces of cowdung on his clothes and they were also torn here and there. But he quickly reminded himself that Kŭnnyŏn couldn't see, and tried to figure out what to say to her, looking up at the ceiling. He swallowed many times, but he could not think of a word to say. He felt as if he had never known how to speak in all his life.

Suddenly he felt weak when it crossed his mind that she might already know he was a cripple. He looked outside dispiritedly as he imagined Kŭnnyŏn saying, "Who would marry someone like you?"

The leaves of the squash and the gourd vines that wound around the hedge, of the corn stalks and apricot trees and the bush clover that stretched upward toward the sky, all shook freely and blithely in the breeze. He felt somehow less free than those plants and trees, and he sighed till his whole body shook.

At last Ch'ilsŏng emerged from his yard with firm resolution and, after pacing in front of Kŭnnyŏn's house several times, pushed open the bush clover gate and strode in.

The door to the dirt-floored room was shut, and only a bush clover broom lay in the yard. When he opened the door a cat jumped out, mewing. He was so frightened that his heart throbbed wildly. He stepped on to the dirt floor and after much hesitation opened the door of the inner room. Only heavy air moved out toward him; Kŭnnyŏn was not there. He suspected at once that she had gotten married already, and searched the kitchen and the backyard. As he was about to give up and turn back, he heard the bush clover gate open. Frightened, he ran to a post and stepped close to the straw mat stored behind it. The door of the kitchen opened noisily and Kŭnnyŏn came in with the wooden laundry basin. He felt faint and weak. He felt as if Kŭnnyŏn could see and would come up to him; as if she was not blind, but could always open her eyelids and see with her starry eyes. Feeling he was about to suffocate any moment, he suppressed his breath and went behind the straw mat. But his breath came in wilder pants, and he felt as if the straw mat would block his nostrils and make him swoon.

Kŭnnyŏn went out into the backyard. Hearing the dragging of her shoes, he stuck out his head, peered about, and tried to move his feet; but his whole body twitched convulsively and he could not move a step. He thought of giving up and going home. He felt as if his body had been made of stone. But then the hedge rustled as Kŭnnyŏn spread laundry on it and he remembered "Kŭnnyŏn is going to marry a man in town!" His feet began to move in wild staggering.

Kŭnnyŏn, in the middle of spreading a piece of laundry on the hedge, sharply turned her face and halted. Ch'ilsŏng dared not look at Kŭnnyŏn but stood there like one out of his wits.

"Who is it?"

Silence.

"Who is it?" Kŭnnyŏn's voice was trembling. Ch'ilsŏng thought he had to say something, anything, but his lips refused to move. At long last he moved forward one step.

"Oh, it's you." Kŭnnyŏn moved close to the hedge and bowed her head. Her softly closed eyelids were tremulous. Ch'ilsŏng became a little bolder as Kŭnnyŏn recognized him. He began to worry about the outside now, and he kept looking out.

"Go away! My mother will be back soon." Kŭnnyŏn spoke decisively. Her voice was the same as when she was a child.

"I heard you're going to get married. You must be happy."

"What foolish talk. Go away!" Kŭnnyŏn, fingering her laundry, sighed softly. White flesh peeped from between the rents in her thin blouse. Ch'ilsŏng stepped close to her unawares.

"Oh, Mother!" Kŭnnyŏn shouted, grasping the hedge. Ch'ilsŏng became fearful and thought of retreating. He felt faint and the ground swirled before him.

"My mother's coming."

Ch'ilsŏng opened his eyes at the sound of Kŭnnyŏn's trembling voice. The thick braid of glossy black hair on her back smelt intensely of Kŭnnyŏn. Ch'ilsŏng pressed Kŭnnyŏn's foot with his foot. Kŭnnyŏn blushed and, withdrawing her foot, moved away. The laundry in her hand fell limply to the ground.

Ch'ilsŏng feared that she might pick up a stone and hit him, but Kŭnnyŏn stepped close to the hedge and just fingered the bush clover twigs. Her hair ribbon blew in the breeze. She did not say another word, but just fingered the twigs of the hedge.

"I'll give you sweets and . . . and clothes, too. You won't get married, will you, if I do?"

Kŭnnyŏn kept silent for a long time and then, raising her head a little, said, "Who cares for sweets?" and laughed softly.

Ch'ilsŏng also laughed and asked again, "You won't, will you?"

"How do I know? My father knows."

Ch'ilsŏng was at a loss for words at that. So he just stood there like a fool.

"Get out at once." Kŭnnyŏn turned her face toward him. She had thick eyelashes over softly closed eyes, and hanging at the tips of her eyelashes were drops of anxiety.

"Well, are you going to marry, then?"

Kŭnnyŏn dropped her head and rolled a stone with the tip of her shoe. Ch'ilsŏng felt like crying.

"You won't? Promise?"

Kŭnnyŏn, instead of answering, sighed and turned away. The baby cried just then. Ch'ilsŏng, startled, ran out.

When he got home, he saw Ch'il-un tying the baby with a strip of cloth. She was rolling on the floor of the kitchen. The baby moved her thin limbs wildly and struggled. Ch'il-un hit her as if she had been a dead fish.

"Are you going to sleep or not? If you won't sleep, then I'll kill you." He waved a fist at the baby, his nose dripping from both nostrils. The baby shook like a leaf and tears kept flowing out of her closed eyes.

"Yes! Close your eyes like that and sleep!" Ch'il-un lay down beside the baby and squeezed his side with one hand.

"Mother, it hurts here so much, I can't carry the baby any more. I can't," Ch'il-un murmured, snuffling. Presently, drowsiness filled his eyes and he fell asleep. Ch'ilsŏng looked down at his brother absently and stepped onto the dirt floor.

"Mama!" The baby he thought was sleeping opened her round eyes and looked up at her brother. Ch'ilsŏng got frightened. Unconsciously he lifted a foot and raised an eyebrow, as if to kick her. The baby twisted her thin lips and closed her eyes.

"Mama! Mama!" the baby's mouth was calling and tears were running down her cheeks. Ch'ilsŏng went into the room, paced it in a circle a few times and came out into the backyard. Hoping Kŭnnyŏn was still standing in her yard, he carefully parted the brushwood of the hedge and peeped in. Kŭnnyŏn was not there; only the laundered clothes lay spread over the hedge.

He came into the room and, looking up at the beggar's sack hanging on the wall, thought about how he would buy material for Kŭnnyŏn's clothes. He thought to himself, who knows but that might show his feelings to Kŭnnyŏn and her parents, too? He slung his sack over his shoulder sideways and, putting the straw hat on his head, went outside. Passing the kitchen, he caught sight of the baby lapping up something. When he looked around he saw that the baby was drinking her own urine beside the stove.

"You! Dirty thing!" Ch'ilsŏng growled and went out to the street. It was hot, as if he had stepped into hot water. Taking the new highway, he arranged his clothes and hat and tried to walk with dignity. He thought he would have to look more like a gentleman from now on. He coughed a solemn false cough and tried to walk slowly. Well, if he walked like that the children wouldn't pester him or the grown-ups make fun of him. He recalled Kŭnnyŏn's face as he had this thought. He looked back stealthily, but his village was already out of sight and only the Indian millet field filled his view. As he walked near the field the smell of young Indian millet leaves floated past and sweat ran down his back. He jerked his body once or twice and looked in no particular direction.

The burnt mountain that shone green beyond the Indian millet field looked so close that it seemed he could reach its top if he moved only a few steps. It was the same mountain that he could see at leisure from the window of his house, and it was also the mountain that he could look at while trying to walk inconspicuously past an Indian millet field like this.

He exhaled a deep sigh. Whenever he looked at the mountain he felt his torn mind compose itself, and recalled things from his childhood he had quite forgotten.

One spring day when mist was rising from the distant mountain, he woke up in the morning and from his window he saw his friends going up the mountain in single file with A-frame racks on their backs and long staffs stuck sideways across their A-frames. He envied them so much that he sighed and looked at them like a mindless boy, thinking, when will I be all right again and able to go up the mountain to gather wood like those boys, with a staff stuck in the A-frame slung over my back? And he thought that when he grew up he would climb the mountain and split thick boughs and bring down more wood than the A-frame could hold.

He sneered at himself when he recalled that thought. All the joints in his bones ached, and his heart contracted. He shook his head a couple of times and trudged on. Before his eyes was only Kŭnnyŏn now.

Two days later.

Ch'ilsŏng was standing at the entrance of the town of Songhwa, six miles from his village. He could not earn much by begging in the town near his village, so he had roamed on to Songhwa. After two days and nights of begging he at last managed to buy some cotton material for Kŭnnyŏn's dress and was going back home.

He thought of spending that night somewhere, but decided to start homeward at once because he wanted to give the gift to Kŭnnyŏn quickly, and also because he was worried about Kŭnnyŏn's rumored marriage.

The starless sky and the furry-soft darkness dazed his eyes, but for some reason his mind was at rest, and a certain degree of hope brightened his eyes. He could distinctly discern the mountains and the waters, as if they lived in his mind's eye, and even the pebbles on the highway seemed to be amicably inviting him to play with them.

He thought he liked the road at night much more than in the daytime, when cars ran past raising dust and endless pedestrians walked on it. So he walked on, without feeling any pain in his legs. When he halted his steps, the smell of the mountain welcomed him and the running brook whispered to him. The smell of mud also wafted up to him from the rice paddy, and when mountain birds resumed singing, the distant glow of lamps seemed to float up and fly away.

Every time he breathed, the fabric for Kŭnnyŏn's clothes touched his chest like the skin of a girl and made his flesh thrill down to the toes. "How shall I give it to her?" He opened his mouth unconsciously and made as if to mouth something. He pictured himself standing face to face with Kŭnnyŏn. "When I give her this cloth, Kŭnnyŏn will blossom with smiles to the tips of her thick eyelashes!" His heart pumped noisily.

Raindrops began to fall as dawn broke in the eastern sky. He became frightened and started to run, but the rain came thicker and the wind scattered it with a sound like the fluttering of a flock of sparrows.

He hesitated over what to do for a while, and turned his steps toward a village that showed its dim outline through the thick screen of rain. If it hadn't been for Kŭnnyŏn's cloth he would have marched on, rain or no rain, but he feared that the precious fabric would get wet from the rain, so he decided to seek shelter in the nearby village.

When he looked back after walking a good while the highway could be seen distinctly, and for some reason he felt unwilling to move, but he forced himself on.

When he reached the village, a smell of wet straw invaded his nostrils and as he walked past a privy the stink stung them. He stepped under the eaves of a house. He felt chilly all over and his eyes were tired, so he moved next to the wall and crouched down beside it. An image of the spindly tree at the entrance of his village flitted before his eyes. Kŭnnyŏn appeared before him. He opened his eyes wide.

Day had dawned amid the rain. The distant mountain could be seen, the cluster of roofs revealed itself, and water dripped from the eaves noisily. He mustered his courage, stood up, and looked around.

He saw that the house he was standing by looked like a rich man's. The walls were of cement, and the roof was of dark, baked tiles; the wooden gate was large and studded with nails with heads as big as his fists. He felt his frozen heart thaw.

The marble nameplate looked dignified. Surrounded by the sound of raindrops, Ch'ilsŏng looked at the nameplate hard, and kept on thinking.

"Maybe this is a lucky day for me. Maybe I can get a good breakfast at this house, and some rice or money too." He squeezed his eyes shut and thought, "Shall I pretend to be blind, too? Maybe that would make me look more pitiful and they might give me more rice and money." He tried to keep his eyes shut but his eyelids itched and his eyelashes trembled, and the marble nameplate criss-crossed his view, so that at last he opened his eyes.

"What shall I do? Maybe my clothes are too clean." He ran at once toward the muddy spot where he had been squatting. He felt even more chilly, and his lips trembled. As he was about to peep in through the crack between the two panels of the gate he heard footsteps and quickly moved aside. The gate opened with a loud squeak. As always when people looked at him, Ch'ilsŏng dropped his head and stood uneasily.

"Who is it?" It was a thick voice. Ch'ilsŏng looked up. The man had long, narrow horizontal eyes and looked like a servant, clad in black clothes.

"I . . . want some food."

"So early in the morning?" the man muttered to himself and turned back toward the main building.

"This is a charitable house. Other people would have tried to chase me away first." Ch'ilsŏng congratulated himself and looked in.

The elevated building with the wooden porch attached looked like the master's study; to one side of it was a small gate, and beyond the gate the living-room floor of the inner quarters could be glimpsed. Stretching from the left of the study up to the front gate was a room that looked like a storehouse, and in front of it lay stacks of straw. Yellowish water dripped from the straw stacks. In the spacious front yard water flowed forcefully in a stream, creating a furrow.

"I'll have to go in there to get some food," he thought, and began walking awkwardly toward the inner gate. When he stepped over the threshold of the middle gate, a dog shot out from the inner kitchen like an arrow. When it growled at him, Ch'ilsŏng stepped back one step and clucked his tongue to appease it. The dog bared its sharp teeth and, jumping up, pulled at the beggar's sack with its teeth. He shouted and ran out past the middle gate. He hoped someone was in the study to call the dog back, but no sound came from there. The dog rolled its eyes and, raising its forefeet, tried to jump up to his face. Ch'ilsŏng held his begging sack with his teeth and kept bending and stretching his body. But the dog did not abate its attack, and Ch'ilsŏng had to make a further retreat. The dog followed him to the main gate and, when Ch'ilsŏng hesitated to make an exit, ran up to him and pulled at his trouser leg with its teeth. Ch'ilsŏng screamed and ran. The man came out from inside.

"C'mon, c'mon."

The dog ignored the call and kept barking with its sharp muzzle. Ch'ilsŏng looked back at the dog with murder in his eyes. The man beckoned to the dog with his hand. The dog slowly retreated with backward steps, still keeping its eyes on Ch'ilsŏng.

Ch'ilsŏng suddenly felt nauseated and a chill ran down his spine. He felt feverish all at once. He looked for the dog but it was not there. Instead, the big, ugly gate blocked his view impudently. He thought of knocking on it again, but he shuddered to think of encountering the dog again. He gave up and staggered on.

The rain whipped him mercilessly, while the wind and the sounds of the trees shaking and the water flowing in the ditch almost split his eardrums. On the surface of the muddy water that flowed in swirls floated whitish straw, and leaves whirled swiftly like green birds.

The wet clothes clung to his body mercilessly and the tempestuous wind made him pant for breath. He looked around, hoping to find something, but all the gates of the houses were tightly shut and breakfast smoke rose from the chimneys. He hoped to find an empty house or a water mill, but before his heavy eyes the dog kept jumping up and down, and he felt as if it were following him. The trouser leg torn by the dog flapped as he walked and disclosed his yellow, withered leg. The rain dripping from his tattered straw hat, worn low over his eyes, felt as salty on his lips as tears. He suddenly felt like crying when he thought of the material getting wet.

He stood still. The rain was so thick that he could not discern where the mountain was and where the brook, while through the madly flapping grain stalks a loud, heavy sound like a huge animal roaring shook the earth.

He ardently wished to advance, but his feet refused to move. He looked back, to note that he had almost passed the village. He moved toward the two or three houses at the end of the village, but kept gazing at the field, as if he had some unfinished business.

It was not the first time that he had been chased away by a dog; and countless times he had been abused and persecuted by men, too. But somehow he felt an uncontrollable fury today.

"Why are you standing there like that?"

He looked back in surprise to find that he was standing before a small building which apparently was a water-mill. The man who was looking at him with outstretched neck looked between forty and fifty, and Ch'ilsŏng could instantly tell that he was a cripple and a beggar like himself. The man grinned. He did not feel like going in, but entered after some hesitation. With a strong smell of rice husks came also the stink of horse droppings.

"Come over here. Oh, your clothes are all wet."

The man raised himself leaning on his crutches, spread the straw mat he had been sitting on, and sat down on one corner of it. Ch'ilsŏng quickly noted the man's gray hair and beard. He feared that the man might try to take away his earnings.

"You must be cold because of those wet clothes. Here, put on my old jacket and take them off and dry them." The man searched his bundle and said, "Here it is. Come on."

Ch'ilsŏng looked back. It was a dark, western jacket patched in several places. He envied the man such a good garment and looked directly into his smiling eyes. The man did not look like one who would try to snatch away other beggars' earnings. Ch'ilsŏng dropped his glance and looked at the water dripping from his sleeves. The man walked toward him, leaning on his crutch.

"Why are you standing there like that? Put this on."

"Oh, no." Ch'ilsŏng retreated one step and looked at the western jacket. His heart throbbed before a garment the like of which he had never worn in his life.

"Oh, aren't you a stubborn fellow! Then come here and sit on this mat." The man led him by the hand and made him sit on the straw mat. The man pretended not to notice Ch'ilsŏng's twisted legs.

"Have you eaten anything for breakfast?"

Ch'ilsŏng was fearful lest the man wanted a share in any food he might have in his sack, and cast a glance at the sack. It was dripping also.

"No."

After a silence, the man murmured, "Then you've got to eat something."

He searched his bundle for a while. "Here. Eat this, though it's only a trifle." He took out and spread before Ch'ilsŏng something wrapped in a piece of newspaper. Inside the newspaper was some half dried-up boiled millet.

His appetite suddenly whetted by the sight of food, Ch'ilsŏng stretched out his hand to take it, but his hand did not work. It just shook. The man noticed it and placed the paper on Ch'ilsŏng's raised knees close to his mouth, saying, "I'm sorry there's so little."

Shyness weighed heavily on his eyelids, so he looked down, sniffed to hide his embarrassment, and sucked in the millet on the paper placed on his raised knees. The smell of printer's ink spread in his mouth and the slightly spoiled millet tasted sweeter the more he chewed it. As he smacked his lips over the last grain, his tongue yearned for more. His ears felt itchy and hot.

The man regretted there was no more. Ch'ilsŏng took his mouth away from the newspaper and smiled at him. The man smiled, too, and turning his eyes caught sight of Ch'ilsŏng's leg.

"Oh, you're bleeding! You must have hurt yourself!" He stooped down to look at it. Ch'ilsŏng felt the pain reviving and looked at it, too. His trouser leg was soaked red with blood and his leg had begun to bleed once more. Suddenly he felt a pain in his bowels, and bent his leg and raised his head. He felt as if he were smelling the fishy smell of wet dogs in the wind.

"I got bitten by a dog."

"Oh, have you been to that tile-roofed house? The house that raises those bloody dogs? And there's more than one, too. Let me look at it. You mustn't leave a dog bite unattended."

The man grasped his leg. Ch'ilsŏng quickly pulled away but felt a smarting sensation across the bridge of his nose. He twitched his nose a couple of times. Tears ran down his cheeks. The man noticed that, and laughed and patted him on the back.

"Are you crying? If one were to cry at every . . . Well, you mustn't cry."

Ch'ilsŏng raised his head quickly to look at the man. The man's eyes were full of fury. When his eyes traveled to his leg again, Ch'ilsŏng felt heavy in the chest and dry in his throat. He dropped his head and, scooping up soft dust that lay piled on the floor, rubbed it on the wound.

"Oh, no! Don't ever do that again. Leave it alone if you don't have any ointment. Don't rub dirt on wounds again. That makes them fester."

Ch'ilsŏng bent his leg from embarrassment and looked out. The man was sunk in thought again.

Wind whipped in the rain, and the countless spiders' webs hanging from the ceiling swayed like smoke. The leaves of the willow tree shook like a frightened child and muddy water ran along the earth in a torrent. He looked up, startled to see a big bat covered with white chaff flapping its wings threateningly.

"Are you a born cripple?" the man asked suddenly. Ch'ilsŏng bowed his head and, after much hesitation, answered, "No."

"Then it was because of an illness. Did you get any treatment?"

Ch'ilsŏng looked long at his legs again, hesitating. At last he muttered, "No. None at all."

"Ugh, in this world sound legs get broken. It's nothing unusual not to get treatment for illness." The man laughed into the void. The laughter made Ch'ilsŏng shudder. He glanced at the man. As the man looked out at the road with fiercely dilated eyes, blue veins bulged on his forehead and his lips were clenched shut. "Oh, I curse myself to think what a fool I was! I should have fought till death! What a damned stupid fool I was!"

Ch'ilsŏng pricked up his ears and tried to understand the meaning of the man's words, but could not make it out. The man looked back at Ch'ilsŏng. The two or three thin wrinkles under his eyes reminded Ch'ilsŏng of his own father.

"Listen, my boy. I was the head of a family once. I was a model worker in a factory, too. A first-rate engineer. After my leg was broken I was thrown out of the factory, and my woman ran away and the children cried from hunger. My parents died of sorrow. Oh, there's no use talking about it."

The man stared at Ch'ilsŏng. Ch'ilsŏng's heart pounded for some reason and he could not meet the man's eyes, so he looked at his broken leg, and at the mute earth under that leg.

Outside it was misty with drizzling rain, and the distant mountain looked tearful. The croaking of frogs gave him the illusion of being in his own village, and he fancied himself looking at Kŭnnyŏn's back under the locust tree. Ch'ilsŏng got up.

"I've got to go home."

The man got up, too.

"Oh, do you have a home? Then go."

When Ch'ilsŏng raised his head the man came near him and arranged his straw hat for him, smiling. Ch'ilsŏng felt like leaning on him as if he were his mother.

"Goodbye. Hope to see you again."

Instead of answering, Ch'ilsŏng smiled at him and left. When he looked back after a long time the man was standing there before the mill, absently. Ch'ilsŏng wiped away his tears with his fist and looked back again.

The patches of millet and Indian millet fields were flooded with rain, and the stalks were half sunk under water. A frog croaked, and he thought to himself this was going to be a lean year again. The croaking of the frog sounded like the heavy groan of a man.

It began to drizzle again. His clothes that got wet once more and the rain weighing down his eyelashes made his heart heavy with swirling indefinable misgivings.

When he reached his village the rain thickened again and the wind also began to blow. Even the locust tree that always looked cool seemed gloomy under the scowling sky, and the low mountains screening the back of the village looked dim through the rain. His steps faltered when the hedges of the houses and the vegetable gardens came into view, and when he thought that Kŭnnyŏn might be going to the well below the mountain with the water jar on her head.

When he arrived home his mother came out to meet him with eyes full of tears.

"Oh, you bad boy! Where have you been all this while? Didn't you ever think your mother'd be waiting?" Taking the sack from him, his mother wept. Ch'ilsŏng didn't answer, but came into the room where the floor was more than half covered with bowls and basins for catching the rain leaking from the ceiling. The water hit the bowls and basins rhythmically. Ch'ilsŏng stood there and didn't know what to do. He shivered and shook more severely from cold than when he had been walking.

Ch'il-un and the baby were lying on the floor, and the baby's head was wrapped round with some whitish cloth. On their small bodies too the water fell.

"Sit down somewhere. Oh, I roamed the town all night last night searching for you. I even looked into taverns and bars. You bad boy, why didn't you tell me you'd be away if you weren't coming back at night?"

His mother wept aloud now. Since she had lost her husband she leaned on her crippled son as the pillar of the family. Ch'il-un woke up from the noise.

"Oh, it's Brother! Brother's back!" He jumped up, rubbing his eyes. Swarms of flies flew up, and the baby fretted. Ch'il-un rubbed his eyes with both hands and tried to look at his brother but couldn't, so he rubbed harder.

"Oh, son, don't. That will hurt you more. Oh, the children have been sick while you were away and made me so worried. And Ch'il-un's got those sore eyes, too. I wonder what's come over this village. Everybody, young and old, has sore eyes."

None of these words came to Ch'ilsŏng's ears. He dearly wished to lie down somewhere where water did not fall and go to sleep. Ch'il-un broke out crying from irritation and then, going out the back door, urinated and washed his eyes with the urine.

"Wet your eyes well. Not just the lids but the eyeballs, too. Look how he wants to look at you. He asked for his brother all day yesterday." His mother wept again. Ch'ilsŏng moved aside to avoid the water dripping on his back. This time water dropped on his nose and ran down to his lips. He struck his nose angrily and swore.

"Oh, why should it rain now? And the wind! What fierce wind! It will break all the millet stalks. Oh, God, what can be done?" She raised her clasped hands as if in prayer. Her hair was all matted with the rain, and her eyes were bloodshot, the eyelids blue-black and sunken. Her soiled clothes were stained with rain.

Ch'ilsŏng sat down on the sill and closed his eyes. His eyes felt unbearably sore and his eyelashes stung his eyeballs. As he rolled his eyes a couple of times, he suddenly recalled the water-mill.

"Yesterday the dike of Kaettong's rice paddy broke and everything was swept away. Oh, what a dreadful curse is that wind! What's going to happen to *our* field?"

His mother ran outside. Ch'il-un, crying, tried to follow her but tripped on the doorsill, fell down on the ground and screamed. Ch'ilsŏng raised his eyebrows. "I'll kill that thing!"

His mother quickly picked up Ch'il-un to take him out of her older son's sight and walked around in and out, casting anxious eyes toward their field.

Ch'ilsŏng did not want to see his worried mother, so he turned aside and closed his eyes. Startled, he opened his eyes. The baby, who had been lying in a corner of the room drawing quick breaths, tried to get up and fell down repeatedly, weeping. She kept rubbing her head on the straw mat and fretfully scratched the cloth wound round her head, making a sound that made him feel creepy.

Ch'ilsŏng tried not to open his eyes but he could not help opening them and catching sight of the baby's yellow fingers tearing at her head. He wished the baby dead, and closed his eyes.

Wind blew more fiercely. One could hear the branches of the apricot tree breaking, and also a sound like a pillar toppling that shook the back door. Ch'il-un came into the room and lay down.

"Brother, get me some eye medicine tomorrow. Kaettong's father bought him eye medicine from the town and his eyes are all right now."

Ch'ilsŏng listened to his brother in silence and thought of the fabric inside his shirt. The thought that he should have bought eye medicine instead crossed his mind but quickly disappeared, and he tried to think of a way to give the cloth to Kŭnnyŏn.

A match struck in the kitchen and soon his mother came in.

"Water got into the stove, up to the top. What can I do? The little ones haven't had anything yet, either. How hungry you all must be!" She went out and came running back presently.

"The dike broke in Kŭnnyŏn's rice paddy, too. The strongest dike in the neighborhood. Oh, what's going to happen to ours?"

Ch'ilsŏng's eyes became dilated.

"Oh, why doesn't this little girl go to sleep? Don't tear at your head like that! That little girl hasn't slept a wink for days. Kaettong's mother told me rat skin's good for sores so I killed one and plastered its skin on her head, but she keeps tearing at it like that. I guess it itches because it's healing. Don't you think so?" His mother seemed to want some reassuring concurrence. But Ch'ilsŏng didn't want to hear about anything except Kŭnnyŏn. He asked patiently, "Then everything's swept away in their rice fields?"

"Yes! Oh my milk's dried up." Looking at the fretting baby, his mother massaged her breasts. They were limp.

The baby panted more urgently and her hands tried to reach her head but dropped down tiredly. His mother listened again to the sound of the wind.

"Oh, our millet will all be swept away now! Our field can't escape a flood if Kŭnnyŏn's field got swept away. Oh, Kŭnnyŏn's lucky she doesn't have to live through this. She got married yesterday."

"What?" Ch'ilsŏng screamed. The precious fabric kept inside his shirt struck his skin like a rock. His mother looked at her son, startled.

"Mum, look at that!" Ch'il-un jumped up and groaned. They all looked.

The cloth wrapped around the baby's head was about half torn off, and maggots as big as rice grains were crawling out of it.

"Oh, God! What happened? What *happened?*" His mother went over to the baby and snatched away the cloth. The rat skin came away and from it dropped masses of maggots bathed in blood.

"Baby! My baby! Wake up! Oh, wake up!" Hearing his mother's scream, Ch'ilsŏng ran outside frenziedly.

The rain poured down fiercely and the wind stormed madly, and the sky, torn mercilessly by the lightning, roared with thunder.

Ch'ilsŏng glared up at the sky.

Pierrot

Hwang Sun-wŏn

Born in 1915, Hwang Sun-wŏn is one of the most respected masters of fiction in Korea. And he fully merits this respect, too. Through the decades when being a writer meant writing trivial popular novels or starving, Hwang Sun-wŏn steadily refused to compromise, and adhered stubbornly to his artistic vision.

Hwang Sun-wŏn's stories deal with the timeless elements of life in Korea. He pursues, through a series of illuminating and suggestive images, the meaning of being a Korean and living in Korea. The tired old troupe leader in "Pierrot" (1951) is one such image, although here the particular circumstance of the Korean War makes him somewhat more typical of the '50s decade than his other images. As in "Pierrot," in most of his stories the harsh circumstances of life, rather than being indicted or attacked, are mournfully gazed upon with lyrical tenderness and quiet resignation. The focus of attention, in other words, is not the circumstances themselves but the characters' emotional reactions to them. This is why Hwang Sun-wŏn is a genuinely Korean author, and why he represents so strongly the main tradition of Korean literature.

In his longer works he exhibits a more ambitious historical perspective, examining the meaning of Korea's past history and the problem of what attitude to take toward the heritage of the nation's checkered past.

After a writing career that spanned five decades and after many years of teaching creative writing at a university, Hwang is now living in quiet retirement.

As had happened in Taegu, in Pusan also we came to be beholden for our shelter to a lawyer's family.

I sent my family on ahead of me for refuge, and when I followed them to Pusan later, I found that my family had not come down to Pusan but had stopped in Taegu. The reason was that it cost less to live in Taegu than in Pusan. So I went up to Taegu on Christmas day. My wife and children were living in a rented space in the great mansion of a lawyer next to the burned-out courthouse, which stood like a skeleton. The nest of my beloved wife and darling children was a shed in a corner of the spacious garden of this majestic mansion.

It was much colder in Taegu than in Pusan. As the room was built for storage, with the only door facing north, not a ray of sunshine strayed into it all day. It was chilly and sinister, so much so that the children all went out as soon as day broke, although it was freezing cold outside. But we deemed ourselves lucky. It was fortunate that we had among our acquaintance a friend of this family, so that we could obtain some kind of shelter, which was needless to say a great good fortune for refugees like us.

There were some rules we had to observe in this house. By decree of the mother-in-law of the lawyer, we were forbidden to draw water from the well in the inner yard after dusk, or in the morning before they did, or to do laundry of whatever kind in the inner yard, where there was a well and also tap water. The prohibition against drawing water in the morning was no inconvenience to us. As we ate only twice a day, we needed to draw water only late in the morning for late breakfast, after the lawyer's family had all finished breakfast. It was the same with laundry. We had only to carry water to the outer yard and wash our things there. But on days when we had used up our water, if somebody got thirsty at night, especially if any of the children got thirsty, it was painful not to have any water. Well, people don't die or get ill because of one night's thirst.

There was another prohibition decreed by this august old lady, and that concerned the use of the lavatory. We were forbidden to use the one in the inner yard, so my wife had to build makeshift facilities in a corner of the garden behind the bushes. It was hidden from view by straw matting hung like a curtain. It was very embarrassing for grown-ups to use this crude latrine in the daytime, but we were not in a position to complain about such small inconveniences.

It did not take too long for us to perceive that the household was managed entirely by the mother-in-law of the lawyer. My wife was informed by the maid of the house that, as the lawyer's wife was the only child of this old lady, she had come to live with her daughter and son-in-law when the daughter married, and from the first governed the whole household. The children had a separate room to themselves, and the old lady occupied a big heated-floor room alone, from whence she reigned. Nobody in that family ate in the morning until after the old lady had finished her breakfast.

The old lady's hobby was playing cards with friends, and for that purpose they met in one of their homes in turn, and they also went to Buddhist temples in a group to offer prayers every now and then. We could often see the old lady going out in a silk dress, and she looked so erect and trim that one could hardly think of her as nearing sixty. Her friends who frequently visited the house were all well-dressed and well-groomed women who did not look as if they had ever known hardship in their lives. Maybe life is something that should be lived with at least that much decency.

About ten days after I joined my family, we woke up one morning to find that one of the rubber shoes of my eight-year-old daughter Sŏn-a had disappeared. It was in vain that we searched everywhere nearby. The whole family covered every square inch of the spacious garden. It could not have been stolen, because if anybody meant to steal shoes why should he have taken only Sŏn-a's, and only one shoe at that? So we had to conclude that the shepherd dog of the house had carried it away and left it somewhere far off.

Although we were extremely short of money, we couldn't let our daughter go around barefoot in winter, so my wife went out to buy a pair of shoes. When she came back with a new pair, she recounted what she had heard at the shoe shop: sometimes one shoe is stolen by someone who has a sick member in the family, in the belief that the sickness would be transferred to the owner of the shoe, if he or she is of the same age as the sick person and the shoe is disposed of in a certain manner. Then my wife said that a child of the lawyer who was about Sŏn-a's age had been ill in bed for several days.

When she said that she looked worried, and angry, and also sad.

I shook my head and said that could not be the case. But I, too, could not help having an anxious and angry feeling in my heart. Granted that it was a foolish superstition, and granted that we were people of no consequence at all; still, if one loves one's own child, one should know that other people's children are equally dear to their parents. Moreover, Sŏn-a was the most fragile of our four children. If she were to get ill in refugee life like this, there would be no way to bring her back to health at all.

A few days of anxiety and uneasiness passed. We heard that the sick child of the lawyer was well again. And our Sŏn-a did not take ill. The disappearance of the shoe must have been the shepherd dog's doing. The old lady, who spent many days praying to Buddha in the temple, could not have done anything so inhuman as that.

It was a few days later.

When I got home my wife was sitting alone in the cold, dark room and told me in a voice heavy with anxiety that the old lady of the house told her that we must vacate the room. The reason was that they needed the room (which was in fact a shed) to store coal. But my wife had heard a different story from the housemaid.

At midday, a large group of friends of the old lady came to play cards, as often happened. One of the old women caught sight of the straw mat screen behind the bush in the corner of the garden. Why don't people's eyes grow dim as they should with old age? She went up to it to see what it was. When she found out what was behind, she spat with vehemence and complained ferociously about the monstrosity of the thing. She ran up to the old lady of the house at once and blamed her very loudly for letting people defecate in the garden. So the old lady of the house herself began cursing the uncivilized paupers who wore human masks but were not fit to be treated as human beings. She went on to declare that since her house was not a refugee asylum she would order us out at once. Then she went to my wife and ordered her to vacate the room. But she could not very well tell my wife that we had to leave the house because we had made a latrine in the garden, so she gave a different reason—that they needed our room to store coal. Well, that proved the verity of the old lady's saying that human beings should so behave as to be worthy of being regarded as human beings, because it was the old lady herself who had forbidden us to use the facilities of the house and thereby forced us to relieve ourselves in the garden behind the straw mat screen. After all, she had not forgotten that as human beings we had to relieve ourselves and could not but resort to such an uncivilized method, however reluctant we might have been to do so. And moreover, she made it clear to us herself that our room was no room for human beings to dwell in, but a shed for storing things like coal.

So this was how the shabby Hwang Sun-wŏn family, evicted from the shed in the lawyer's mansion, drifted to Pusan at last around the end of March, after a few more attempts at securing shelter in Taegu.

We had planned to stay with my sister-in-law's family in her rented room for a while until we could rent a room for ourselves. I had seen that the room the family was living in had space to accommodate a few more people.

This house happened to be a lawyer's house, too. It was located at the rear of the Kyŏngnam Middle School. It was a pretty big house of mixed Japanese and western style, and my sister-in-law and her children were using a room of about one hundred and twenty square feet. As there was an old cabinet and a small table to one side of the room, usable space consisted of only about ninety square feet, but that was enough for my sister-in-law and her three children and the six members of our family.

When we came to Pusan, however, we found that another family was already living with my sister-in-law. It consisted of a mother and two children. The husband of this lady was an army judge advocate stationed at the front. Originally the lawyer had promised to give this family a separate room, but later on he said he needed to keep the other room for guests, so this lady and her children came to live in the room my sister-in-law was occupying. That had caused no inconvenience, as both families consisted of women and children (my brother-in-law had gone to the United States for technical training and was now staying in Tokyo because the war made it impossible for him to return home). Moreover, the acquaintance of my sister-in-law who had helped her rent this room from the lawyer and this lady's husband were both in the legal profession, so my sister-in-law and the lady became good friends very soon.

But the convenience did not last long. The landlord suddenly demanded that they vacate the room. The reason was that they needed the room for the maid. The strange thing was that the demand had been made on the very day the transfer of my sister-in-law's acquaintance, in respect for whose position the lawyer had rented the room to my sister-in-law, was unofficially decided. My sister-in-law learned of the transfer a few days later when it was officially announced, but the lawyer could have obtained the information easily enough through private channels in legal circles. It is rather extraordinary that the decision on the transfer and the demand to vacate the room had been made on the same day, but I suppose it is only proper to regard it as a coincidence. A man of such prominent social position would not have behaved so hastily and impolitely from a calculation of immediate advantage. So that was the state the room was in before we got to Pusan.

What could we do? Needless to say, we were not so rich as to be able to stay at an inn. After lengthy deliberations we decided to take lodgings in separate groups. It was decided that I should sleep with my aged parents in their one hundred and eighty square feet room in Nampodong, inhabited by nineteen people of three families, and our two eldest children were sent away to where their maternal grandfather's family of six lived in a forty square foot room, while the two younger children and my wife could do nothing but stay with my sister-in-law.

I had to hear every day from my wife or from my older children who had been to see my wife how fierce was the demand of the landlord for evacuation of the room. While in Taegu, we had heard that many of the refugees had left Pusan, so we thought we'd be able to rent a room if we tried hard enough. It was true that Pusan was not so crowded as when I first came last winter, but there were still no rooms. My wife and I searched everywhere and inquired of everybody we knew, but it was all in vain.

The demand for eviction was so persistent that the lady who had been living in that room with my sister-in-law moved away to her husband's uncle's. And early in the morning after that a tempest broke out in the lawyer's residence.

While everybody was still in bed, the door of the room was thrust open with great force, and there stood the lawyer himself with fierce glaring eyes. He thundered in an angry voice, "Do you behave like this and yet call yourselves human beings? Get out of my house at once. Go to an inn if you don't have anywhere to go. Human beings must know how to behave. If you don't leave this house this very day I will settle the matter legally."

My wife and her sister could not keep silent at that. They declared that they could not go out in the streets to live, or go to an inn. The two grown-up daughters of the house came to support their father, and his wife and eldest son were also mobilized. The eldest son of the house, who was said to be attending a law college in Seoul, threatened to use his fists, but the old lawyer dissuaded him and led him away, perhaps having determined that such violence would work to their disadvantage if the matter were brought to court.

I listened to this report from my wife in a corner of the room in Nampodong inhabited by nineteen people. That we were not worthy of being looked upon as human beings was no surprise, our worthlessness in that regard having been settled quite beyond doubt by the old lady in Taegu; and that the landlord would deal with the matter legally was perhaps natural, since he was a lawyer. But we could not very well go and stay at an inn. If we could afford that, we would have done it long before. As to the reflection that we did not behave properly, I know there may be truth in it, because refugees cannot very well afford to behave well all the time. But we had not really been all that shameless. What my sister-in-law had spent for mending the flooring of the room was as good as paying nearly twenty thousand won rent a month, and only the day before we had told the lawyer's wife that we could give her some key money when we managed to sell all our remaining clothes. The lady of the house then said that it was not because they wanted money that they were demanding the room back, but because they needed the room to give to the maid. My wife then asked the lady to let her provide space in the room for the maid of the house, but they still refused. There was no helping it. My wife had to ask her to give her some time until she could rent a room. As the maid has been mentioned, I might as well note here that the woman who was working as a maid in that house had told my wife and my sister-in-law that she was a not-too-distant relative of the family who had come for a visit and was staying in the house to help with the household work; that in this house no maid ever stayed beyond a couple of months, that the current servant was an old woman who was now away on a visit to the country to see her son, and that this room had never been used by people but as a sort of storage room. Anyway, my sister-in-law knew that an old woman worked as a maid in the house. Well, the judgment that we did not know how to behave all derives from our lack of ability to rent a room.

My wife then said solemnly, with a sad and tearful face, as if she had made a grave decision, that all our family should live together in the room from that night. Her reason was that, since our situation was at its worst, it would be better for the family to live together until we could rent a room. I hesitated to agree with her.

I thought of the law student. A young man who had threatened women with his fists would not let me alone. But how could a man with a weak constitution, nearing forty, confront a young man in his twenties? But at the same time how could I, as head of the family, leave wife and children in that kind of plight, however much of a weakling I am acknowledged to be? Of course it was not that my wife wanted me to protect her from the brute force of that young man. On the contrary, if she had thought of that she would never have suggested that we live together in that room. My wife only thought of my poor old parents, who slept almost every night sitting up because of me, so she suggested that the family keep together until a room could be found, as the state of things had reached a point that could not get worse.

I went to school. The school at which I had been teaching in Seoul had moved down to Pusan, and had begun to hold classes every other day in a park. This was one of the school days. I asked several colleagues who had come down to Pusan before me to look for a room for me. Although I knew it was not a very proper thing to do, I even asked some of my senior students to look out for a vacant room for me.

In the afternoon I sat in a tea-room without drinking any tea and asked some friends to help me out of this plight.

Toward evening I went out to drink cheap rice wine in one of the makeshift liquor stalls that stood in a row along the quay. I emptied one bowl. I looked up to notice that a couple of sailing vessels were anchored beyond the bulwark. Oh, the sea was always good to look at. Right in front of my eyes gulls kept darting up and down. Oh, that was a lovely sight, too.

But in fact I was not in a mood to appreciate the poetic beauty of the sea and the gulls. I felt as if a fishbone were stuck in my throat. That fishbone was the thought that from now on I had to go to the lawyer's house, and consequently to confront the law student. I had never seen this young man, but I had once seen the lawyer himself when he was pruning trees in the garden. He looked past forty, but his well-combed hair was as glossy and black as a young man's, and he was of a sturdy constitution. I thought that if the son took after his father he must be well-built and strong. I was rather unwilling to meet him.

I gulped down another bowl of wine. I had had many a fist fight myself when in my twenties. My face bore numerous souvenirs of those battles. My nose had bled many a time and I also made other noses bleed not a few times. Once I had broken a man's two front teeth, and received in return a scar like a vaccination mark on the crown of my head. To be frank, at the height of my youth I had never lost in an even battle. But after thirty I had always avoided a confrontation of fists. Today, nearing forty, I begin to have fears at the mere thought of a fight. I emptied another wine bowl. But if challenged, I could not just sit cringing in a corner. There is such a thing as self-defense. Yes. I will rise to the challenge. After this long interval, I will exhibit my finesse as of old times. A fight cannot be won with physical strength alone. With the help of alcohol, I made plans about how to tackle the young man according to his various possible methods of attack. I pictured the scene in which I knocked my adversary down, and got excited. It was not before my pocket was emptied and dusk covered the entire quay that I left the liquor stall.

Nothing happened that night. Nothing happened the next day, or the day after that. In the meanwhile the woman who had been working as maid went back to her home town and the old servant woman of the house returned from the country. She was a really old woman, her hair all gray and her back bent. This old woman cooked, washed and cleaned all day.

Once, I saw my wife and my sister-in-law whispering in a corner. When I asked what it was about, they told me that the old servant woman wanted to sell secretly two bottles of soy sauce belonging to the lawyer's household because she was in need of money to settle an old debt for medicine to a herb doctor, and the lawyer's family would not pay her her salary. I tried to figure out to myself whether this kind of stealing would constitute a crime in the eyes of the law.

On the evening of the fourth day after I moved to this house I talked it over with my wife and, in the hope that the landlord might accept a compromise, decided that my wife would go to the lady of the house to pay her one month's rent and plead for mercy. The problem was the amount of rent to take. We reckoned that twenty or thirty thousand won would never do, so we thought of offering forty thousand won, but at last decided on fifty thousand from desperation. We didn't know how we could pay fifty thousand won a month for the room and manage to live, but we had heard that the current price of rooms was ten thousand won per twenty square feet, and we knew that some people demanded to have a room vacated with the ulterior purpose of

raising the rent. Moreover, we thought anything would be better than
to have the matter brought to court as the lawyer had threatened, and to
be thrown out into the streets. So we decided to try to reach an agreement about the room by any means, and then go out and work hard
with our minds at ease to earn a living. And in fact we were already
engaged in trade. My wife was going to the Kukje Market with what
remained of our clothes, and the two older children were trading with
the American Army troops. The fifty thousand won in question was
taken out of my wife's business capital.

My wife went into the living room and returned after a short while.
The money was not in her hands, so we thought a compromise had
been reached. But my wife said no. They still insisted on our vacating
the room. The master of the house and the eldest son slept in a one
hundred and sixty square foot room; and in the main room the master's
wife and the younger son slept; so I suppose they could not very well
say they wanted the room back because the house was too crowded.
The lady of the house said that she had to have the room back because
her grown-up daughters could hardly sleep because of the snoring of
the old servant woman. Then my wife suggested that we make space in
our room for the old servant woman to sleep. The lady still insisted on
having the room back. She further said that a friend of her daughter
offered to make a present of a gold wrist-watch if her family could rent
the room, but they had said no.

I felt a chill in my liver. A gold wrist-watch! That was certainly not
a trifle. So I asked my wife what she had done with the money, and she
said she just put it before the lady of the house, suggesting that she buy
books for her daughters with it. Our ardent hope was that the money
would not be returned. But the next day the money was returned.

The following night, it happened. I always stayed away from the
room in the daytime, spending the time mostly in the room where my
parents lived, except for teaching at school every other day. Most of
the refugees in Pusan went out to the market to sell cigarettes, leaving
only children in their shelters. My parents also sold cigarettes in the
market. So in my parents' room I waited for my older children to
return, to go with them to the Kukje Market to pick my wife up so we
could return home in a group. Thus it went that night.

When we got back in the evening, we found two strapping girls
standing majestically in our room. They were the daughters of the
lawyer. We could not discern which was the older of the two, but

anyway we heard that the older daughter was a high school senior and the younger daughter a high school freshman. The two said they would sleep in our room that night. I wondered to myself which of the two girls was the one who had a friend who would make a present of a gold wrist-watch for renting the room. I felt I had to escape from the scene.

But before I had time to do so, the two big girls declared to no one in particular that the room would have to be vacated within a couple of days and, after giving me a look, went out. It does not matter whether the look was of contempt, derision, or whatever. Anyway, I had to admit to myself that the tactics of these girls had much more effect on me than a few boxes on my ears from their older brother would have been.

Well, anyway, every morning when I went out of the house I always wished I wouldn't have to return.

The next day was a school day. When I opened the belled door of the entrance porch and stepped out, the lawyer was there pruning box-wood trees in a stooping posture beside some flaming red camellia blossoms. Even at a fleeting glance one could perceive that he cherished and carefully tended the garden plants. It was an elegant hobby. Maybe life is something that should be lived with at least that much elegance and leisure. I escaped from the porch as if pursued.

At school I again asked my colleagues to look for a room for me. I also asked some upperclass students to help me with this problem. After school I again sat in a tea-room without drinking any tea and begged my friends for help.

Then in Nampodong I waited for my older children to return. The children came back after dark. I thought my wife was sure to have gone home by herself because we were so late. We decided to go straight home. The road from Nampodong to the Kyŏngnam Middle School was dark.

We pushed at the iron gate. It was locked from inside. We peeped in and saw that our room was not lighted. I thought my wife must still be in the market waiting for us, and my sister-in-law had turned off the light to put her children to sleep. We decided to wait for my wife so we could all go in together, and I led the children to the footbridge over a ditch where my wife must pass on her way home, and crouched down.

My second son crouched down beside me. My eldest son also sat beside me. But my wife did not come for a long time. Nam-a, my second son, began to nod from sleepiness although it was early in the evening. What he did must be tiring for a boy his age. I turned my eyes to the ditch. I took out a cigarette. The match did not light. Rain began to drip.

Tong-a, my eldest son, stood up and walked to the house. In a little while he came running back and said that my wife was already back home and that the gate was open. He said he heard his mother's voice from our room when he drew near the gate.

When we arrived we learned that the light in our room was out for reasons we had not guessed. The electricity in this house was on a special line so that the house had power all day and all night, and all the other rooms in the house were brightly lit even now. For a while we sat silently in the darkness.

My sister-in-law said, as if to herself, that she would leave the room tomorrow even if she had to sleep under the bridge. She said that though the landlord's family had always been harsh to the children, of late it had become well-nigh unbearable. If my sister-in-law's seven-year-old and my six-year-old began to sing or went out in the hall to go to the toilet, someone in the landlord's family never failed to shout at them not to be noisy. If the children in our room joined in when the seven-year-old son of the lawyer marched in the hall singing a military march, they were reprimanded for making noise. What was still more painful to see was the keen anguish of my girl, Sŏn-a, at the least noise her younger brother and her cousin made, for fear they would be scolded by the landlord's family.

My sister-in-law wept in the darkness, suppressing her voice. I felt fire burning in my chest, too. This was a different kind of anger from what I felt when one of Sŏn-a's rubber shoes was stolen. But whatever tactics they adopted, we could only endure and seek ways of minimizing the pain they produced.

So the countermeasure we thought up was to leave the room vacant during the daytime from the next day. My two younger children were to stay at Nampodong, and my sister-in-law was to spend the day with her children where her parents were living and return alone in the evening to prepare dinner. Only after we had thus set up our plans did we swallow cold food in the darkness.

I spent the whole day next day in my parents' room in Nampodong with Sŏn-a and Kyŏng-a. I was relieved that the day had brightened up. It had rained the night before.

My wife came to us before dark, but the older children had not come back although it was already dark. Kyŏng-a said he was sleepy and fell asleep in his mother's arms.

The two older children came back only after it was completely dark. They said it was hard to get a ride on the tram lately. The two children excitedly took out of the secret pockets in their clothes cigarette and chewing-gum packets with deft hands before their parents and grandparents. Their deft hands gave me sorrow. I averted my eyes.

We came out into the street. I was carrying the sleeping Kyŏng-a on my back, and my wife carried her bundle on her head. We walked up the wide street in front of the Tong-a Theater. My eldest son Tong-a walked close to me and showed off his conversational skill in English, telling me that he could easily make purchases if he walked up to GIs and said "Please sall to me." I corrected him, saying that it was not "sall to me" but "sell to me." Tong-a is a fifth grader. I would have to send him to school so that he could finish primary school and enter middle school. But the boy had already begun to learn English conversation. And the father corrects him, too.

Nam-a also walked up to my side and began telling me about the clever boy he had met that day. When the lad was in danger of being caught, Nam-a said, he sprawled on his back in a nearby rice paddy. It was a flooded rice paddy. The lad, sunk in water up to his ears, kicked all four limbs, rolled his eyeballs and moved his mouth wildly. The boy had a few GI bucks hidden in his shirt. The men who were going to nab him looked at the sight for some time and then poked his belly a few times with a rather worried expression. The boy took no notice of it, but kept on rolling his eyes and moving his mouth wildly. Maybe they thought he was an epileptic. The men went away. Hearing that, it struck me that my Nam-a, who was chatting away like this beside me, would also have to learn how to fake an epileptic fit to guard a few military bucks.

We turned to the right at the Pusŏnggyo Bridge. The road along the ditch was dark. Stars twinkled in the sky but the road was dark.

Nam-a suddenly suggested that we all sing together. I was going to say no, but Sŏn-a, who was walking beside her mother, began singing as if she had been waiting for the opportunity. "Stepping over the dead bodies of our comrades . . ." It was the military march the lawyer's son could sing but our children could not sing along with him in that house. I recalled how Sŏn-a always tried to prevent her younger brother from singing and making noise in the lawyer's house. I did not have the heart to tell her not to sing. Nam-a and Tong-a joined her.

As soon as the march was over, Nam-a began to sing the cycling song and to run in the dark, pretending to be riding a bicycle. How come he's so sprightly tonight, when he was so sleepy yesterday? Could it be that he had luck with his trade today? "Look out, you oldster over there, or you'll get run over!" Nam-a's bicycle now turned toward us and swept past between his father and mother. This oldster of a father had to dodge to avoid being run over.

That made Kyŏng-a on my back wake up. He joined his sister in singing "Come, sweet, pretty butterfly." Sŏn-a waved her arms in tune to her song, like a butterfly fluttering in the dark.

When his sister's song was over, Kyŏng-a, now wide awake, began to sing "Beautiful wild rabbit." He began the wild rabbit jump, too. Not content with jumping on my back, he climbed onto my shoulders and jumped, sitting on my neck. "Whither are you jumping like that? I'm going over that hill by myself and I'll come back with lots and lots of chestnuts." Kyŏng-a continued jumping until he finished the song.

Trying hard not to totter under Kyŏng-a's gyrations, I thought, if he is a rabbit, then his mother and father are rabbits, too. But his father rabbit, far from jumping over the hill and coming back with lots and lots of chestnuts, is staggering under his slight weight, as if walking straight were a great and formidable feat.

Then I suddenly thought of the word "pierrot." Oh yes, I am performing a circus act now with Kyŏng-a on my shoulders. Well then, Kyŏng-a is also performing a circus act on my shoulders. Sŏn-a was also acting the butterfly in this circus. Nam-a was the trick cyclist. And it would be a sad circus if Nam-a had to put on an epileptic fit in order to guard a few military bucks, like the little lad he saw today. Tong-a's "please sall to me" is also a circus act, and their deft putting away and taking out of cigarette and chewing-gun packets are all polished circus routines. So they are the little pierrots of the Hwang Sun-wŏn Circus Troupe, and I am their master of ceremonies. Our stage today is this Pumindong road beside the ditch.

Pierrot Tong-a began to sing "Sorrento." Yes, show off all your accomplishments. I do not know whether, when you look back on today's circus performance many years later, you will grieve or laugh over it. And you, also, do not have to know whether your father and mother witnessed your circus acts today with tears or with laughter. I only wish, my dear little pierrots, that when each of you has his own circus troupe, you will not have to repeat this kind of circus on this kind of stage with your young pierrots. Oh, excuse me, ladies and gentlemen, it was just the maundering of an old clown. Well then, shall we listen to Pierrot Tong-a's solo?

My wife, who had been walking a few feet behind me, came up to me and placed an arm around my waist. This wife of the leader must have thought her troupe leader husband's circus act was in danger. I grasped my wife's hand by way of telling her not to worry. At that moment, Pierrot Tong-a's solo abruptly stopped in the middle of the last bar. We were already at the entrance of the alley leading to the lawyer's house.

Well, ladies and gentlemen, that will have to be the end of today's program. I am ashamed to have shown you such a poor circus, owing to lack of rehearsal. But tomorrow we may be able to present you with something better. Thank you so much for your kind attention. I thank you all on behalf of the entire troupe. Well then, a warm good night to you all.

Eroica Symphony

Park Yong-sook

Park Yong-sook, born in 1934, is interested in both literature and the fine arts, and has written art and music criticism as well as literary works. He made his literary debut in 1959, at the age of twenty-five.

As an author his main concern was at first the inner reality of man's unconscious, and he used the stream-of-unconsciousness technique extensively. But from the late 1960s he became more interested in the meaning of history, and has written works retracing the historical process in an attempt to probe into the meaning of historical experience and its relation to the reality of today. "Eroica Symphony" (1965), an essayistic short story, is delightful for the tentative tone of its philosophical reverie and the innocence of its romance. From the viewpoint of strict realism, the story has considerable gaps and improbabilities, but it is true to its internal logic, and we watch the two sweethearts with sympathetic concern, even though the man's actions, if he existed in real life, might well have been regarded as outlandish.

Since the 1980s Park Yong-sook has stayed away from creative writing and devoted his energies to fine art criticism, and he is currently a professor of fine arts and a director of a fine art gallery in downtown Seoul.

Men carry such heavy burdens! Some of the load is acquired by individuals for their own purposes, but most of the burdens we shoulder have been there from even before we were born, so that in fact a man struggles through life with the load he has inherited. Some, of course, add burdens of their own invention. At first glance, this kind of man may look very stupid because he makes his already heavy load heavier. But these men, although they seem stupid, may not necessarily be so. It may really be that they are wiser.

Be that as it may, we are born into the world to find, on first opening our eyes, many burdens, whose utility we do not know, scattered about in mountainous heaps all over the place. As we grow up, we learn the use of these loads one by one. Some are heirlooms of our own ancestors, some are remnants left by Westerners, but at all events these loads tend to become bulkier as time passes and centuries go by. So much so that the earlier you lived, the lighter the load you were burdened with. Of course, you might say that our wisdom grows and thereby we learn how to discriminate among the burdens, but anyway it is more troublesome than having fewer of them to deal with. In any case, in all periods people worry a lot about how to dispose of their ever-increasing burdens. For, however hard you may try, you are never able to shoulder all of the load you have inherited. But, of course, the burdens do not go away because you try to avoid them. No. In fact, no man can keep completely away from these burdensome inheritances. Therein lies man's fate. The loads are too heavy to shoulder in their entirety, but one can't simply refuse to shoulder them. What on earth, really, are these loads for? But with the lapse of ages, people have stopped even pondering this point. They just take it for granted that the loads are there because that's the way things are, and they live among the piled-up loads they do not understand the meaning of.

While engaged in living, it sometimes happens that they discover from among these burdens something they need. But most people go no further than imitating other men, as do apes captured in the jungles. Let a man wash his face in a basin, and an ape would do the same. Why does the man wash his face in a basin and put on an apron? The ape does not know. Likewise, men ordinarily regard their enormous inherited burdens as an ape would. Now let me talk about one of our many burdens, that which is called music.

As I understand it, there has never before been a time when music has pervaded our everyday life as much as it does these days. Music flows into our ears any time, anywhere, whether we are walking on the street, entering town, stepping into rooms or whatever. It is like living all the time in music except when we lose consciousness. It didn't use to be that way until some five or six years ago. If we wanted to listen to music, we had to go to a stereo parlor or buy records. In those cases it was mostly Western classical music we heard. But the circumstances changed 180 degrees with the importation of popular music from the United States, where it was booming. Classical music lost its sway and instead pop music reigns. Moreover, people don't have to go to a stereo parlor to listen to music any more. They only need a good pair of ears to be visited by music all the time. As apes put on skirts in imitation of men, so do men shake their bodies to pop music rhythm, as other men do.

There was a controversy once over whether pop music is music or not. The more conservative people, who preferred classical music, were of the opinion that pop music is not music, but young people, who liked it, argued that it is modern music. Anyway, as in all such cases, conflict does not lead to any clear-cut conclusion, unlike in the case of boxing matches. So the argument becomes inconclusive, and people go on listening to pop tunes, not knowing whether they are music or mere vulgar worldly noise. In short, pop music has been imposed on men, an added burden.

It is true that in many cities there are still stereo parlors in existence patronized by music lovers, but the atmosphere of such places is not so soothing as in former times. There aren't any commentators to explain the pieces, nor do they always play request records promptly enough for busy people. It is a recent phenomenon, but city tea-rooms are increasingly taking on the function of stereo parlors. Come to think of it, it is a welcome phenomenon, indicating that tea-rooms are recovering their proper function, which had been abandoned in the destitute days of the Korean War. That may be a proof, also, of the fact that living has become less strenuous to a certain degree in recent times.

The story I want to tell here is about a disc jockey in one of these tea-rooms. Disc jockey is a new kind of job that has been proliferating recently in Korea. The job is taking root in radio and television stations, and also in stereo parlors and tea-rooms. This new occupation is having its day since the advent of pop music. A disc jockey is not exactly a professional; he's just a worker. There is the English word "technician," but the word is alien to Korean ears. However that may be, it is a dignified job, having an expertise of its own. Of course, all jobs have a certain dignity when the workers become experts, but the disc jockey ideally should have more dignity than other workers. Thanks to the invention of the record player, performers do not have to come before the audience to give them music. The disc jockey performs this function. Therefore, since the disc jockey takes the place of hundreds of great musicians, he or she has to be dignified. But with the emergence of pop music, dignity has collapsed and the disc jockeys have degenerated into mere wage earners. Perhaps inevitably, as pop music has fallen into the hands of uncultured people and become a commodity instead of an art, the disc jockey booths of tea-rooms have become quite like box offices of cinema houses. Because the masses do not know much about dignity, they do not demand it of disc jockeys. Disc jockeying is a job, and that suffices.

The jockey's booth in this tea-room has quite a number of records, including a decent selection of classical records; this place is rather highbrow, for a tea-room. Most of the disc jockeys in tea-rooms are men, but in this tea-room the jockey is a woman of about twenty-two or three. She did not study music in college or anything; she does her work with some slight knowledge of music. She comes to work at one o'clock in the afternoon, and from then on until eleven o'clock at night she picks out records requested, puts them on the stereo and adjusts the volume.

Records requested are ordinarily of popular music, so they are not hard to pick out. The English used for titles is not difficult. But some customers request classical orchestral music in German, and may even specify the opus number and name the orchestra too. Ordinarily, classics are not played in tea-rooms, but in early mornings or late at night such requests are granted. To handle such cases, disc jockeys must have at least some elementary knowledge of German and some basic knowledge about classical music.

It is the same with adjusting the volume. As the interior decoration of tea-rooms must change with the seasons, so the volume should be adjusted according to the time of day. Different kinds of customers patronize the tea-room at different hours. So adjusting the volume is a task that requires sensibility, because it is part of the job of beautifying a dull, frustrating day with music. This is not an easy task, whatever anybody might have to say to the contrary, just as the manager's task of changing the interior decoration is not an easy one. Whether it be hard or easy, it is not a mere job; it requires and leads to self-discipline.

The term is rarely encountered these days, but there is such a thing as "the tea way." Our ancestors practiced the way of tea as a means of self-discipline. From the blending of tea flavors and selection of utensils to the brewing and drinking of tea and handling of tea sets, the mood, the arrangement of the room in which to drink tea . . . Come to think of it, tea serving is not a simple matter. We say, practice the way, but it is not so much a matter of learning the rules as of awakening to the true way of life and attaining self-discovery through the simple ceremony of drinking tea. Thus, when one has mastered the decorum of tea serving one has comprehended the essence of life. That is to say, in current phraseology, one has become a refined man. But modern tea-rooms care very little about this tea way. They are more like market-places. The tea-room owners may not be particularly to blame for this phenomenon, for it is a trend of the times. It is like the ape putting on an apron in imitation of human beings, or people making a clumsy imitation of picking up the load left behind by others, not knowing its real purpose.

Coming back to our Miss B, she is, anyway, burdened with this load. It is a pity she is so thin, but her profile, seen through the window of the jockey's booth, is impressive, consisting of sharply defined features. She is always sitting before the table with a somber expression— something unusual in girls of her age. One might say she is past the easily excitable age, but her somberness is not entirely due to maturity.

She has been occupying this same post for about three years now, long enough to make her feel bored. The cause of her gloom may be attributed to this boredom more than to anything else. She is a disc jockey, just as other people are other things according to their work. The obligatory adjustment of volume, the invariable record rack like a dust-coated bookcase, the request notes with the names of some silly popular songs in childish hands submitted by immature teenagers. So she often feels like the shopkeeper of a small sweetshop. Just as at the thrusting of pennies, at the presentation of request notes she dispenses the commodity on the stereo mechanically. It is like selling sweets. But music is not for selling, at least originally it was not. What is most precious to men they keep or give to others free of charge.

Music is priceless. You give music freely, and wait for the spiritual transformation in the hearer till he or she is completely of one mind with you. But in this upside-down age art has become a commercial item, and therefore its original function as the soul's tonic has been negated. Anyway, disc jockeys are not responsible for this. But the phenomenon furnishes an important factor in making Miss B bored and depressed. In the end, you might say that she has no firm principles to live by. Most people, whether they live entirely apart from or completely involved in the affairs of the world, usually rely on other people's opinions rather than on their own for value judgments. It is the same in Miss B's case. Although she is a disc jockey, she really doesn't know what to think of classical and pop music. Since most cultured people value the classics highly, she thinks that classics are valuable, and since frivolous people tend to like pop music, she takes pop music to be of trifling value.

In this regard, Miss B is not an exception. Even though her financial circumstances do not allow her to be aristocratic, she has inherited the feminine rules of conduct of the nobility; but she does not know the meaning of the whole set of virtues of aristocratic women. Miss B sits at her desk in the jockey's box. As moneyed commoners try to buy knighthood, so ignorant common men outside the box ogle her. Notes requesting a rendezvous; notes saying "I love you"; notes praising her beauty; notes saying the writers want to be her friends; notes expressing respect; all sorts of trash keep invading her section of the tea-room. On receiving these notes, she hesitates, as a nobleman hesitates about whether to sell his title for money or not.

Originally, Western classical music had been the home entertainment of Western noblemen. It could be heard only on court stages and in the salons of titled ladies. Through that music, the Western aristocracy reflected on life and discovered themselves. Then, with the decline of aristocracy and the rise of commoners, music was taken out of the chambers of lordly manor houses. The uncultured people did not know how to use this thing, although they took it over from the nobility; they just dragged it here and there and let it tear apart. Just as common men do not know what to do with a title of nobility, music was of no use to common men. If there was music, it was no longer music reflecting life, but music taking our thoughts away from life. No, they cannot think deeply about life. Therefore, they evade life. It is the same with Miss B. Like the commoner in the "Tale of a Nobleman," she abides by aristocratic rules of conduct, but it is without enthusiasm, without a feeling of inner reward. That means that men are, after all, slaves of the loads they have inherited. Although invisible, the knot is tight that binds her to her inherited burden. She does not comprehend the meaning of her burden, nor the reason for her enslavement to it.

When baffled by such a mystery, men usually resort to liquor, gambling or sex; but in the case of women, especially unmarried girls like Miss B, when trapped in labyrinths like this, they look for a thread called marriage. In such circumstances, a girl is likely to marry before she knows exactly what she is doing. But anything done as an escape from something is likely to bring regret and grief afterwards. It is a different question if one is prepared to meet this sorrow and regret. Anyway, this was how Miss B felt at about that time. That was why she was always so gloomy.

Then, one spring day, she became interested in a regular male customer of her tea-room. He looked about thirty, and he had been a patron of this tea-room for a couple of years now. But it was only recently that she came to feel any interest in him. Oh, it was not that she had been entirely unaware of his existence until now. She just thought that he used this tea-room like anyone else—for appointments or relaxation. But, recently, she had begun to sense something unusual about him. First of all, he was always alone. He sometimes came in the late afternoon, around the end of office hours, and sometimes dropped in for an hour or two in the late evening. For days he would come every day, but at other times he would come at intervals of several days.

Most people who come to tea-rooms have definite purposes of their own. Apart from those who come to meet people by appointment, many come to listen to music or to flirt with waitresses and hostesses. There are some people, too, who have no definite occupation and come to tea-rooms to kill time. At first she thought he belonged to one of these types. But however you might look at it, he could not be classified into any of these types. Since he spent an hour or two by himself every time, he was definitely not coming to meet somebody. Neither did he have any close contacts with the hostess or the waitresses; he never talked to anybody from the time he stepped into the tea-room till he left, except to order tea. Sometimes he looked like someone who came to this tea-room in order to avoid talking to people.

Or was he out of work? But most jobless people visit tea-rooms in the daytime. Well then, finally, did he come to this tea-room to listen to music? That seemed most likely. But not quite. Music lovers usually request classical music. There had never been a request for classical music made during the hours he stayed in this tea-room. In Miss B's judgment, one cannot call anyone who does not ask for classical music a music lover.

One might say he just sat there. His profile, when he smoked, looked very lonely. But when he was not smoking, his eyes seemed to be pondering over something very deeply, so that one felt a certain isolating intensity in his eyes. The eyes of a police detective intent on a case? But his eyes were not that insistent. What did he do? Anyway, he did not look like an ordinary man. But she began to feel more keenly interested in him once she recognized the songs he requested—or, rather, his handwriting.

Having worked in the record booth several years, she came to discern most of the hands of regular patrons. For a long time now she had noticed requests written in an uncommonly handsome script. In most cases one can guess at the degree of learning of a man by his handwriting. But, unfortunately, the music requested in that handsome script was not elegant classical music but frivolous pop songs or cinema theme music. So she had been feeling sorry for the man who must be very learned but had very little appreciation of music. Then one day she found that the hand belonged to none other than this man. The music he requested included:

The Lost Sun (theme music of a domestic film)
Exodus (theme song of the film)
One Fine Day (from Puccini's *Madame Butterfly*)
Go Down, Moses (Negro spiritual)
Phaedra (theme music of the film)
He's Got the Whole World in His Hand (spiritual)
Guitar Twist (jazz)
Let's Go (jazz)
Autumn Leaves (pop song)
El Cid (theme music of the film)
Theme of Love (theme music of *Ben Hur*)

One evening she picked out all the records he had requested and played them consecutively. As the second song started, he suddenly poured an intense gaze on Miss B. She could not describe it even to herself, but they were such impressive eyes. They looked grateful, puzzled, no—anyway it was an expression that one could come up with only in moments of truth. As she went on playing the records, his expression grew more somber and he looked away. When all the music had been played, his eyes became lustrous again and he stared at her.

Miss B did not know how to cope with a moment like that, so she became flustered and dropped her glance. Then he smiled at Miss B and made a slight bow. Confused, Miss B also nodded in response.

Thereafter, whenever the man came in Miss B played several songs from his earlier requests before he even asked for them, upon which he would pay silent regard with his eyes. His face and manner testified that he was an unusual man, but she could not comprehend why he patronized this noisy tea-room. And why did he request pop music such as teenagers favor? What did he do for a living? Was he married? The more interested she became in him, the more enveloped in mystery did he seem. Then, early one summer evening, she received a note in his hand. It was not a request for music. It was a personal note.

"I'll be waiting for you in front of the Tŏksu Palace tomorrow morning at ten."

On receiving this note, she lost her composure. It was not the first time she had received notes of this kind from patrons, but she always thought them ridiculous and threw them into the rubbish bin, because they were written by people who seemed as though they'd do such childish things. But this kind of note from this man was utterly unexpected. She had never imagined it could happen. So she was confused, but maybe she was also bemused with delight, as if something long awaited had at last arrived,

The next morning there was a slight rain. After much hesitation, Miss B set out from her house carrying an umbrella and wearing rain boots. Somehow she felt that an appointment with him was sacred, unbreakable. When she got off the bus in front of the palace grounds he was standing at the gate already, and he watched her approach. Perhaps because of the rain, his garments looked shabby. The worn and torn plastic umbrella with which he was protecting himself from the rain did not help his appearance much. They did not exchange any overt greetings when they met. He just gave Miss B a silent smile.

"Let's go in," he suggested.

What does he want to do in the ancient palace on a rainy day? But Miss B had no choice but to follow him. All of a sudden thunder struck and rain began to pour in torrents. The pouring rain splashed their legs, and through the tear in the plastic dome of his umbrella water leaked onto his face. Miss B looked at him anxiously, but they were not sufficiently acquainted yet for Miss B to remark on it. He seemed slightly embarrassed, too, for he kept turning his umbrella to prevent the tear from letting rain fall on his face. The morning was still early; there weren't many people in the well-swept palace grounds. Only the two people were walking in the rain. They reached the National Museum building.

"Shall we go into the museum?" he asked. Miss B nodded. Stepping into the museum, he asked again, "Shall I act as commentator?"

Miss B nodded again. Then the man, as if they had been long-time friends or old sweethearts, or rather as if they were teacher and student, began to explain the relics, utterly unabashed. From pottery to paintings, Buddha images and decorative jewelry of royalty, his explanation was fluent. His commentary was concise and systematic, too. He divided history into dynastic periods and then wittily explained the transition of thoughts and ideas. Also, he drew freely from the East and West and ancient and modern worlds in interpreting the pattern on a piece of pottery. Moreover, his explanation was enthusiastic, unlike the mechanical commentaries of tourist guides. Miss B felt a little displeased. What kind of man is this? Isn't he showing off his knowledge? Perhaps he looked to Miss B like one of those streetcorner missionaries who wail phrases from the Bible.

When they stepped out of the exit onto the stairs after spending quite some time inside, they saw a young American man and woman who looked like tourists taking shelter from the rain. They were people they had passed inside the museum a while ago. Maybe they had found nothing to interest them particularly. They had come out soon. The rain was pouring down more fiercely than before. The ditch below was overflowing with muddy yellow water. A pair of blue-eyed people. They looked like the incarnation of vitality to Miss B and the man. The rain pouring down cruelly. And the muddy ditch-water overflowing noisily. The trees and lawns and flowers that brave, nay, that enjoy the fierce rain; everything seemed so youthful. The man, who had been silent for some time, asked abruptly,

"Do you know today is a special day?"

She kept silent to indicate her ignorance. She looked at him in surprise. She couldn't recall that it was any kind of a special day.

"This is the seventh day of the seventh month, by the lunar calendar."*

It was only then that she said,

"Oh, today's the day the two heavenly lovers meet—the two stars in the old legend."

He smiled significantly.

"Well, here we have rain, sure enough," the woman remarked.

"Yes. Tears of too much joy, too much joy!" he repeated, his cheeks flushed red as if with the reflected delight of the heavenly lovers.

They parted like that that day. It was really a stupid encounter, come to think of it. When a man and a woman meet, they ordinarily go to drink tea, have lunch, or see films and thus try to avoid serious conversation. From this conventional viewpoint, their date had been very silly indeed. But the more Miss B puzzled over what kind of a man he was, the more interested she became in him.

There arose a great confusion in her world of common sense after the day of her visit to the museum. The image of that man in the museum, the image of that man listening to pop music in this tea-room, the two images she could not harmonize into one, however hard she tried.

"Does he work at the museum?" she wondered, but she discarded the idea at once. That he did not was evident from the way the ticket man talked to him.

"Then, is he a researcher in archaeology? A professor of archaeology?" But the next moment she brushed aside that idea, too. Would a cultured archaeology professor listen to pop songs? She simply could not make him out. He continued to come to the tea-room after their visit to the museum. But his attitude was not at all different from what it had been. He would be sitting there, smoking and staring into space, and even when his request music was played he made no sign of recognition. But then, after the piece was finished, he would turn toward Miss B and nod. That was all.

---

*The seventh day of the seventh month by the lunar calendar is the day on which, legend has it, the two stars who are heavenly lovers are granted their once-a-year rendezvous. The lovers, who were a shepherd and a weaving girl, were separated by the order of the king of the sky because they neglected their work from being too deeply engrossed in love. They were exiled separately to stars located far apart, and the legend also has it that on the day of their meeting, magpies build a bridge across the sky for the lovers to meet, and it rains on that day because the reunited lovers shed tears of joy. The day is not a folk holiday and often goes by unnoticed in modern city life. [Translator]

A month after that, they met again at the Tŏksu Palace. A sunny day in the Tŏksu Palace is very pleasant. After the bustle in the streets, it is an entirely new environment when you step into the palace. Coming out of the art gallery, they took shelter from the hot sun on the shaded benches. In front of them, stone seals were spouting thin streams of water. This fountain is a mere toy compared with the more sumptuous ones in the West, but to the young people on the bench it gave the joy of youth. Somewhere a cicada chirped, as if unaware of the fact that it was in the heart of the city. At last the man, who had been looking around the royal courtyard, began a conversation.

"Here in this palace is modern history."

Miss B, puzzled at this unexpected topic, asked,

"What do you mean?"

Then he began explaining the two different styles of architecture on either side of them—the stone museum building on the one hand and the ancient wooden royal audience hall on the other. He called the Western-style stone building the male and the traditional Korean-style building the female. It made Miss B laugh. Then he began to explain heatedly why they were male and female respectively. First of all, the stone building is made of heavy material, so it gives a feeling of massiveness and we feel a strength as of muscles in it. When you quarry stones, you dig them with rough equipment from steep mountains. And the lines of stone structures are all straight lines. Straight lines are sharp and therefore challenging, looking as if they were about to pierce you. Moreover, there is always something incomplete about straight lines; it is expected that straight lines will act unceasingly, to complement their incompleteness. That is to say, Western architecture embodies the element of the progressive and the innovative, which are masculine attributes.

In contrast, the ancient palace is built of wood, so massiveness is absent from it. Instead, the softness of wood reminds one of the soft flesh of females. Besides, in dealing with wooden materials, their natural grain is utilized to the fullest; and they are gathered not from steep dangerous cliffs, but from verdant forests. And then the curve of the eaves bends so softly that, unlike the challenging straight line, it is almost too perfect and complete. So, unlike the stone structure, these elements suggest peace, timelessness, and conservatism, which are feminine characteristics.

Then there are other elements like color, and use of accessories such as nails, and other matters pertaining to construction technique; but these are the most important factors.

"So modern history is how the male came to wed the female."

Then the woman laughed and said,

"Oh, do males come to wed females? I thought females married into the males' houses."

He laughed also.

"Oh, because the female is so shy and dignified, the male, being too impatient, just jumped in."

"Isn't that like a thief?"

"Well, women often call men thieves."

"Oh, what an awful thing to say!" She laughed at the absurdity of his remark. Sobering, she said, as if to score after a lost point, "But modern girls aren't like that."

"How do you mean?"

"They aren't so shy as to wait for the men to take the initiative. Far from it, they are aggressive like men."

Then he suddenly became very excited and said,

"Are they, really?"

"Yes. Really."

"Then that's our future."

He seemed intoxicated, as if he was picturing something exhilarating before his eyes. But Miss B became gloomy because of the sudden change of subject. Rather, his lengthy disquisition from the first was not of keen interest to her. People ordinarily are not strongly interested in anything that does not directly concern them, even if it was an urgent problem of the times. So Miss B turned to a topic that she had been anxious to explore.

"Do you like jazz?"

He looked uneasy, like one awakened from a reverie and, turning a little toward Miss B, said,

"No, I like classical music."

"Classical music?" she retorted in surprise.

"Yes. In music, the most important thing is the tradition from Bach to Beethoven. After that everything is a mere variation of what had already been written."

"But you always request pop music?" she inquired, at a loss.

He smiled queerly and said,

"No, I always requested classical music."

"What? You requested classical music? Then what about *Let's Go* and *Guitar Twist*?"

"Oh, those are jazz, to be sure, but when I request them, each of them becomes a movement in a classical symphony. There is a phrase, you know, like 'eight chords making up the universe.' That is to say, the pop songs are each a chord. Well, what shall I say the universe is? For me, I'd say it is the *Eroica Symphony*."

"*Eroica Symphony*? Beethoven's?"

"Yes. *Eroica Symphony*. Hahaha."

He laughed a bold laugh like a boastful, middle-aged libertine. But it seemed to Miss B that behind the laughter there lurked the truth of the man. Miss B, affected by his hearty laughter, was drawn into it and found herself laughing, forgetting her original intention in bringing up the topic.

A man's and a woman's feelings become a shade more delicate when they part without any promise of a next meeting. It was the same with Miss B, so she felt strangely emotional now and then. But, just as his reasons for frequenting this tea-room had been uncertain, Miss B's reasons for meeting the man were also obscure. They were not sweethearts, they had no definite business to discuss, and of course they were not instructor and pupil. Maybe we could call them apprentice sweethearts. But that might be the secret thought of Miss B alone. When people meet, especially when a man and a woman meet, there has to be a plausible reason. Modern people, especially, need rational reasons. To be sure, there must be a reason for Miss B's meeting that man. But she couldn't put into words her reasons for seeing that particular man.

So the feeling of boredom she had been experiencing up to now changed into a misgiving. When one is unsure about the true character of another person, one has such anxious feelings. That is to say, when a person one is dealing with is not comprehended, the person becomes a burden. We might say that Miss B had now acquired a burden in addition to all the burdens she already bore. People try to understand one another in order that the other party will not become an added burden to them. When they have comprehended one another, people say they have "seen" each other.

To "see each other" means that the two people's consciousness takes one seat. The place where the consciousness of one and the other can sit together—when they find that common seat, the two cease to be burdens to each other. In the case of Miss B, she had not yet found that common seat for herself and the man. When they have not found that seat people become anxious, and in order to get away from the anxiety they unceasingly challenge the other party and search for the common seat.

So with Miss B. She wanted to know all about the man. But what really is this thing called knowing? Is it knowing his social status? His living environment? His appearance? His income? His propensity for spending? His hobby? His taste? The knowledge of these things is not enough to enable one to find the human being's ultimate seat. Or rather, the seat must exist somewhere underneath all these. Anyway, Miss B wanted to discover this man's ultimate seat. So she diligently thought about him.

He did not appear in the tea-room again after their last date, but she kept thinking of him. As days went by, the thought of the Eroica Symphony occupied her more persistently. Most people who request music do so for the sake of a memory connected with the music. That means that by hearing a piece of music they bring to mind the specific person, event, or place connected with the melody. But when a man requests pop music as a portion of a symphony, he must be thinking of the meaning of the music itself. So she thought about the meaning of the pieces on his request notes one by one. For example, Puccini's "One Fine Day" is an aria from the opera *Madame Butterfly*, in which a Japanese girl is betrayed by an American sailor. Then, what on earth was that man looking for in that music? In this manner, Miss B kept pondering.

Perhaps summer is the best season for tea-rooms. However scorching hot it may be outside, inside the tea-room the air conditioner cools the air and there are cold beverages in plenty. The waves foaming with white teeth, the wind that sweeps up the waves that break with a roar, and the young naked bodies rushing into the blue water—if this is the seashore in summer, then tea-rooms are beaches inside the city. Even so, the small disc jockey's room, walled by glass on all sides, looks enclosed. Moreover, as the man who constantly occupies her mind has not given a hint of his existence for over a month, there is nothing noteworthy about her life these days.

One early autumn evening, when the fierce heat had begun to subside, the long-awaited man made his appearance suddenly. Miss B's gladness was expressed in her reproachful look, but she *was* glad, to be sure. But the man, without even ordering a cup of tea, hurriedly scribbled a note, sent it to the record booth, and disappeared immediately. The note said simply, "Ten o'clock tomorrow morning at the front gate of Tŏksu Palace."

Sometimes meeting people can be a bothersome affair, but really there is no greater pleasure on earth. Our pleasure in meeting people is numbed by our being surrounded by people on all sides from birth. It can easily be imagined, the delight of meeting a fellow human being on a desert island. Our feeling when we meet strangers in daily life may be anxiety, expectation, or impatience. At any rate, meeting people can be a greatly rewarding experience. We often feel unsettled when we step into a shop to have a suit made, to buy a pair of shoes, or purchase a daily commodity or fancy goods; but these moments are not unsettling because we are going to meet things. They are so because we are going to acquire things we will be using or wearing when we meet people. One need not describe in words the anxious, heart-throbbing expectation of two young people meeting!

Miss B stepped into the open air with a pounding heart. Continuously feeling a thrill running through her body, she hastened to the place of appointment. The sky was high and there wasn't a speck of cloud visible. When she stepped onto T'aepyŏngro, she saw a bustling crowd densely lining both sides of the street. What had happened? But such a thing was far from having any importance to her at the moment. When she had come near Tŏksu Palace, though, she was made aware that this noisy crowd had something to do with her own personal affairs. Nothing was on the road, but people were struggling against each other for a better view. And she became aware that she could not cross the road lined by crowds on both sides.

In front of the crowd, policemen and military police were strictly forbidding crossing, and mounted policemen could be seen riding about blowing whistles. Miss B became hot with impatience. But there was nothing she could do. Across the street was the Tŏksu Palace. He must be there waiting for her now. The long hand of her watch ticked past the hour mark. When she recalled that it was Armed Forces Day, she was dismayed.

"For heaven's sake!" she muttered to herself, and stood there behind the crowd, as if lost. The pushing and pushed crowd. The noisy talk, the sound of the whistle; time ticked past.

In the clear blue autumn sky, a bunch of clouds appeared from no-where to brood over the City Hall. At long last, making splitting metallic sounds, jet airplanes began to confound the sky with swallow swoops, and band music could be heard. With the appearance of the army band with an honor guard in front, the crowd became still more noisy and disorderly. The copper-skinned soldiers, the helmets and rucksacks and the guns looking heavy, even cumbersome, to the soldiers with their gloomy ex-pressions, their uniformly angular, undernourished faces—all seemed part of a loaded-down herd of animals. Trucks, combat vehicles, armored cars, guns, mounted soldiers, and military equipment she did not know the names of. Over the heads of the dull, slow procession of the herd, bal-loons of all colors let loose by bored people soared to the sky, as if fleeing for freedom. Rather, they were shouting for freedom, escaping, soaring into the sky far above the City Hall plaza.

It was too painful a trial for Miss B to shrug off as the bad luck of a day. She came back home tired, and unfortunately he did not appear in the tea-room again, so there is no further progress in our story of their romance. But then one day, about a fortnight afterwards, Miss B hap-pened to open an evening paper in her booth. There was a small article under the headline: "_____ Arrested for Violation of National Security Law."* And there was a picture, beside the article, of the man. She looked at it again, unbelieving, but it was undoubtedly his picture. There was no mistake, although she looked at it again and again.

Most women are more shocked by an event itself than at the true and detailed facts of an event. Miss B is not an exception. She experi-enced unspeakable agitation while holding the paper in her hands. With the passing of time, that agitation changed into frustration. She was overwhelmed with a feeling, a conviction that everything had gone wrong. For some time after that she kept falling deeper into a pit of gloom. But every pit has a bottom. When hitting the bottom, one begins to ask questions. Has everything gone wrong now, irrevocably? Why was he arrested? What is this National Security Law? Question after question arose in her mind. And then, after that, a person can't

---

*The military regime that seized power through the 1961 coup devised the so-called National Security Law to arrest and imprison anyone who criticized or opposed it. Therefore, many who were victimized by this law were regarded as heroes by people who chafed under the yoke of military dictatorship. [Translator]

help wandering in a world of ratiocination, searching for the culprit. It was during this stage, while ruminating through the peculiar impressions and memories of him, that she had a sudden flash of insight. A strange ray passed through her brain, making it seem a resonant chamber. Then came the ecstasy of revelation.

"That's it!" she exulted, but if you asked "What's it?" she wouldn't have been able to tell you in well-defined phrases. Still, in her mind, she saw all too clearly the thing which had been vague. The two consciousnesses had found their common seat. She had striven and found the common seat for both of them. Then it became clear to her—the feeling with which he had listened to pop music, and also what pop music is and what classical music is.

Indeed, everything—the tea-room, the player booth, the ranged records—all looked vitalized, like new spring plants. Moreover, all these, instead of being tiresome burdens to her, became her wings.

Our story has to come to an end here. Of course such an extraordinary experience as Miss B's enabled her to love the man truly, and also to begin a new life in which she came to love all human beings; but to tell that story, we would have to go into this case under the National Security Law. That would make a long, tedious story, so as we originally intended we are going to close with the account of Miss B's discovery. For reference, we record here how Miss B in her own way arranged and interpreted the music he requested and made the whole into an Eroica Symphony.

1. The Lost Sun—the sorrow of the loss of one's fatherland and leader.
2. Guitar Twist—chaos, disorder, incoherence.
3. One Fine Day—the breach of faith by Westerners.
4. Phaedra—Fate's stubborn pursuit.
5. Exodus—Escape from repression.
6. Go Down, Moses—the awakening to leadership, the will of the hero.
7. He's Got the Whole World in His Hand—the sense of unity, the will toward synthesis.
8. Autumn Leaves—the sorrow of estrangement.
9. The Theme of Love—self-discipline of the hero to purify love.
10. El Cid—the messiah and the cross.
11. Let's Go—everything's over.

My Idol's Abode

Ch'oe In-hoon

Born in 1936, Ch'oe In-hoon began his writing career early, in 1959. The young writer greatly impressed a few critics and readers from the first with his firm intelligence, keen psychological insight and bold indictment of the irrationalities of society. But he had to wait quite a few years for general recognition, and even now has a more intellectual than general readership.

Ch'oe's main concern as a writer is with the relationship among ideology, social institutions, and the human consciousness. His principal lifelong quest may be defined as a search for a spiritual home. "My Idol's Abode" (1960), an early work, records the failure of a meeting of two souls, a typical encounter of spiritually homeless modern men.

Ch'oe In-hoon has many remarkable gifts, not least among them his keen satirical wit which he employs for scathing attacks on the shams and subterfuges of modern society and institutions. When Ch'oe In-hoon engages in his relentless analysis and exposure he sounds embittered and angry, but we are never made to feel he is angry without cause. He is one of the most penetrating spokesmen of this generation's anguished sense of alienation.

The author also shows a deep concern with the national heritage, and has "rewritten" many Korean classical works, to re-examine thoroughly the values of Korea's past and their effects on Korean people today. In mid-career he tried his hand at writing dramas, and has

produced daring experimental pieces which have earned him high ac-
claim. All in all, Ch'oe In-hoon is a writer for those prepared to face
the naked truth about life and human beings.

~~~

It was shortly after Seoul was recaptured and the government moved back
from Pusan. In Myŏngdong,* damaged by bombs and deserted by the
pre-war crowd, there was a tea-room named "Arisa." We fledgling men
of letters used a corner of the tea-room, which was very snugly recessed
and which we had fondly named "Venus's bosom," as a kind of private
drawing-room, to talk spiritedly or just stare at the ceiling for hours. Mr.
K was our respected mentor and the center of the group. Like other
tea-rooms of that time, coffee at Arisa tasted rather funny and we jokingly
called it "simulated coffee," but in fact we could not very well afford to
order that beverage as rent for occupying the space there.

However, we were not at all daunted by the disapproving glances
from the counter; and in effect, the proprietress for the most part generously overlooked our occupying so much space every day without
adding much to the sales, and even hospitably attended to us. Thus, the
tea-room became our haunt. Mr. K was an established author at the
time, and therefore many renowned figures of the literary circle of that
time came by to the tea-room to talk with him and make requests for
his contributions, much to our envy and admiration. And of course
there were many nameless would-be authors who came for the benefit
of his opinion and advice.

One day I happened to notice, among those who came to the tea-
room on account of Mr. K, one young man who belonged to neither of
those two groups. It was plain that he was not there for business.
Neither was he there for sociable purposes. It was one drizzly July
afternoon when he first appeared in the tea-room. I distinctly remember the date, because something very depressing had occurred that day
and my diary bears a record of the day.

. He paid silent regard to Mr. K with his eyes, strode off to a table a
few yards away, and sat obliquely on the chair, facing Mr. K. His
movement was so mechanical that it affected me strangely. When I
heard later that that was the first time in many years he and Mr. K had

---

*Myŏngdong is a busy fashion and entertainment district in the heart of Seoul.
[Translator]

met, I did not know what to think of such deportment as his. Since Mr. K was of a taciturn disposition and treated everyone more or less equally, I had got into the habit of observing his conversation narrowly to figure out the degree of familiarity and the nature of the relationship between him and his various acquaintances. It gave me childish amusement to whisper my inferences into Mr. K's ears. Mr. K usually simply smiled or chuckled at my observations.

Well, one more surprising thing about this stranger was that Mr. K, who is usually imperturbable, evinced a great change of emotion on seeing him and, walking over to the newcomer, sat down beside him and talked to him earnestly, taking his arm. It was the first time Mr. K had received anyone thus. That could not fail to excite my curiosity.

Who could the stranger be? Although he was one of those who look more mature than his age, it was not difficult to see that he was twenty or more years Mr. K's junior, and although the young man seemed noticeably lacking in diffidence, I could see that he looked up to Mr. K. But that was all that I could figure out about him. I could not suppress my interest and curiosity, and my attention would of itself wander to where they were, even while I was carrying on a conversation with pals at my table. Well, I was somewhat embarrassed by my intense curiosity, as it is not very flattering to one's ego to be so strongly attracted to another, and especially as the other members of my group seemed hardly to notice him. But there was no help for it—he seemed such an extraordinary character.

After that, he came to the tea-room quite frequently. As Mr. K had simply said, in response to my inquiry, "Well, it's someone I know," I remained totally ignorant about him, but I was beginning to think that knowing in the ordinary sense—the usual data about a person implied in the word "knowing"—was unnecessary and irrelevant in the case of that man. I blush to confess this, as it means that I had made of him in my mind a figure of mystery—like perhaps the Count of Monte Cristo in the work by Dumas *père*. However, it was not as if I was a naive idolizer. I had sensibility and discrimination enough to perceive subtle shades of character and nuances of personality, and prided myself on my acuteness in this regard. Well, he may not have been a Count of Monte Cristo, but he was certainly above my measurement, or too complex for my analysis.

When he came into the tea-room he always took a seat at a table or two away from us, and then Mr. K went over to him. He did not take notice of the others in the group in any way. That displeased me. I decided to take no notice of him myself, but then felt ashamed of myself—his eyes, when they met mine by chance, had no pride or arrogance in them. I discovered that I was carrying on an entirely one-sided contention. I suppose the following account will prove to the reader that my hostility or spite was entirely meaningless and that he defied hasty judgment.

From what I have said so far the reader may have imagined a human being who had become corrupt inside and callous on the surface. I was drawing toward roughly that conclusion myself. But it was a misconception. His closed lips, as he turned his eyes quietly toward the window in the middle of a conversation with Mr. K, were not at all those of one who prides himself on having penetrated the last secret of the universe. In other words, had he been an abstract painter, he would not have been one of those who shallowly laugh at the traditional pencil sketch. Oh, no, he's not the fossil remains of an ardent poetic aspiration gone sour, I said to myself, and decided to give up the psychological combat. Once I gave up the struggle I found that I was in a much better position for observing him. Eyes not clouded by the ego—I gained that necessary condition for observation through humility. On my stage there were only two actors—him and Mr. K.

When I beheld the stage as a spectator I was surprised once again by a new discovery. Of the two actors Mr. K seemed to be in the minor role. In worldly terms it was certainly Mr. K whose position was the weightier; but in terms of the mental currents being exchanged between the two, his was the stronger and seemed to tax Mr. K's strength in the reception of it. Having got rid of personal pride, I felt a genuine artistic interest in the relationship between them. Of course, the immaturity of my view prevented my taking into consideration the factor that Mr. K had the handicap of being so many years the young man's senior and so superior in social status that he could not take the role of the challenger, and I noted only the surface phenomena. At that time at any rate my whole concern was on the shift in the uncertain balance between the two as they appeared on my stage.

Once he came to the tea-room on a very dull afternoon. Only Mr. K and I were at our table. Surprisingly, the man threw himself into our "Venus's bosom." He seemed very pleased with something. He sat obliquely in a chair and tapped the floor with his feet, or playfully yawned, making a small O with his mouth in a simulated rabbit's yawn. As was their wont, neither Mr. K nor the young man took any pains to carry on a conversation. But after a while the young man suddenly straightened up, moved close up to Mr. K, and slipping a hand under Mr. K's armpit, said,

"Your eyes are as impressively clear as in the old days. They aren't at all a middle-aged man's. Does that mean you haven't found a woman who'd buy those eyes?"

Then he chuckled. In his chuckle I thought I sensed something unmistakable—something wounded, I was convinced.

After that, he made his appearance in the tea-room only after a good month's absence. Mr. K was not there then. He sat himself down at a table, apparently to wait for Mr. K's appearance, looked out at the darkening streets for a good while, then got up and left the room with a barely perceptible nod to me. My heart bade me "follow," and I hastened out after him. He was standing in the doorway vacantly, stroking his chin with one hand. I went up to him and extended my hand.

The handshake was carried out in silence, and I realized that I was admitted into the company of the actors on stage. I was ecstatic, like when a woman one has fallen in love with at first sight accepts one's approach.

"Haven't we long been friends? I've been convinced of it for a long time now," I said rapturously, but he did not respond in any way. We walked together shoulder to shoulder, and without any explicit agreement both of us were walking into the grounds of the Myŏngdong Catholic chapel. After sitting down on the bench he spoke for the first time.

"In my opinion, those who feel drawn to each other must strive at all costs to prevent becoming friends or lovers."

I smiled, "You mean so as not to become disillusioned?"

"Disillusioned? Well, maybe that's it."

I unfolded to him my impression of him since his first appearance, and the reasons for my being drawn to him. As he listened to me his face became overcast with gloom—or, rather, torment. I became confused.

"I am an accursed man. I am fated to ruin all those who come near me."

But on his face as he said this there hovered a quiet smile. His words did not make me run away from him. On the contrary, they made me trust in him the more deeply.

"If ruin is my fate, then I'll gladly accept it," I said. The dramatic declaration made me excited, and satisfied my yearning for dramatic intensity. I wanted to believe that conversation with him at least was not exchange of dead words for form's sake, but a matter of two souls comparing their call signs. Contemplating his face, on which the thickly leaved trees threw patterns of light and shade intercepting the afternoon sun, I sat bemused. Had I ever met anyone who was so keenly alive to human beings?

My religion at that time was hero-worship. Only, my hero did not wear conventional diadems or medals. My hero was rather a man of depth of character and humane attractiveness. Well, I held no definite doctrine of hero-worship, but it was a faith and a mental disposition. A man possessed by a dark, naked force; a man who failed repeatedly in worldly affairs but who never compromised, and whose intelligence and common sense shielded all the turbulence of emotion inside—such was roughly the portrait of my hero. The young man's face and mood seemed to satisfy the outlines of this portrait, and so, summoning my courage, I approached him aggressively. Thus we became friends.

He appeared in the tea-room every Wednesday between six and seven o'clock. But Mr. K did not know that we had become friends. The man did not show any mark of intimacy with me before the others, and thus Mr. K had failed to notice the development of our acquaintance. I didn't take any particular notice of him in front of others, either. Like lovers who choose to remain unacknowledged before the public, we feigned indifference before the others.

Since the development of my acquaintance with him I had discovered many unusual things about him. When we met, we always used to come out of the tea-room and head toward a bench in front of the Catholic chapel. One day, as we were rounding a corner and heading up the hill, I found I had run out of cigarettes, and retraced a few steps to stop at a cigarette stall. I tarried a few minutes, to wait for my change, and then headed up the hill once more, looking for him on the spot where we parted. He was not there. I walked quickly to the bench he and I always took, but he was not there either. I waited for a long time but he did not appear.

When we met the next time I did not say a word in reproach, and he did not say a word in apology, either. This is a trivial instance, but typical of his ways. Far from seeming a defect, such personal habits seemed to me the eccentricity of a genuine artist. Well, that proves how complete his conquest of me was.

One day he became serious and said, "I really must confess."

"What it is?" was all I could say, in anxious expectation.

"I'm going to tell you something that will make you want to flee from me for dear life."

"You want to get rid of me? Well, go ahead. There's no telling the effect of a tale without hearing it first."

He was silent for a long time. It almost seemed as if he was going to remain silent till the end of his life. But he began, and told me the following story:

"My home is W— city, way up north on the west coast. I was a high school freshman the year the Korean War broke out. My father was a surgeon, and had a private practice before the liberation, but after the liberation the communist government pressured him into closing his private clinic and becoming a salaried doctor in the provincial hospital. The air was always gloomy at our home, and I think it was because of my father's dissatisfaction with a lot of the things he had to endure at work. But my father's ideological anguish did not draw my concern, as I was besieged with a problem of my own.

"I was at the age when Zola's 'Nana' could absolutely enthrall me. Because the repressive policy which is characteristic of controlled societies extended to the area of publication also, there were very few books from which a boy my age, just beginning to be awakened to sex, could get enlightenment on the subject. The 'Nana' that cast such a thrall on me was of course not a North Korean publication but a Japanese translation published by Japan's 'New Wave' publisher. I found the book in a secondhand bookshop and purchased it with money coaxed out of my mother. The used book was very expensive. The night I made the book mine I stayed up all night to read it through. The reason I bought the book was a passage that had caught my eyes and made my heart leap when I was leafing through it casually in the bookstore. Come to think of it, one may say that the eroticism in 'Nana' is mild compared with the eroticism in such works as 'Lady Chatterley's Lover,' but to me at that time it was a dream world that surpassed my imaginative capacity. The prostitute's eroticism in the book was to me not sex but song. My knowledge of carnal transactions had been almost blank, as it was impossible to hope to be instructed by books, and as I had no friends who could supply me with so-called dirty sexual knowledge. For me, it was the summit of ecstasy to read that Nana stripped herself naked before the man in front of the mantlepiece. I caressed Nana's entire body delineated in print. When I closed my eyes her naked body loomed before me. I was intoxicated in that dream, and I walked on clouds. I caressed the imagined body with my mind's eye, and biological desire had no part in it. I believe that it was the purest love of a man for a woman.

"Then there appeared before me a real live woman. There was a half-Korean and half-western style wooden house in the residential area on the slope of a hill that I had to pass on my way to school every day. One morning I saw a woman coming out of the house. I just walked past her, but when I rounded a corner of the street a hot lump shot up from my chest and exploded in my throat. I stretched my neck and looked at the gate of the house. The woman was not there. But on my retina was inscribed a distinct outline of her face, which resembled a sweet briar. A nameless grief assaulted me and I turned my gaze toward the sea quickly. In the sky above the sea were huge lumps of dark clouds which gleamed ominously with the reflected glare of the sea.

"I saw the woman a few more times after that. I think she was about twenty or slightly older. The woman became one with Nana in my imagination, and I was Georges. She sometimes came out of her house wearing a light dress and carrying a parasol, or sometimes she wore a wide-brimmed summer hat.

"I did not dream that I could ever become personally acquainted with her. My only hope was that she would not disappear, but stay where my eyes could sometimes light on her. One day I saw the woman walking with a stalwart young man. Perhaps taking courage at the fact that the street was deserted, the woman halted to pick something off his hair. It's not what she removed that was important, but rather that the gesture was an expression of fondness. I felt a sorrow like one betrayed. I resolved never to pass that house again. From the next day I picked a much longer road to school.

"The war broke out about a week after that event. Before people had had time to worry about the gravity of the danger, bombing began. The townspeople hastily fled to a suburb to escape the bombing, and life became completely topsy-turvy. Huge bombers flew across the cobalt-blue sky and flew away after smoothly discharging bombs. The silver-gray airplanes flying through the light, cottonwool clouds, sending reverberations through the sky, presented a languorous beauty, like silver-gray fish swimming in a crystal-clear lake. To me at least they presented such beauty. I did not dislike the war. And there was a very good reason for it, too. The war released me from school. School had been my prison for a long time. School meant the distasteful lessons in ideology and rigorous physical training.

"The war had chased people away from the city. I, who had till then been indifferent to the city, felt a sudden friendliness and freedom in it, as if it had become mine and only mine—our family could not flee, because my father had to treat the wounded. I sauntered around the courtyard of the Catholic chapel with leisurely steps, frowned or smiled or folded my arms, all quite as I liked, and there was no one to say anything about it. I strolled the streets, in my imagination crowding buildings and squares with people and events of my own creation and delighting in or mourning their imagined happiness or sorrow. It was an indescribably sweet exercise. I steered myself toward the woman's house. The gate was locked, an empty basket lay a little way from it, and only silence could be heard from the house. I hid myself in a recess and watched for nearly two hours, but no one either entered or left the house. It was the same the next day. I retraced my steps home heavily.

" 'You mustn't wander around in this dangerous city. You must stay quietly at home and go into the dug-out shelter when the air raid signal sounds,' Father warned me, and scolded Mother for not keeping me at home, but there was nothing Mother could do, short of literally tying me down, to make me stay at home.

"The next day there was the largest-scale air raid since the outbreak of the war. Bombers, which came in sets of four, came and went and dropped bombs. The neighborhood of my home and the woman's house had escaped bombing till then, but we were not spared that day. After the raid ceased I slipped out of the air-raid shelter and looked in the direction of her house, but I saw the entire area thereabouts befogged with black smoke. I found myself frantically running toward her house. Tears were streaming down my cheeks as I ran. Arriving there, I saw that half of her house had disappeared, and flames were rising from what must be the kitchen. Looking carefully, I saw that the house was not on fire but that the flames came from the house next to it, which was on fire. Courage rose in me and I jumped on to the porch of that house. Where the hall ended, there was a woman lying on her back, pressed under a huge column.

"I could not help screaming when I saw her face. It was a terrible face, all besmirched with blood, and gaping. Her hand waved to me in supplication. I shot out of the house like lightning, ran all the way home, and jumped into my bed to forget everything. I lay still until sundown, racked by chills and a headache, but jumped out of bed after dark. When I reached the spot again I saw corpses being carried out of the house on stretchers.

"'A column fell on her. She could have lived if only she'd been discovered earlier.' I heard the words dimly, and fainted away."

He paused when he got that far in the story. Then he resumed. "I didn't realize what it meant for me then. My family all escaped south safely. But from then on there grew in my heart a secret torment. Had I removed the column, or summoned people, she would have lived. The men's words, 'she could have lived if discovered earlier,' haunted me like a curse. I don't know why I did such a foolish thing at that time. But the fact remains that I knowingly left a human being to writhe with pain for hours and to die. And that human being was my beloved. The woman still lives in my heart and accuses me of cruelty. Ah, I'm a murderer, a murderer!"

He sobbed, pressing his forehead on the back of the bench.

All my questions were answered.

I sat there speechless, with my hand upon his shoulder, feeling the veil of mystery lifting from around him. He was tormented by this secret sorrow! Compassion welled up in my heart, and I added pressure to my hand on his shoulder, cursing life for its cruel tricks.

From that day till the next time we met I racked my brains trying to think of a way of relieving him from the burden of that memory. But I could think of nothing more original than a few days' trip. When I suggested it to him, he looked thoughtful for quite a while and then accepted my invitation, saying that I might pick him up at his home on the day we were to leave.

I set out in search of his house with a small suitcase in one hand and the directions to his home in the other. After wandering for quite a while I found the house which bore the address he had inscribed on the map. I was much taken aback by the sign on the brick house which said "St. Mary's Neuropsychiatric Clinic." I recalled that he had said his father was a doctor. At the reception desk sat a thin, bespectacled man who looked up at me when I went in, laying aside the balance in his hand. I put my suitcase down beside the sofa in the hall and said,

"I've come to see somebody."

"Yes? Is it a patient?"

"No."

"Then an employee? Who?"

"No, I came to see the director's . . ."

"The director's away."

"No, it's not the director."

I realized how foolishly I had been stammering and gave his name, adding that I believed he was the director's son. The clerk grinned at once.

"I see. Well, I suppose you add one more to the list of his dupes. He's an in-patient. If you want to see him you must see his doctor first."

The clerk led me to the room with a "Consultation" sign on it and opened the door for me. A doctor who looked about forty glanced up from a thick book he was reading. I was completely at a loss.

"I'm in charge of everything concerning the patients while the director's away," the doctor said.

I told the doctor that I was a friend of the young man, and that I had decided to go on a trip with him to help relieve him of a tormenting memory.

"We do sometimes permit patients to take trips, but first tell me what kind of acquaintance you have with him," was the doctor's response.

After briefly narrating the history of my friendship with his patient, I asked, "But how did he come to be hospitalized so suddenly?" and then felt surprised as I remembered that the hospital address was what my friend had given me as his home address.

"Well, he became an in-patient about three months ago."

"What?"

I was astonished. It was less than three months since I had first met him. The doctor sighed and said, "I see you're one of his victims."

"What do you mean, victims?"

There was nothing I could do but grow more and more amazed at every utterance of the doctor's. The doctor explained, "I mean that story about the woman who died during the bombing."

"Yes, I know that story. Well, it's no wonder you know it, as part of your patient's history."

"Well, it's not something I detected as a doctor. To tell you the truth, I'm one of his dupes myself."

"You?" I exclaimed in confusion, and pursued, "I don't understand. Please explain."

The doctor nodded and offered me a cigarette, lighting one up himself.

"I will. I'll begin with the conclusion. That story is a complete fiction. He's never been anywhere north of Seoul. He was born and raised in Seoul throughout his life."

Something exploded in my head. I could not believe it. His tormented expression as he recounted the story, and the faultless narrative! Why should he unfold such a fiction to everyone he met, and why should he feign such preposterous grief?

"His illness is a very intricate mixture of many complexes. There is no single name for it, but it is a kind of exhibitionism. Megalomania, Oedipal complex, delusions of heroism and other disorders are very complexly woven in his psyche. That imaginary tale is a manifestation of that illness. He thinks that fiction solves his many problems."

"But he looks perfectly normal, except for the invention of that story."

"That's exactly why his is a difficult case. He is one of the almost incurable cases."

The doctor told me further that Mr. K also sometimes came by the hospital, and that the hospital had been permitting him to seek out Mr. K in town, as Mr. K had a great deal of influence on him.

I kept on smoking. My chest tightened. I felt like one kicked hard in the behind after being dragged around by a cunning, invisible foe.

"Would you like to see him?"

I still had too much lingering attachment to resist the offer. I nodded. The door opened after a while and he walked in. He was completely unperturbed to see me. I exclaimed to myself, "So this was it!" I realized at last that I had mistaken the meaningless unconcern of a man out of his right mind for the lofty indifference of a true artist.

He smiled generously at me and said, "I suppose you've been given an introduction to Freud by our revered doctor. That story, I admit, is a fiction. But what if it is? Are you, too, one of those who think it's a harmless joke to make friends love-sick by writing sham love letters, but insanity to create a fiction to show what damage the war has done to us? Do you think I am a mental case, too? Have I done anything till the other day that made me look suspicious in your eyes? Wasn't it I myself who gave you the address of this hospital? Have you ever heard of a criminal giving his address to a detective?"

As I remained speechless with confusion at his eloquent outburst, the doctor replied for me, "Doesn't it prove the criminal to be abnormal, that he gave his address to the detective?"

That logical answer was a truly incisive surprise attack. The man's dignified face blanched instantly and then became flushed. Glaring at the doctor, he shouted, "What, you cunning swindler! You dare pretend to correct human minds with your bits of Freud? Let me out of here at once! And refund all the money you squeezed out of me! You dare say I'm mad? Make me a university professor, and I'll explain Hegel's logic for hours on end. And you!" He turned to me. "Is this all your friendship means? You bow to the diagnosis of a quack doctor like that? It's you who are to be pitied. I pity you! Please get out of here. I don't want any pity or affection from fools."

The solid friendship between him and me in which I had such complete faith evaporated before my eyes like a mist and he became a total stranger again. I saw an impassable gulf gaping between us. I wasn't sure any more who was sane and who insane. I was afraid I was going mad. A berserk desire to kick and smash up everything swirled inside me. I could not stay still any more. I pushed open the door and ran outside. I swept past Mr. K's surprised face which I glimpsed as he was coming in the gate as I went out, and I heard my former friend's guffaw and derision, "There, look at that! A self-styled first-rate intellectual of this country making a hasty retreat before the divine authority of common sense! My friend, my old pal!"

I ran, not knowing where to go, with the suitcase in my hand. Passersby who saw me must have thought me a mental patient escaping from the hospital. As I ran, in the endless desert of my brain only sand swirled up in a whirlwind.

The Rainy Spell

Yoon Heung-gil

Yoon Heung-gil, born in 1942, is an author who eludes classification. It is not because he has intentionally rejected the dominant literary trends. In fact, he has treated many of the themes other contemporary authors favored—the problem of social injustice, economic inequality, abuse of human rights, and the aftermaths of national division. But there is always more to savor in his stories than in the average writer's, even when he treats the same subject. While indignation predominates in the works of other writers, pity runs stronger in his stories. And his characters are always fuller. Having experienced excruciating emotional and psychological conflicts all through his penurious childhood and adolescence, Yoon has an acute understanding of the worms that gnaw at the root of the human psyche and man's innumerable compensatory mechanisms. Thus, even his villains have some redeeming qualities, and his heroes, human weaknesses. This, together with his verbal wit, irony, and inimitable handling of his native Cholla-do dialect, constitute his charm. After taking us through numerous pitfalls and trials that lie in ambush for humanity, Yoon offers a possibility of meaningful survival.

"The Rainy Spell," first published in 1978, is still rated as one of the finest short stories to deal with the Korean War experience. Because it was a war in which a homogeneous race slaughtered each other, the Korean War left a wound in the Korean psyche that is still not completely healed after half a century. The momentous encounter

153

between the two grandmothers with sons in the opposing war camps is
innocently reported by a child who gets caught up in the grown-ups'
games of hate. The final reconciliation between the women holds out a
hope for healing and transcendence.

~~~

1

The rain that had started to pour from the day after we reaped the last
pea-pods showed no sign of letting up even after many days. The rain
came sometimes in fine powdery drops, or in hard, fierce balls, threatening to pierce the roof. Tonight, rain enveloped the pitch darkness
like a dripping-wet mop.

It must have been somewhere right outside the village. My guess is
that it came from somewhere around the empty house beside the river-
bank which was used for storing funeral palanquins. The house always
struck me as an eerie place, and even dogs would bark in long, dismal,
fox-like howls when going near it. But it might have come in reality
from a place much farther than the empty house. The distant howling
of dogs filled the silence following the thinning rain. As if that far-off
howling had been a military signal, all the village dogs that had managed to survive the war began to bark in turn. Their barking was
unusually fierce that night.

That evening we were all gathered in the guest room occupied by
my maternal grandmother, because she was greatly disturbed by something and we had to comfort and reassure her. But Mother and Maternal Aunt's efforts to say something comforting ceased after the dogs
began to bark outside. Stealing glances at Grandmother, they repeatedly turned their eyes towards the darkness beyond, separated from the
room only by the door panelled with gauze mosquito netting. An obscure moth with tremulous wings had been crawling up and down the
doorpost for a long time now.

"Just wait and see. It won't be long before we'll know for sure. Just
wait and see if I'm ever wrong," Grandmother murmured in a sunken
voice. She was shelling peas from the pods. The peas would be cooked
with the rice for breakfast the next morning. Sitting with her lap full of

damp pea-pods, she shelled the peas with sure, experienced hands—
first breaking off the tip and slitting open the pod, then running her
finger through it. When the bright green peas slid out to one side,
Grandmother cupped them in her palm and poured them into the bamboo basket at her knee, and dropped the empty pod into her lap.

Mother and Aunt, who lost the chance to make a rejoinder, exchanged awkward glances. Outside, the rain grew noisy again, and the
dogs barked more fiercely, as if in competition. The night grew still
stormier, and from the direction of the storage platform came the clatter of metal hitting the cement floor. The tin pail hung on the wall must
have fallen down. A sudden gust of wind and rain rushed into the
room, rattling the door and blowing out the kerosene lamp that had
been flickering precariously. The room sank under the sudden flood of
darkness and sticky humidity. The moth's wings also stopped quiver-
ing. A dog began to bark three or four houses beyond ours in the alley.
Our dog Wŏlly, who had kept silent till then, growled. The wild com-
motion of the dogs, which had begun at the entrance of the village, was
coming nearer and nearer our house.

"Light that lamp," Grandmother said. "Light the lamp, I said. Didn't
you hear me?" Feeling about the room in the dark, Grandmother made
a rustling noise. "What evil weather!"

I groped about the room, found a match, and lit the kerosene lamp.
Mother trimmed the wick. A strip of sooty smoke curled upward and
drew a round shadow on the ceiling.

"It's always wet like this around this time of the year." Mother
spoke in an effort to lessen the uneasiness created by the weather.

"It's all because of the weather. It's because of this weather that
you're worrying yourself sick for no reason," Aunt also put in. Aunt
had graduated from a high school in Seoul before the war broke out,
when my mother's family lived in Seoul.

"No. It isn't for no reason. You don't know. When has my dream
ever predicted wrong?" Grandmother shook her head left and right.
But even as her head shook, her hands worked surely and steadily.

"I don't believe in dreams. Only the day before yesterday we received Kiljun's letter saying he's well and strong."

"That's right. You read yourself where Kiljun said he's bored these
days because there aren't any battles."

"All that's of no use. I knew three or four days beforehand when
your father died. Only, that time, it was a thumb instead of a tooth.

That time I'd dreamed my thumb just came loose and disappeared."

Oh, the hateful account of that dream again! Doesn't Grandmother ever get tired of talking about that dream? Ever since she woke up at dawn, Grandmother had kept murmuring about her dream, her eyes vague and clouded. Continually moving her sunken, almost toothless mouth, she kept hinting that there was an inauspicious force rushing towards her. She had only seven teeth left in all; she had dreamed that a large iron pincer from out of nowhere forced itself into her mouth, yanked the strongest of the seven, and fled. The first thing Grandmother did as soon as she woke up from her dream was to feel in her mouth and check the number of her teeth. Then she ordered Aunt to bring a mirror and checked the number again with her eyes. Still not content, she made me come right up to her face and demanded repeated assurances from me. No matter how often anybody looked in, there were seven teeth in her mouth, just as before. Moreover, the lower canine tooth that she treasured as a substitute for a grinder was as soundly in its place as ever.

But Grandmother wouldn't give credence to anybody's testimony. It seemed that to her it was out of the question that the canine tooth could remain there as if nothing had happened. Her thoughts strayed from reality and dwelled only in her dream. She refused to believe that her daughters and son-in-law were telling the truth, and she even doubted the eyesight of her grandson, whom she always praised highly for being good at threading needles. Not only did she distrust the mirror, but she even disbelieved her own fingers, which had made a tactile survey of the teeth inside her mouth.

Grandmother had spent the whole long summer's day muttering about her dream. It taxed all of our nerves to distraction. The first one to break down and mention my maternal uncle's name was my mother. When Mother incautiously mentioned the name of her brother, who was serving at the front as a major and commander of a platoon in the Republic's army, Grandmother's flabby cheeks convulsed in a spasm. Aunt cast a reproachful look at her older sister. Grandmother, however, ignored Mother's words. Having judged that there was no other way of setting the old woman's mind at ease, Aunt also began talking about Uncle before long. But Grandmother never uttered her only son's name even once. She just kept on talking about that hateful dream.

As darkness began to set in, it became difficult to tell who was being comforted and who was giving comfort. As the night deepened,

Grandmother's words became more and more darkly suggestive, as if she were under a spell, and her face even took on an expression of triumphant self-confidence. Mother and Aunt, on the other hand, fidgeted uneasily and gazed vacantly at the pea-pods they had brought in to shell. In the end, all work was handed over to Grandmother, and Mother and Aunt could do nothing but listen to the endless incantatory muttering of the old woman.

Rain was pouring down like a wet mop over the whole surface of the village. The three or four dogs that were lucky enough to survive the war mercilessly tore the shroud of darkness, filling every space with their shrill howling. Grandmother kept on shelling with expert hands, putting the bright green peas into the bamboo basket and the empty pods back into her lap. Our dog Wŏlly, who received no kindly attention from anyone these difficult, gloomy days, began barking in surprisingly furious and ringing tones. Just then we could hear footsteps rounding the walls of the house next door. These were not the footsteps of just one person. There seemed to be three, or at least two. Someone must have stepped on a puddle; there was a splashing sound, and hard upon it came a grumbling about the terrible weather.

Who could those people be? Who would dare trudge through the village in this pouring rain in the depth of the night? Even though the war front had receded to the north, it was still a dangerous time. Communist guerrillas still occasionally invaded and set fire to the town police station. No one with any sense of propriety ever visited other people's houses after dark, unless on some emergency. To which house, then, could those people be going at this time of the night? What mischief might they be brewing, tramping the night streets in a group?

Mother grabbed hold of Aunt's hand. With her hand in her sister's keeping, Aunt stared into the darkness beyond, which was visible through the gauze panels of the door. Underneath the wooden porch adjoining the inner room, Wŏlly was barking desperately. Even Grandmother, whose hearing was not very good, had already realized that the band of men had stopped in front of the twig gate of our house and was hesitating there.

"Here they are at last. Here they are," Grandmother murmured in a parched voice.

"Sunku!" Someone called Father's name from beyond the twig gate. "Sunku, are you in?"

In the inner room Paternal Grandmother let out short, raspy coughs.

We could hear Father stirring to go out. Hearing that, Mother whispered in a frightened voice towards the inner room. "I'll slip out and see what's going on. You stay where you are and pretend you're dead."

But Father was already in the hall. Putting on his shoes, Father bade us to heed Mother's words. Wŏlly, who had been yelping frantically, suddenly ceased barking with a sharp groan. Father must have done something to him. Crossing the yard, Father spoke cautiously, "Who is it?"

"It's me, the village head."

"Why, what brings you here in the middle of the night?"

The bell attached to the twig gate tinkled. We could hear the men exchanging a few words. Then there was silence again outside, and only the vigorous dripping of rain filled our ears. Mother, who had been standing irresolutely in the room, could bear it no longer and threw open the door. She rushed outside, and Aunt followed her quickly. In the inner room Paternal Grandmother emitted a few hoarse coughs. Right beside me Maternal Grandmother was shelling peas steadily, completely absorbed in the work. Running her finger through the pod, she murmured, "It won't shake me a bit. I knew we were going to have some tidings today or tomorrow. I knew it for a long time. I'm all prepared."

I couldn't sit still. After some inner struggle, I left Maternal Grandmother alone and stole out of the room. Even on the dirt veranda I could hear her parched voice saying, "I'm not shaken, not I."

It was much darker outside than I had thought. Each time I moved my legs, Wŏlly's wet, furry, smelly body hit my inner thighs. The dog kept groaning and licking my hand. The rain was heavier than I had expected. It bathed my face and soaked my hemp shirt, and made me drenched as a rat that has fallen into a water-jar. Wŏlly gave up following me and retreated, growling fearfully. The grown-ups' contours were visible only when I drew quite close to the twig gate. It looked as if whatever information they had brought was passed on. In spite of the pouring rain, the grown-ups just stood still. I could dimly see the heads of two men covered with military waterproof cloth and the familiar face of the village head who stood facing us. Father and Aunt were supporting Mother's trembling, sinking body. After a long silence the village head spoke.

"Please give your mother-in-law my sincere condolences."

Then one of the two men wrapped in waterproof cloth spoke. He hesitated a great deal, as if extremely reluctant to speak. His voice, therefore, sounded very shy.

"I really don't know what to say. We're just as grieved as any of his family. It was an errand we'd have been glad to be spared. Goodbye, then, sir. We have to go back now."

"Thank you. Be careful in the dark," Father said.

They slipped through the twig gate, picking their way with their flashlights. A sob escaped from Mother. Aunt reproached her. Then Mother began to cry a little louder. Without saying a word, Father walked ahead towards the house. Aunt followed, supporting Mother, whispering to her "Please take hold of yourself. What will Mother do if you cry like this? Try to think of Mother, Mother!"

My mother covered her mouth with her hand. In this way, she managed to control her sobs when she stepped into the room.

Father, who had reached the room before any of us, was kneeling awkwardly before Maternal Grandmother, like one guilty, and was turning something over in his hand. It was the wet piece of paper that the village head must have handed over to him. Father was dripping water like just-hung laundry. But it was not only Father. All of us who had been outside, including myself, were making puddles on the floor with water dripping from our clothes. The thin summer clothes of Mother and Aunt were clinging to their skin, and revealed their bodies inside as if they were naked.

"I told you," Maternal Grandmother murmured again, as if to herself. "See?"

For some time now I had been watching Grandmother's moves with great uneasiness. I was paying more attention now to her working hands than to her incessantly moving sunken mouth. I had noticed a change in the movement of her hands. It seemed that no one except me noticed the change. As before, she was working with lowered eyes, but when we returned to the room from outside, Grandmother's two gaunt arms were trembling slightly. Moreover, she was unconsciously dropping the freshly shelled peas into her skirt that was filled with empty pods. I was afraid she would keep on making the mistake, and repeatedly looked out for a chance to give her a hint. But each time I tried, I found I could not open my mouth, so oppressive was the silence in the room. I could do nothing but watch her shaking, wrinkled fingertips even though I knew she would be dropping the empty pods, good only for fuel, into the bamboo basket that ought to hold shelled peas.

"Haven't I been telling you all along we'd have some tidings today, for sure?" Grandmother, whose hitherto pale face was momentarily flushed and looked ten years younger, murmured again. But as she broke the tip of another pod and ran her finger through it, she instantly turned ashen pale, like a corpse, and aged ten years more in the selfsame posture. Grandmother was in a strange state of excitement. We could feel it from the way she swallowed till her entire throat trembled.

"I knew several days beforehand when your father died. I suppose you resented me, thinking this old woman mutters ill-omened words as a pastime, having nothing to do besides eating. But what do you say now? I'd like to know what you think of my premonitions. Do they still sound to you like the prattle of an old woman? You mustn't think that of me, you mustn't. Even though I can't see and hear as well as you, I don't go around jabbering empty words. You're greatly mistaken if you think old women have nothing better to do than wasting precious food and babbling. To this day my dreams have never been wrong. Whenever we had a calamity coming, my dreams have always predicted it."

Sitting fully erect, with her head held upright, she reproached her daughters for not having acknowledged her prescience. Her face was again flushed red. As she looked at her daughters, her bloodshot eyes seemed to glow with triumph. She seemed overcome by an irresistible desire to brag about the accuracy of her prophecy. As I gazed at her ridiculously triumphant expression, something like a spell hit me: my maternal grandmother suddenly looked to me like a weird, dreadful being. I could not help giving credence to her assertion that she had always, like an inspired prophet, unerringly predicted the approach of tragedy. Grandmother had gained her victory in the battle declared by herself, and she seemed still to have abundant energy left over after the battle to upbraid us for any imagined slight to her authority. This aspect of Grandmother left a deep, ineradicable impression on me, as if she had been a being of inscrutable, unapproachable power.

Mother's sobbing was rising by imperceptible degrees. It began as thin as a thread, so that the other people in the room hardly perceived it at first. But as no one tried to stop her, even when her sobbing rose considerably, she began at last to cry with full force. A mosquito had alighted on the nape of Aunt's bloodlessly pale neck and was sucking blood. But Aunt did not stir. She sat there like one out of her wits, even though the mosquito sucked until its belly was round and pink as a cherry. The door of the room stood open. Even though mosquitoes swarmed in through the open door, nobody bothered to close it.

One could clearly guess at the progress of the people covered with military waterproof cloth by the shifting direction of the dogs' barking. Receding from the moment the men left, the barking moved further and further to the end of the village, and at last died down entirely. A black insect was disturbing the air of the room, flying around unchecked. At last, after it zipped through the room several times and almost put out the lamp, it was caught in my hand. It was a mole-cricket. It writhed between my thumb and forefinger and tried to get loose. Straining its strong forelegs which it used to dig up earth, it tried to break my grip. But of what use were all its desperate struggles? Its life and death were completely at my mercy. I could kill it or let it live just as I liked. I began to put more and more pressure on the two fingers holding the insect. Just then I heard Grandmother murmur again.

"I'm not shaken. I knew all along this would happen. I'm all right."

Then, Mother's sobs reached their peak, and the whole room was filled with the painful, drawn-out lament that seemed to gnaw into our very bones.

"Poor Jun, poor, poor Jun, what a fool you were to volunteer when others went into hiding to dodge conscription! Poor Jun, poor Jun, why didn't you listen to me when I told you not to become an officer? Now, what are we to do? What are we to do?" Her voice prolonged the words and trailed off into moans whenever she uttered the name of the dead man.

The heart-rending sobs of Mother, which filled the room in no time, soon spread into the yard steeped in darkness, and on the film of her sobs piled, layer upon layer, the shrieking rain of the long rainy season.

2

Gŏnji-san always looked dignified, standing tall surrounded by a host of lesser mountains and hills and piercing the sky with the tip of its peak. There was a time, however, when this stately mountain took on a ridiculous aspect. For a time Gŏnji-san became a place where grown-ups gathered at night to play with fire. Sometimes we could see mist rising from the top of the mountain even in broad daylight. What an enormous amount of water must have been made there by the grown-ups at night! Having experienced the bitter humiliation of making the round of the village wearing a rice winnowing basket over my head as punishment for bed-wetting, I could not help looking with suspicion at the running brook in the village that started from the mountain. The rustic, taciturn and dignified mountain looked absurd, suddenly sending up smoke and fire. For grown-ups' play, it was childish and silly, but peaceful and tranquil. I had not then realized the relationship between the signal fire and the massacres. I could not have understood why, time after time, immediately after flames rose up from the mountain, there was a street battle in town and one of the villages was laid waste. But even had I understood the implications, the result would have been the same. In spite of my ridiculous thoughts on beholding the signal fire for the first time, Gŏnji-san shortly regained its dignified repose in my eyes and became even dearer to me.

One day, I found upon arising that thick black clouds had coiled around the mountain from its waist up. The rain had halted, but anyone could tell from the dark cloud completely covering the eastern sky around Gŏnji-san that an even bigger batch of rain than any we'd had was making preparations for an assault. From time to time, lightning darted out from the dark corner of the sky and pierced Gŏnji-san as sharply as the bamboo lance that I once saw a man thrusting into another man's chest on the village road beside the dike. And each time thunder shook heaven and earth, like a wail sent out by the pierced mountain, I could very well imagine what the pain of being impaled by darting lightning must be like, and did not at all think the mountain cowardly for sending out such a miserable scream. It was clear that Gŏnji-san was being tortured by the sky from early morning.

I could tell Maternal Grandmother's approach even with my eyes closed. When she walked, her footsteps made no sound but only her skirt rustled. Like a weightless person's, her walk was light and careful. Having approached so carefully, she emitted a strange smell. It was a very strange smell, such as one can sniff in the corners of an old, old chest, or an antique, or a deep pond of stagnant water. I could feel the careful approach of my grandmother, from a smell like that of ancient dust and the rustle of her skirt.

I was lying in the adjacent room, pretending to be asleep. From the time I began to regard my grandmother as an awesome being, I had got into the habit of pretending to be asleep when she came near. Grandmother seemed to be taking twice her usual care so as not to awaken her grandson from his nap. But I had already inhaled a distasteful fill

of her peculiar smell, and had guessed what she was going to do. And I was not wrong, either. Her gaunt hand fumbled into my underpants.*
"Now let me feel my jewel," she would have said at other times. She would also have said, "This one's round as an apple, just like his maternal uncle's." But today, she did not say a word. She only silently moved her fingers, and felt my groin. This nameless act, which began from the time Mother's family came to live with us as refugees, was a big trial to me, and a very insulting experience. I'd dare anybody to claim I'm not telling the truth when I say I have never admitted my maternal grandmother's encroaching hand into my underpants without great displeasure. I don't know if there would be any seven-year-old who would willingly consent to be treated like a baby; for my part, I had prided myself for being a big boy with a sound judgment equal to any grown-up's, and such an act of Grandmother's was a severe blow to my self-esteem. But there was no shaking her off, as I knew such a refusal would grieve her deeply, so I could not but endure the insult.

Taking her hand off my groin, Grandmother sighed deeply. I could feel her gaze lingering on my face for a long time after her hand left my body.

"Poor thing!"

Leaving the two muttered words behind, she moved away. I opened my eyes a slit and peeped at Grandmother's back as she receded noise-lessly, her wrinkled cotton skirt trailing behind her. I don't know whom she may have meant in her lamentation just now. There were too many poor things around me. There was, of course, my maternal uncle who had just been killed in a battle at the front. And to tell the truth, I myself was also very much of a poor thing. Since the incident of having accepted a Western sweet as a bribe from a police detective, I had been cooped up in the house for over a month now in penance, anxiously watching the moods of my father, who held command of housebound penance, and of Paternal Grandmother, in whose hands

---

*This and what follows should not be taken as a sexual play. Because in Korea only males could carry on the family line, it was not unusual for grandmothers to feel their infant grandsons' sexual organs, to assure themselves that the lineage is secure, and feel great pride if the grandsons had strong and healthy reproductive organs. It was unusual, however, for grandmothers to feel the organs of grandsons as old as age seven, so the grandmother's act here would indicate how critical is her sense of her family line ending. The fact that the grandson is her heir only on the distaff side also adds to the pathos of the whole act. [Translator]

alone rested the power of forgiveness. But maybe the poorest thing of all was Maternal Grandmother herself. She looked completely worn out as she sat on the edge of the living-room floor. There was not a trace of the stubborn, awesome being we glimpsed on the night the notification came from the front. Today she was simply a shabby, withered old woman gazing vacantly at the distant mountain. My joy at being freed from her unwelcome hand turned to gloom at the sight of her pitiful figure.

For a few days after we learned of the death of my maternal uncle, the house was in chaos. Everyone was grieving, but my mother's grief was most out of control. Mother had tied her forehead with a white strip of cloth, as we children did on school sports days, and was bed-ridden with grief. She sat up from time to time to cry for a while, striking the floor with her palm uttering loud lamentations, and then collapsed back on the bedding. At mealtimes, however, she sat up to eat hurriedly the bowl of barley Aunt brought in to her. As soon as she finished eating, she thrust away the meal tray and cried out with loud lamentations and sank back on her bedding. Lying on her back, she would repeatedly mutter that her family ought to adopt a son to continue the line.

Aunt's behavior was in sharp contrast to Mother's. From first to last, she did not shed a drop of tear, nor did she exchange a word with anybody. She didn't eat a thing, either. Moreover, she silently took over all of Mother's work, and cooked, washed dishes, and did the laundry. Until I saw her flop backwards on the third day while trying to lift up a water pail beside the well in the backyard, I had been thinking that Aunt must surely be eating something secretly in the bamboo grove behind the house or in the dark kitchen. I had set my heart at rest thinking that Aunt, who had unbelievably strong will-power and sometimes completely confounded our expectations, would surely not go three days without eating a morsel.

But Mother and Aunt were not our greatest worry. What made us most uneasy was the discord between my paternal and maternal grand-mothers. When my mother's family, which had moved to Seoul to give my uncle and aunt the benefit of education in the capital, suddenly appeared before us one day as refugees carrying bundles, it was my paternal grandmother who welcomed the family warmly and made the guest room available for them to move in. We often heard my paternal grandmother express her wish that the two old women could be a companion and support for each other in these harsh times; and, in fact, the two old ladies got along perfectly well, without even a single discord, until that unfortunate day. They got along well even after the Republic's army recovered dominion over the South and my paternal uncle, who had till then been going around flourishing his armband as an officer of the People's Army, fled with the retreating communist forces, and my maternal uncle, who had till then been hiding in a dug-out cave in the bamboo grove, joined the Republic's army. Each victory or defeat in the war thus became a matter of conflicting emotions for the two old ladies.

The discord between the two old ladies began with that incident of my accepting the gift of a Western sweet from a stranger which incurred the fury of Paternal Grandmother, who branded me a butcher of men who had sold his uncle for a sweet and, therefore, one not worthy to be treated as a human being. Maternal Grandmother earned the displeasure of her counterpart by protecting and defending me. The decisive rupture between the two grandmothers came on the day after we received the death notice of my maternal uncle. It was my maternal grandmother who started the provocation. On that afternoon, too, the weather was sinister. Forked lightning darted out of the clouds, repeatedly impaling the crown of Gŏnji-san. Maternal Grandmother, who had been watching the sky standing at the edge of the living-room floor, suddenly began to utter dreadful curses.

"Pour on! Pour on! Pour on and sweep away all the reds hiding between the rocks! Strike on, and burn to soot all the reds clinging to the trees! Pour on, strike on! That's right! Thank you, God!"

All the family rushed into the living-room, but everyone was so stupefied that no one could say a word to check Grandmother's torrential curses. She continued to pour out vehement curses towards Gŏnji-san, which was said to be teeming with communist partisans, as if she could distinctly visualize red partisans being struck dead one after another by lightning.

"Has that old hag gone stark mad, or turned into a devil?"

The door of the inner room opened with a clatter and out came Paternal Grandmother, her face distorted with fury. I realized belatedly that there was one person in the house who could be Maternal Grandmother's match, and became tense.

"Whose house does she think this is, that she dares put on such horseplay?"

Maternal Grandmother looked around with vague eyes, like one violently shaken awake from sleepwalking.

"This is too good a spectacle for only a family audience, isn't it? I've heard of good deeds being repaid with poison, but I can't believe what I'm witnessing today. A fine display of gratitude this is, to one who gave you shelter from bombs! If you mean to go crazy, do so at least with a clean conscience. If you harbor such base ingratitude, lightning will strike you!"

After thus subduing the other with imperious reproof, Paternal Grandmother continued her upbraiding.

"Do you think your curses will bring your dead son back and kill living people? Don't you imagine such a thing! Life and death are meted out by Heaven, and Heaven only. One lives as long as one's allotted to live by Heaven. And it's because of one's own sins that a child dies before oneself. It's because of sins in an earlier life that a parent has to see a child die and endure the sorrow. It's your own fate that your son died. There's nobody to blame for it. You ought to know shame by now. Aren't you in your sixties?"

"All right. Granted it's because of my sins* that I've lost my son. Is it because you're a blessed woman that you reared a son like that?"

"Listen to that! Hasn't she really gone raving mad? What do you mean, 'a son like that'? What's wrong with my son?"

"Think. You'll know if you're not a fool."

"Because you have no son left to offer you sacrifice after your death, you wish the same for everyone!"

"Stop it, both of you!" Father shouted.

"Wait and see. My Sunchŏl isn't such a fool! You might not rest content until something happens to him, but Sunchŏl can slip through showers without getting wet!"

"Stop it, please!" Father shouted again.

Mother had been pinching Maternal Grandmother's thigh all along.

"Did you hear what your mother-in-law said? She, who's an in-law

---

*This is not to be taken as the maternal grandmother's admission of having committed sins needing expiation. It is rather an announcement of her resolution to accept her suffering and sorrow in resignation. According to Buddhist theory of metempsychosis, one pays for one's sins in an after-life, and thus there is no escaping the consequences of one's acts. This theory is often used by Koreans to "justify" and to reconcile themselves to their unmerited sufferings for which there can be no explanation in terms of universal justice of reward and punishment. [Translator]

after all, calls me a woman without a son to offer me sacrifices after my death. Isn't it misfortune enough to have given up an only son for the country, without being despised by an in-law? What mad words can a woman not utter, a woman who's just lost a son? Does she have to reproach me thus for foolish words uttered in madness of grief, and flaunt before me her possession of many sons? Answer me, if you have a mouth to speak!"

Maternal Grandmother appealed to Mother, and Mother, with a tearful face, kept winking a pleading eye at Maternal Grandmother and pinching her leg. Paternal Grandmother, for her part, appealed to Father:

"Be careful how you judge, son! Is it wrong of me to rebuke an old woman who's praying for your brother's death? Must you, too, blame me? She may be your mother-in-law, but she's an enemy to me, and I can't live with her under the same roof! If you don't throw her out at once, I'm going to leave this house!"

"All right! I'm leaving! I would hate to live in this house any longer! I'd rather die out in the streets than stay a minute longer in a communist's hou . . ."

Maternal Grandmother's hoarse voice stopped dead. She slowly turned her head and vacantly gazed at my father. Finishing the word "house" weakly and at length, she looked at Mother this time. Lastly, she gazed at me intently for quite a while, and shook her head left and right. Then she suddenly dropped her head. Her downward-bent gaze sank heavily on a bamboo basket. Silently pulling the bamboo basket toward her knee, she picked up a pea-pod with a motion as silent as if she had been a shadow. Her face was as grey as a corpse's, and remained so from then on.

The turmoil created by Maternal Grandmother's words shook up the whole house. When the word "communist" came out of Maternal Grandmother's mouth, all the family members doubted their ears, and stood still in stupefaction. They could hardly breathe, and could only watch her slowly-moving hands. "Communist" was a forbidden word among us, ever since we became a marked house in the village, watched by the police on account of my paternal uncle. This taboo was as strictly observed as the taboo against eating salty shrimp pickles during scrofula. Oh, to trespass such a solemn taboo! Maternal Grandmother's mistake was a fatal one, which no amount of apology would render forgivable. The amazement of the family members was beyond description, but the one most shocked by the utterance was none other than she who said it. Maternal Grandmother did not offer any apologies. It was partly because all apologies were useless, but more likely because she tried to expiate her transgression by silently enduring all the censure of her in-law counterpart. No words can describe the fury of my paternal grandmother. She jumped up and down madly, foamed at the mouth, and almost fainted away. Then she tried to wrest an assurance from Father that he would expel Maternal Grandmother and Aunt from the house, and even Mother if she seemed sympathetic to them.

"You must drive them out this very day. And be sure to open all their bags before they step out of the gate. My silver hair-slide is missing, and it's not hard to guess who took it."

Aunt silently walked away to the guest room. After pouring out her fill of abuses, Paternal Grandmother lay down from exhaustion. The silence that ensued was soon shattered by the outburst of Mother's weeping. Instantly, Father's command fell like thunder.

"Shut up!"

Silence was a more unbearable torture than noisy unrest. Father strode out of the house. Maternal Grandmother remained on the living-room floor deep into the night, shelling peas with her gaunt, shaky hands. Father came back home only at dawn, dead drunk and reeking of sour alcohol.

Incandescent sparks of lightning kept piercing the crown of Gŏnji-san, thickly enfolded in black clouds. The signal fire which rose up almost every night from the mountain could not be seen any more since the rainy season began. Maternal Grandmother, who turned her eyes from time to time towards the mountain, looked pitifully lonely as she sat on the edge of the living-room floor. She did not say a word today, even though lightning struck today just as on that other day. Ever since that unhappy quarrel with her in-law, she hardly opened her mouth. She kept moving her hands incessantly, the bamboo basket at her knee, as if shelling peas were the one and only task left for her in the world till her dying day.

3

A boy, who had recently come to live in our village as a refugee from the North, came over to where we were playing, accompanied by a man wearing a straw hat. The boy's face was all scabby. Pointing at me with his hand that had been scratching his bare, dirt-stained belly, he said a few words to the man. The man gave me an attentive stare from beneath the wide-brimmed straw hat which concealed a good part of his face. The boy from the North took what the strange man gave him from out of his pocket and sprinted away like a fleeing hare. The tall man with the straw hat walked up to me directly. His dark, tanned skin, his sharp, penetrating eyes, and his unhesitating stride somehow overpowered me.

"What a fine boy!"

The stranger's eyes seemed to narrow and, surprisingly, contrary to what I had expected from my first impression, a friendly smile filled his face. The man stroked my head a few times.

"You'd be a really good boy if you give straight answers to my questions."

The man's attitude made me extremely uneasy. I could not look into his eyes, so I opened and closed my hands for no reason and stood there with my head lowered. In my palm was my paternal grandmother's silver hair-slide, which I had rubbed against a stone mortar into a giant nail, and which earned me victory over all the neighborhood boys in nail fights.

"Your father's name is Kim Sunku, isn't it?"

The man unbuttoned his white tieless shirt.

"Then Kim Sunchŏl must be your uncle, isn't he?"

The man took off his straw hat. I had not said a word till then. But the man went on ingratiatingly. "That's right. Answer my questions like the clever boy you are!"

The man waved his straw hat as if it were a fan, holding open his tieless shirt to ventilate his body.

"I'm your uncle's friend. We're very close friends, but it's been a long time since we met last. I have something very important to discuss with your uncle. Will you tell me where he is?"

The man, whom I had just met for the first time in my life, used the standard Seoul dialect meticulously, like Aunt.

"Oh, isn't it hot! It's very hot here. Shall we go over there where it's breezy and have a little chat?"

He forbade the other children to follow. When we reached the shade of a tree on the hill behind the village, where other children couldn't see us, the man halted and fumbled in his pocket.

"I've got a very important message to convey to your uncle. If you tell me where he is, I'll give you these," the man said holding out in his palm five flat pieces of something wrapped in silver paper. He unwrapped one of them and stuck it in front of my nose.

"Have you ever tasted anything like this?" The dark-brown colored thing gave off a delicious aroma.

"These are chocolates. I'll give them to you if you just answer my questions straight."

I took a great deal of care not to let my eyes rest on the strange treat. But I could not stop my mouth from watering.

"There's nothing to be shy about. It's natural for good boys to get rewards. Now, won't you tell me? If only you tell me what I've asked, I'll be happy to let you have these delicious chocolates."

I don't know what it was that made me hesitate. Was it because I was undecided about the ethical propriety of accepting such a gift? Or was it the shyness of a country boy in front of a stranger, a shyness common to most country boys my age? I don't remember distinctly. But I think I remained standing there mute for quite a while.

"Don't you want them?" the man pressed me. "You're sure you don't want them?" The man showed an expression of regret. "Well then, there's no helping it. I did very much want to see you acting like a good boy and give you these delicious things. I myself don't need these sweets. Here, look. I'll just have to throw them away, even though that's not what I want to do with them."

Unbelievably, the man really threw one of them onto the ground carelessly. He not only threw it down but stepped on it and crushed it. Casting a glance at me, he threw one more on the ground.

"I thought you were a bright boy. I'm really sorry."

He crushed the third one under his foot. Only two pieces of the sweet remained on his palm. It was evident that he was quite capable of crushing the remaining two into the ground. The man suddenly chuckled loudly.

"You're crying? Poor boy! Hey, lad, it's not too late yet. You just think carefully. Hasn't your uncle been to the house? When was it?"

It was at that moment that I felt I was powerless to fend off the sophisticated tactics of a grown-up. Then, as I thought that this man might really be a friend of my uncle, my heart felt a good deal lighter.

The first few words were the most difficult to utter. Once I began, however, I related what had happened as smoothly as reeling yarn off a spool.

My paternal aunt who lived some eight miles off came to visit us, walking the entire distance under the broiling July sun. There was no reason for me to attach any special meaning to Aunt's visit, as she had come several times to our house without prior announcement to stay for a day or two even in those days of unrest. But things began to look very different when Mother, who had gone into the inner room with Aunt, sprang out of the room with a pale complexion. Instead of sending me, as was usual, she ran out herself to fetch Father. Father, who had been weeding in the rice paddies, ran directly into the inner room with his muddy clothes and feet, without stopping to wash himself at the well. Mother, who returned hard upon his heels, fastened the twig gate shut even though it was broad daylight. Everybody seemed slightly out of their right senses. The whole family, except Maternal Grandmother, Maternal Aunt and me, was gathered in the inner room and seemed to be discussing something momentous. Around sunset, the three of us who had been left out were given a bowl of cold rice each. As I finished my meal, I saw that Father had changed into clean clothes. I looked suspiciously at Father's back as he stepped out of the twig gate into the alley paved with darkness.

"You go to sleep early," Mother told me, as she spread my mattress right beside where Paternal Grandmother was sitting. It seemed that everyone was bent on pushing me to go to sleep, even though it was still early in the night.

"Wouldn't it be better to have him sleep in the other room?" Paternal Aunt asked Mother, pointing her chin at me.

"I think it'll be all right," Paternal Grandmother said, "he sleeps soundly once he falls asleep."

"You must be dead tired from playing all day long. You must sleep like a log until tomorrow morning, and not open your eyes a bit all through the night. You understand?" Mother instructed me.

I knew that Father had not gone out for a friendly visit. It was obvious that he went out on important business. I wanted to stay wide awake until Father returned. I was determined to find out the important business of grown-ups from which I was being excluded. To that end, it was necessary to pretend to obey the grown-ups' orders to go to sleep at once. I listened attentively for the least sound in the room, fighting back the sleep that overwhelmed me as soon as I lay down and closed my eyes. But no one said anything of any significance. And, before the important event of Father's arrival, I had fallen fast asleep.

I was awakened by a dull thud on the floor of the room.

"My God! Isn't that a bomb?"

I heard Paternal Grandmother's frightened voice. The two bulks that were blocking my sight were the seated figures of Father and Mother. Dull lamplight seeped dimly through the opening between them.

"Undo your waistband, too," Father said to someone imperiously. The person seemed to hesitate a little, but there came a rustle from beyond.

"*Two* pistols!"

"My God!" Mother and Grandmother softly exclaimed simultaneously. Sleep had completely left me, and a chill slid down my spine like a snake. Even though I knew nobody was paying any attention to me, I realized it was unsafe to let the grownups know I was awake; so I had to take painstaking care in moving my glance inch by inch. I concentrated all my efforts on finding out what was happening in the small space visible to me.

"Has Tongman gone to sleep without knowing I was coming?"

As it seemed that Father was about to turn to me, I closed my eyes quickly. The shadow that had been shielding my face moved aside quickly, and lamplight pricked my eyelids.

"We kept him in the dark," Mother said proudly, as if that had been some meritorious deed.

"Don't worry. Once he falls asleep, a team of horses couldn't kick him awake," Grandmother insisted.

There was a short silence in the room. It seemed that nobody dared open his mouth. But my ears were brimming with the thick voice of the man who had sneaked into the house in the dark, carrying pistols and hand grenades. If that man is really my uncle, whose whereabouts the whole family had been fretting to know, his voice had, regrettably, become so rough as to be unrecognizable to me at first. His voice didn't use to be as rough as a clay pot that has been carelessly handled on pebbles, or so gloomy that nothing seemed capable of cheering it up. As far back as I could remember, my uncle chuckled heartily at the slightest joke, even though his elders might frown on such manners, and rarely remained aloof from disputes but always tried to involve others in them. He was easily excited or moved. But, no matter how I reckoned, there was no one but my uncle who could be the owner of that voice I had just heard. I imagined my uncle's face and form, which must have become as rough as the voice. Then, suddenly, I felt an uncontrollable itch in the hollows of my knees. The itch spread instantly to my entire body, as if I had been lying on ant-infested grass: I had an irresistible urge to scratch the middle of my back or my armpits or between my toes, places where my hands could not reach while I lay flat on my back. On top of it all, my throat tickled with an imminent cough, and my mouth filled with water.

Grandmother seemed most anxious to know what Uncle's life on the mountain was like. She heaped question after question on how he fared on the mountain. To all her questions Uncle answered barely a word or two, and seemed irked by the necessity of saying even that much. But Grandmother seemed not to notice Uncle's mood, and asked endless questions.

"You say there are many others besides you, but they must all be men. Who cooks rice and soup at each mealtime?"

"We do."

"You make preserves and season vegetables, too?"

"Yes."

"How on earth! If only I could be there with you I'd prepare your food with proper seasoning!"

No response.

"Do they taste all right?"

"Yes."

"I know they couldn't, but I can't help asking all the same."

"They're all right."

"Do you skip meals often, because you move around here and there?"

"No."

"Promise me you won't eat raw rice, however hungry you may get. You'd get diarrhea. If you do, what could you do in the depths of the mountain? You can't call a doctor or get medicine. Do pay attention, won't you?"

"Don't worry."

"And since it's in the depths of the mountain, it must be cold as January at night, even in summer like this. Do each of you have a quilt to cover your middle at night?"

"Of course."

"Padded with cotton wool?"

No response.

"Don't stay in the cold too long. And, for frostbite, eggplant stems are the best remedy. You boil the stems and soak your hands and feet in the fluid. That takes out the frostbite at once. If I were beside you . . ."

"Please don't worry!"

"How can I help it? It tears my heart to see your frostbitten hands and feet. The times are rough, but for you, my darling last-born, to get so frostbitten like that!"

"Please, Mother, stop!" Uncle sighed with impatience.

"Do, Mother, that's enough," Father chimed in cautiously.

"Do you mean I shouldn't worry, even though my son's hands are frostbitten?" Grandmother raised her voice angrily. Such things were of the utmost importance to her. But Father also raised his voice.

"It's going to be daybreak soon, and you keep wasting time with your useless questions! How can you worry about preserves and quilts when his life's at stake?"

Grandmother was silenced. Of course she had many more questions, but a certain tone in Father's rebuke silenced her, stubborn as she was.

"What are you going to do now?" Father asked, after a pregnant silence. It was directed at Uncle.

"About what?"

"Are you going back to the mountain and stay there?"

When Uncle was silent, Father asked him if he would consider giving himself up to the police. Father slowly began his persuasion, as if it were something he had carefully considered for a long time. Father emphasized again and again the misery of a hunted existence. Citing as an example a certain young man who had delivered himself up to the police and was now living quietly on his own farm, Father recommended urgently that Uncle do the same. He repeated again and again that otherwise Uncle would die a dog's death. A dog's death, a dog's death, a dog's death, a dog's death.

"Why do you keep saying it's a dog's death?" Uncle retorted sullenly. Uncle swore that before long the People's Army would win back the South. Vowing that he had only to remain alive until that day, he even recommended that Father should so conduct himself as not to get hurt when the government changed. Listening to his talk, I was struck once again by the great change in my uncle. His speech was fluent. In the old days, Uncle was never able to talk so logically. Because he had difficulty getting his points across by logical arguments, he often used to resort to the aid of his fists in his sanguine impatience.

Uncle began to collect things, saying that he must go up the mountain before sunrise. It must have been the pistols and hand grenades that he gathered up. Everybody moved at once.

"I won't let you go, never, now that you're in my house!"

I opened my eyes at last. In that sudden turmoil, nobody paid any attention to me, so I slowly sat up. Uncle's face was covered all over with a bushy beard. Father and Aunt were on either side almost hugging Uncle, who sat leaning against the wall on the warmer part of the floor. Grandmother snatched Uncle's arm from Aunt and, shaking it to and fro, entreated, "Because your brother told me lies, I thought you were staying comfortably somewhere. I thought you spent your days sitting on a chair in a town office somewhere doing things like giving hell to harsh cops. But now that I know the truth I won't let you go back to such a dreadful place! I'd die first rather than let you go!"

Grandmother wept, stroking Uncle's cheek with her palm.

"I'd let you go if I could go with you and look after you day and night, but since it seems I can't, I'll tie you down in this room and not let you out of my sight day or night. Why can't you stay at home, farm the land, get married and let me hold your children before I die?"

Aunt spoke for the first time in my hearing that night and talked to Uncle about the joys of married life, and Mother assented in support of her sister-in-law. Father talked again. He explained in minute detail the drift of the war, and tried to make Uncle realize that he was being deceived by the empty promises of the communists. Father said further that as he knew a couple of people in the police there would be ways to get Uncle released without suffering bodily harm. But Uncle at long last opened his mouth only to say, "Are you, too, trying to trick me into it?" and shook off Father's hand.

"What do you mean, trick you?"

"I've heard all about it." Uncle said that the police slaughtered all the people who, after being decoyed by promises of pardon in printed handbills, went down the mountain to surrender. Uncle said that promises of unconditional pardon and freedom were screaming lies and tricks.

"And you, too, are trying to push me into the trap?"

"What?" Father's arm shot up in the air. The next moment there was the sound of a sharp slap on Uncle's cheek. Father panted furiously and glared at Uncle, as if he would have liked to tear him apart.

"How dare you strike my poor boy!" Grandmother wept aloud, shielding Uncle with her body. Father pulled the tobacco box towards him. His hands shook as he rolled up the green tobacco. Uncle dropped his head.

A cock crowed. At the sound Uncle lifted his head in fright and looked around at the members of the family. The short summer's night was about to end.

"I've killed people," he murmured huskily, like one who had just set down a heavy load he had carried a long, long way. "Many, many people."

Thus began Uncle's wavering toward self-surrender. It was a long persuasion that Father carried out that night, and his patience in delivering it was truly remarkable. At last everything was settled as Father had planned, and it was agreed that Uncle was to remain in hiding for a couple of days until Father obtained assurance from the police for Uncle's safety. Uncle was to go into the dug-out cave in the bamboo grove that Maternal Uncle had used for hiding during the communist occupation.

Everything was settled, and all that remained to be done was for everybody to snatch a wink of sleep before it was broad daylight. But that instant Uncle, who was about to pull off his shirt, suddenly bent forward and pressed his ear to the floor. Grandmother almost jumped from fright.

"What is it?"

"Ssh!"

Uncle put his forefinger on his lips and eyed the door of the room. Everybody's face stiffened, and all listened attentively for noise from outside.

"Someone's there."

My ears caught no sound. There was the distant chirping of grass insects, but I could hear nothing like a human sound. But Uncle had his ear still glued to the floor and didn't seem likely to get up. For a while I heard only the loud pounding of my heart in that suffocating tension, but I caught the sound, the one Uncle must have heard. The sound, which was definitely not that of a pounding heart, was footsteps treading the ground with long intervals in between. The steps were so soft and careful that it was hard to tell if they were coming toward us or receding.

"Who's that outside?"

Father's voice was low, but the reprimand was severe. Then the sound of the movement stopped altogether. Suddenly it occurred to me that it was a familiar tread, of someone I knew very well. I quickly ransacked my brain, trying to figure out who it might be. The footsteps began again. They seemed to be moving a little faster this time. Uncle's body shot up erect. Within the blink of an eye the dark shape jumped over my seated form. The back door fell to the ground with a shattering sound, and Uncle's big bulk rushed away in the dark. He had already crossed the bamboo grove. His movement was so swift that nobody had time to say a word.

I came out through the frame of the back door that Uncle had knocked down to the ground. I ran past the kitchen into the inner yard. I wasn't at all afraid, even though I was alone. I surveyed everything within the twig fence, from the yard and kitchen garden down to the gates, but I could see nothing. When my eyes fell on the unlighted guest room, however, I caught the half-opened door of that room closing noiselessly, shutting out the dim, whitish glare of the morning. I savored the discovery with rapture. It was indeed a familiar tread, of one I knew very well.

"I'd have packed things for him to take if I'd known it would come to this! I didn't feed him a morsel, nor give him one clean garment! If only I'd known! How could I have not fed him one bowl of warm rice! If only I'd known!" Paternal Grandmother wailed, beating her chest. Paternal Aunt grasped my hand tightly and pulled me to one corner. Then she whispered into my ear.

"You mustn't tell anyone your uncle's been home. Do you understand? If you talk about such things to anybody all of us must go to jail. Do you hear?"

Village people were surrounding my house, standing in multiple ranks in front of the gate. They were whispering things to each other and trying to look over the gate into the house. The wailing of women that I could hear from as far as the hill behind the village was coming from my house. As I approached, all eyes turned on me. Villagers exchanged meaningful glances among themselves, pointing their chins at me, and whispered again. The palisade of people suddenly parted in two, as if to make way. A strange man walked out ahead, and my father followed. One step behind him I could see the man with the straw hat. He was holding, coiled around his hand, the rope that bound both my father's hands behind his back. On seeing me, he grinned and winked. Father halted in front of me. His eyes seemed yearning to say something to me, but he silently resumed walking. At the gate Mother, Paternal Aunt and Paternal Grandmother were wailing and crying, repeatedly collapsing and sinking to the ground. Only then did pain begin to rise in me. During the entire day while I was ransacking the village to find the boy from the North who had conducted the man with the straw hat to me, the pain assailed me sometimes with a sense of betrayal, or a terrible fury, or an unbearable sorrow that stung my eyes and stabbed my heart. The man with the straw hat had sworn to me that he would never tell anybody what I would tell him. It was the first mortal treachery I had experienced at the hands of a grown-up.

From that night Maternal Grandmother became my sole protectress and friend. Between us there was the shared secret of sinners. It could have been that secret which gave the two of us the strength to support each other through many persecutions. Paternal Grandmother was a woman of very strong temper. If she so much as caught sight of me, she started back as if she had stepped on a snake, and she refused not only to talk to me but even to let me have my meals in the inner room with the family.

Father returned home after spending seven full days at the police station. My mother, who made frequent trips to town to take Father his food, sniffed and sobbed and sprinkled salt again and again on his head when he stepped into the gate. Father's good-looking face had changed a great deal in those seven days. His eyes were sunken, his cheekbones stood out, and his face, which had become pale blue like newly bleached cotton, looked indescribably shabby. But what hurt me most of all was the look of pain that appeared on Father's face whenever he moved his right leg with a limping lurch. On the night he returned, he ate no less than three cakes of raw bean curd which, along with the sprinkling of salt, was believed to be a good preventive against a second trip to the police station. Father had always been taciturn, but he uttered not a single word that day. From time to time he gazed vacantly at my face and seemed about to say something, but each time he withdrew his gaze silently. I was fully resolved never to run away should Father decide to give me a flogging, even if I were to die under his switch. And there, within his easy reach, were the wooden pillow and the lamp-pole. I felt I could not withdraw from Father's sight without receiving my due punishment. I waited, solemnly kneeling before him. But Father did not utter a word about what had passed. He only issued this command before lying down to sleep.

"Tongman, if you ever so much as step an inch out of the gate from tomorrow, I'll break your legs."

Ah, how happily I'd have closed my eyes for good, if Father had wielded his switch like mad that night, leaving these as my last words, "Father, I deserve to die."

4

The rainy front stayed on. The sky sometimes feigned benevolence by suspending the rain in the morning or afternoon, but its frown did not relax at all; rather, the pressure of the iron-grey clouds increased, and malicious showers poured down fitfully, as if suddenly remembering. Everything between the sky and the earth was so saturated with water that if you pressed a fingertip on any wall or floor, water seeped out in response. All the world was a puddle and a slough. Because of the rain-soaked earth, the well water was no better than slops, and you could not drink a single drop of it without boiling it for a long time.

Even amid such persistent rain there was an attack by communist partisans under cover of night. Though there was a good five miles' distance between our village and the town, we could distinctly hear the noise of bullets like corn popping. Father, who had been up on the hill behind the village in spite of the rain, said that he could see a scarlet flame shooting up in the night sky even from that distance. The detailed news of the surprise attack spread through the village in less than a day.

One villager, who had been to town to ascertain the safety of his brother's family, came by with our neighbor, Chinku's father, to give important advice to Father. As soon as he sat down on the edge of the living-room floor, he gave a vociferous report of his survey in the town, not knowing that Paternal Grandmother was listening in the inner room beyond a paper-panelled door. He said that houses in the vicinity of the police station had suffered much damage, and that the red partisans who made the attack had been severely beaten. According to him, only a handful of partisans made the retreat to the mountains alive. What was most shocking in his report was his description of the corpses of partisans that he said lay scattered throughout the town. He described in vivid detail the hideous shapes of the corpses covered by straw mats. For example, there was one corpse whose limbs were all torn off. He said another had sixteen or seventeen bullet holes. The description that attracted my interest was of a corpse that was thrown in the ditch folded almost in half, the backside inward. I was surprised to learn that a man's body could be folded over, like a pocketknife, with the back inside. I couldn't believe that was possible.

Lastly, he transmitted the news that the corpses were on display in the backyard of the police station, ready to be given to relatives or friends upon request. That was the point of his visit to Father. He recommended by hints that Father had better pay a prompt visit to the town police station. Chinku's father, who came with him, urged the same. Throughout their visit, Father had a look of despair, and he showed great reluctance in following the recommendation of the two men. But when the village head, who was Father's childhood friend, came by later and offered to accompany him to town, he resolved at last to do so.

Paternal Grandmother did not try at all to hide her contempt for Father who left for town in the rain, donning an oil-paper hat cover over his bamboo rain hat. Paternal Grandmother had from the first opposed Father's trip to town. It was her conviction that the trip was entirely unnecessary. She even got furiously angry at her son, who still would not give credence to the decree of Heaven. What Grandmother maintained was simply this: whatever had happened in the town had nothing to do with Uncle; it was the providence of Heaven that Uncle would escape unharmed, no matter what danger he may have run into; Heaven had already appointed the date and even the hour that Uncle was to appear before Grandmother alive and entirely sound. Thus, it was utter nonsense that Father should make the long trip to town to wade through corpses in search of his brother. Grandmother, if no one else, had complete faith in this. Well, she not only had complete faith, but she had made detailed preparations for the happy event, and was waiting with outstretched neck. There was a reason for Grandmother's conviction. Since the unfortunate flight of her younger son, Grandmother's days had been a time of unbearable agony. She couldn't sleep, she couldn't eat, and she fretted all day long, waiting for news of her son. Then one day my paternal aunt, who had come to pay a visit, suggested that she consult a fortune-teller in the village next to hers. Carrying a heavy bundle of rice on her head as fee, Grandmother made the trip to the fortune-teller, reputed to have divine prescience. Late in the evening, Grandmother returned home with a beaming face and summoned all the family to give highest praise to the blind man's foresight and to relate his oracle. Well, the ardently-awaited day, the day that was fated to bring our uncle home at a certain hour, was only a few days ahead of us now.

Father and the head of the village came back from town empty-handed.

That Father's trip had been in vain as good as meant to us that Uncle would be returning home alive. But it was strange that Father remained as taciturn as ever. Father's face showed two very different strands of emotion woven together. His face wore in rapid and irregular succession a look of relief, or a look of bleak despair. It seemed that Father, even if he could regard the absence of Uncle's corpse in the police station yard as an indication that Uncle was still alive, could not rest easy when he thought of the hardships and danger Uncle would have to endure in the future. But Grandmother was not bothered by such considerations. She became triumphant at once, and nearly shouting, declared that it was just as she had told us from the first, that her son Sunchŏl was not an ordinary human being. Then she fell to weeping aloud and, rubbing her palms together heatedly in fervent prayer, with her old worn-out face all muddled by continuously gushing tears, she made full, deep bows in all directions, in token of her gratitude to Heaven and Earth, to Buddha and the mountain spirits, ancestors and household gods. She looked like one gone mad, but her innocent faith and boundless maternal love moved all of our hearts. We all decided to believe. How could we have calmed her down without believing in what she believed? Every member of the family repeatedly recited, solemnly and religiously, the date and the hour that my immortal uncle was destined to return to us. It was only after we realized that daybreak had stolen almost up to the room that we went to bed, to have a preview of our happiness of that day in dreams. It was a long, long day that we lived that day.

Lying on my back in the guest room occupied by my maternal grandmother, I was dimly measuring the density of the rain outside by its dripping sound. The noise, which lifted and resumed and thickened and thinned, tickled my eardrums like the soft tip of a cotton swab. As I was still struggling with a heavy drowsiness on account of the fatigue from the night before, the noise of the rain sounded like a distant whisper in a land of dreams. Still under order of confinement at home, I regarded the long, tedious rain at times as a blessing. Had there been clear sunshine outside to make the fields and hills ablaze with light, wind that shook the trees on the hills, and the cool chirping of cicadas, all the light and sounds of the world might have seemed like a curse to one who had to stay confined indoors without any amusement or distraction. On those occasional afternoons when the rain lifted a bit, I could hear very clearly, while sitting in the room, packs of children noisily galloping through the village streets.

Whenever I pictured the children gleefully drawing willow fish traps in the weedy pools around the river or in the forks of the irrigation ditches, and the silvery-scaled, plump carp they would scoop up, I couldn't help sinking under the misery of a forlorn prisoner. I seemed to have already become a long-forgotten being among my peers. My friends didn't stop by any more at my gate to call me out, even for appearance's sake. I, therefore, disconsolately picked up the blossoms beaten down by the rain under the old persimmon tree beside the twig fence during the hours of envy when all the world seemed to belong to my friends. Thus, I taught myself resignation early in my life. The opening of school was the only hope that I had to cling to. The school, which had closed down because of the war, was to reopen soon, and then Father's order of confinement would lose effect, and my nightmarish house imprisonment would eventually end.

Maternal Grandmother stretched her back, pausing for a moment from shelling peas. Thanks to Grandmother, who kept silently moving her fingers all day long without ever saying a word to anybody, the major portion of the harvested peas had been sorted. But the pods that were still in storage in a corner of the barn showed signs of germinating. The moisture-saturated pods thrust up pale yellow sprouts. The task of shelling the peas before they became inedible fell to Maternal Grandmother. For some reason, all the family seemed to take it for granted that pea shelling was solely and entirely Maternal Grandmother's charge. And she herself seemed to take it for granted as well; she spent all her waking hours shelling the clammy things. Well, it may be more accurate to say that, because she regarded pea shelling as her appointed task and jealously engaged in it, lest someone should take the work away from her, all the others abstained from helping. At any rate, once she sat down with a basket of pea-pods, Maternal Grandmother kept quietly moving her hands, seemingly oblivious to the passage of time. From time to time she poured her heavy sighs into the bamboo basket along with the green peas.

Even though her patience and perseverance were truly extraordinary, sitting thus immobile in one posture seemed to cause her occasional back-aches. Thus, she now pushed the bamboo basket aside and shook her skirt. She rubbed her hands on her skirt and moved close to me. I smelt her peculiar odor in the lukewarm breath that descended on my forehead. I guessed what was forthcoming. Sure enough, a chilly hand that made my body shiver crept into my pants. I had never, even once, felt comfortable lying thus under Maternal Grandmother's gaunt hands.

"It's round as an apple, just like his maternal uncle's."

I knew, without looking, that Maternal Aunt was pulling her summer quilt up to her crown. Aunt had been lying almost continuously for quite some days now on the warmer part of the floor because something was evidently wrong with her respiratory system. Aunt always pulled up her quilt like that whenever Maternal Grandmother mentioned Maternal Uncle.

"Who do you like better, your maternal uncle, or your paternal uncle?"

This was the unreasonable question Maternal Grandmother had got into the habit of posing to me. At first I was extremely disconcerted when she asked me that question. For one thing, it was a question meant for extorting one answer. It was always Maternal Uncle she mentioned first in the question. But my situation did not allow me to pick out either one as my favorite. If I were to tell the truth I would have had to say that I liked both of them. But Maternal Grandmother was demanding that I pick one of the two.

"Do you like your maternal uncle, or your paternal uncle?"

But I knew that the important thing was neither the question nor my answer. I had long ago figured out that the question, posed without any emotion or stress, was simply an introductory remark to her long, rambling discourse. So, it was only the first couple of times that the question threw me into confusion. I therefore lay there silently, pretending not to have heard the question. Then Grandmother would put on an expression of regret.

"I know. The arm always bends inward."*

But it was only for a moment that the look of regret shaded her face. Her face regained equanimity soon enough, and she began her discourse.

"If you are to be really worthy of being Kwŏn Kiljun's nephew, you must first of all know what kind of a person he was. Unless you know what kind of a person your maternal uncle was, you're not fit to claim kinship with him. No, you're not."

---

* "The arm always bends inward" is an expression commonly used in Korea to signify that people always favor their friends and close relatives over strangers and distant kin. In this case, since the boy lives with his paternal uncle and as he belongs with the uncle in the same patrilineal family, which is the primary source of one's identity, he cannot but feel closer kinship to his paternal uncle than to his maternal uncle. [Translator]

The maternal uncle that my maternal grandmother described always wore a football player's uniform. And he dashed about like a thorough-bred on the infinitely vast playground rapidly constructed in my imagination. And he kicked the ball up sky-high, with a perfectly graceful motion. He excelled in studies too, to be sure, but he was a genius in sports. And among sports, football was his specialty; he was the leader of his school football team from middle school to college.

The first time Maternal Grandmother felt pride in her son as a football player was at the very first football match she attended in her life. At the time Maternal Uncle was a high school senior. Maternal Grandmother, who had not wanted her only son to grow up to be a professional athlete, was dumbfounded after the game was over, when hordes of schoolgirls rushed over to her and addressed her as "mother," as if she had been their mother-in-law. Even more amazingly, the girls praised her son to the skies, as if he had been their husband.

She was not one to brook such forwardness in nubile girls, and she chased them away after giving them a smart lecture, but the incident was not altogether displeasing to her. From then on, it became an important task for her to scold away with a stern lecture the schoolgirl fans who besieged her and her son.

"You should've seen your uncle that time . . . that time when the goalkeeper of the opposite team fell backward, struck by the ball your uncle had kicked. That'd have made it easier for you to answer—that you like your maternal uncle better than your paternal one."

Maternal Grandmother was a woman of few words. But once she started talking about her son there was no stopping her. She was putting all her strength into her words, in an effort to implant deep into my heart the image of her splendid son. Sometimes she demanded that I describe my maternal uncle's features, as if afraid I might forget his face.

It is true that my maternal uncle was a splendid young man, worthy of any mother's pride. Even though there were some exaggerations and embellishments in Grandmother's memory, that he was an excellent football player and a much-admired figure are demonstrable truths.

He was a brilliant and handsome man. His face was white as porcelain, and the sharp nosebridge and dark eyebrows gave him a truly distinguished look. His smiles, which revealed two neat rows of clean teeth, and his well-proportioned body exuded refinement and good breeding. Several times we had had him and his friends as guests for a

few days. One time he came with quite a number of them, all carrying
rucksacks. The young men, who said they were on their way to Chiri-
san Mountain, played harmonicas and guitars all night long in the
guest room. That night, one of his friends said he'd give me instruc-
tions on how to kiss girls, and rubbed his coarse jaw on mine and made
me scream and flee from the room. That was when I was five years
old. There was a time also when a beautiful young woman was in the
group. That was the year before the war broke out, and that time also
he and his numerous friends carried on gleefully for five days, incur-
ring the silent displeasure of my paternal grandmother, and putting
Mother in an embarrassing position.

Uncle's friends seemed to be treating him and the young woman
like a royal couple. The group also locked themselves up in the room
for hours at a stretch and seemed to be earnestly discussing something.
Mother explained later on that they were in flight at the time, after a
clash with leftist students with whom they were in long-standing opposition. Except for the period of about a month after the outbreak of the
war, when Maternal Uncle was hiding himself in the dug-out cave in
the bamboo grove behind our house, these were about all the contacts I
had had with him.

My feelings toward my uncle formed through such short encounters
were closer to reverence than love as a kinsman. There were many
things about him that could inspire my adoration. His comely features
and cultured manners and speech had an almost feminine refinement;
but his adroit movements and clear-cut decisiveness, which came from
his almost limitless energy, bespoke manliness itself. The fact that he
was the leader of an organization at such an early age proved him to be
a man of extraordinary qualities, and made him seem even more distinguished in my eyes. To me, the wondrous combination of such diverse
abilities in one human being was an eternal enigma.

My paternal uncle was three years older than my maternal uncle. In
spite of his seniority, however, he was much more immature in his
actions than my maternal uncle. His method of "rewarding" the labors
of the special agents who had been hired to detect illegal home-brew-
ing and clandestine butchery made him famous in the vicinity for a
while. The agents had earned the resentment of the villagers for their
unmerciful vigilance. In the middle of a large gathering of villagers in
the village square, my uncle gave each of the agents a large bucket of
plain water to drink. He termed this a way of rewarding their diligent

labors in detecting clandestine brewing. Each of the agents had to gulp down the enormous amount of water, kneeling and with guns aimed at the napes of their necks. Then they were required to chant, marking time by striking their enormously swollen bellies, "I am the grandson of the yeast! I am the bairn of the cow! My father is an ox! A swine is my mother!" exactly one hundred times. Then they were asked to entertain the villagers with songs—any song. Their hoarse singing, which sounded more like the bellowing of calves, was so miserable that the villagers who had been writhing and giggling all along stopped laughing in the end.

All his actions were comic and preposterous in such a way. There is also the famous anecdote of his "marriage" with the daughter of a small landowner in the neighboring village. With a notorious hoodlum of the village officiating, he "married" the daughter of Mr. Ch'oe in a sham ceremony. The ceremony also took place in the village square, and it was a completely modern, Western-style ceremony, too. To it were invited, or summoned, Mr. Ch'oe and the bride's husband as guests. As soon as the ceremony was over, Uncle handed the bride over to the hoodlum who officiated and went directly up to Mr. Ch'oe. That day Mr. Ch'oe was beaten till he fainted away by the ruffian who kept calling him "father." That was in repayment for the atrocious thrashing he had received at the hands of Mr. Ch'oe's servants on the moonlit night he jumped over the wall of Mr. Ch'oe's house while drunk, after having yearned for his daughter for a long time.

My two uncles were thus antithetical. Whereas my paternal uncle's enlistment in the red army was a blind and impulsive involvement in the whirlwind of events, just like his leap over Mr. Ch'oe's wall in a drunken state, my maternal uncle's activity in the right-wing movement and his volunteering for officership in the Republic's army were decisions grounded firmly on principle and made after careful weighing and examining of the meaning and consequences. Although they had not met often, my two uncles seemed to like each other well enough. If they hadn't, it would have been impossible for my maternal uncle to remain safe in hiding for over a month under the communist rule. Saying that it was only ignorant and poor men like himself who would wear red arm bands, my paternal uncle treated my maternal uncle with respectful courtesy. It may have been an expression of envy and admiration for one who had received a higher education than himself. At any rate, Paternal Uncle frequently bestowed kindly attentions on his in-law relation who had to stay hidden in a cave. To Mother, he explained that his kindly attentions were in consideration of their mutual nephew, and the position of Father and Mother.

But my maternal uncle was different. Even though inwardly he felt warmly towards my paternal uncle who was so cheerful and frank, outwardly he always cast cold glances at his counterpart who went around acting like a playful urchin. His intuition proved right. My paternal uncle, who seemed to have so much affection for my maternal uncle, dispatched his men to the cave in the bamboo grove on that mad dawn of the communists' retreat. It was a few hours after Maternal Uncle, following a hearty supper, had silently disappeared without saying a word to anyone in the family.

I could hear Aunt coughing. Covered with the thin quilt up to her head, and lying still on her back on the warmer part of the floor, she was racked by coughs that constricted her respiratory organs. I could hear Maternal Grandmother murmuring. And I could hear the noise of the thinning and thickening rain.

"He always disliked anything the least bit sloppy. I bet he died as neatly as was his wont in everything. I'm sure only one bullet struck him, in the heart or in the head, so that he died instantly, without writhing or suffering pain."

It seems that Maternal Grandmother was severely shocked by what the villager had recounted thoughtlessly a few days earlier. It may be that the images of variously disfigured corpses went in and out of the guest quarters of our house all night long and disturbed the dreams of an unhappy old woman. It is certainly possible that they did. Maternal Grandmother was praying that her only son had met his death in battle in as neat and peaceful a posture as restful slumber. She prayed ardently that Satan's bullet had struck him in a vital spot, so that he crossed the boundary between this world and the next instantly, not only without bodily pain but also without feeling sorrow at leaving his old, widowed mother without a son in this sorry world. She murmured stubbornly that her son died with all the parts of his body intact, and that he could never have met the fate of those ghosts in ancient tales who had to linger in this world wandering over hills and plains in search of their scattered body parts.

But the voice was weakening perceptibly. Aunt's coughs, on the other hand, became more high-pitched. Grandmother's murmurs were becoming more and more subdued under the continuously intruding noise of the rain.

5

The day appointed by the blind fortune-teller was inexorably approaching. The rain poured on, and everyone was tired. With the exception of Paternal Grandmother, everyone was completely exhausted. Worn out by waiting, and by the rain.

The stepping stones in the river that served as a bridge between our village and the next had sunk long ago under the rising water. After that, a thick rope had been tied across the stream, so that grownups forded the river against the rapid current that came up to the waist by holding onto the rope, and children were carried across piggyback on the grown-ups' shoulders. But, as the water was now deeper than a grown-ups's height, it had become utterly impossible to cross the river. Thus, traffic to town had as good as closed down. There were people who averred they saw things like pigs, oxen, and uprooted pine trees being washed down the river from upstream, but Father brushed off such rumors as nonsense. According to Father, our village was located on the upstream shore of the Sŏmjin River, so that such things could not happen unless there was a great flood. But it was certain that this year's rainy spell was unusually long and heavy. As a consequence traffic to and from the village was tied up, which gave Paternal Grandmother grave worry.

"He's certain to be coming by the road from the town. How terrible it is that the river's so swollen!"

There was a toad that had taken up abode in the dirt veranda of our house for many days despite my manifold persecutions. It seemed to deem itself lucky to have found a shelter at all after having its cave wrecked by the long rain. Pitiable as it was, my mischievousness was aroused by the absurd sight it presented as it dragged its clumsy body around under the wooden floor or on the dirt veranda. On the third day, I turned it bellyside up and, inserting a barley straw in its anus, blew into the straw until its belly was puffed up like a rubber ball. After that it disappeared for an afternoon. But the next morning it was back on the dirt veranda, claiming its right of residence. Squatting on the stepping stone, it gazed vacantly with its protruding eyes at the water dripping from the eaves.

On one of those days, trouble was discovered in the barn. It was not the kind of trouble that broke out suddenly one morning, but rather a gradual development over many days. However, as no one had noticed it, we were all aghast at the discovery. A mist began rising from the bags of barley that had been stored in the barn as soon as they were reaped. As the peas had done some time ago, the grain was now sending up pale yellow sprouts. It was lucky that Father made the discovery when he went in to set mousetraps; otherwise, all the family would have simply had to starve until harvest in the autumn. Suddenly the entire family went around busily, as in the peak farming season. To store the barley bags so as to prevent further damage was a big problem. We installed a storage platform of wooden bars in the barn to provide ventilation space between the floor and the barley bags, and spread the steaming barley on all the level places in the house to let it dry. Wherever I went—bedrooms, kitchen, everywhere—there was barley. I detested barley, and not only because it felt rough in the mouth and gave me tummy aches. It was more on account of a legend Paternal Grandmother had told me.

Once upon a time there lived a boy whose father was ill with a fatal disease. The boy consulted a doctor, who prescribed a concoction made out of people's livers. The boy therefore killed three people he met on his way home—a scholar, a monk and a madman—and made a broth with their livers. Upon drinking it, the father's disease was completely cured. The boy buried the corpses in a sunny place. The next year a strange plant was seen growing on the tomb, and its grain was what we now call barley. The slit in the barley grain is thus the slit the boy made in the bodies of the men for the purpose of taking out their livers.

It was very uncomfortable inside the house with its floors all covered over with such an unpleasant grain. I felt cornered and bound. But Paternal Grandmother was a woman of truly amazing determination. Even in the midst of all the fuss, she simply went on with her plans. First, she ordered Mother to take out of the chest her treasured silk cloth and sew a Korean outfit for Uncle. In her opinion a Korean suit was the most dignified and comfortable garment for indoors. And she made Mother prepare Uncle's favorite dish—fried squash slices—in mountainous heaps, despite Mother's protest that it would get spoiled and become inedible in two days. She seasoned the fern fronds herself, and complained that plants didn't grow as they ought to because the times were hard. All the dishes that spoiled quickly were heavily salted or deep-fried to prevent spoilage. At last the preparations were almost complete. There was enough food to give an ordinary village-scale feast for country people like us.

As she looked around the kitchen, Grandmother's face lit up with the pride of one who has accomplished an important task. Now she had only one more thing to worry about.

"He's sure to be coming by the road from town. How unfortunate it is that the river's so swollen!"

"What's there to worry about? Even if the river's a bit swollen, how could it hinder his coming, if he's destined to come? He knows traffic often gets tied up in the rainy season, so he'll take the stone bridge and come by the circular road."

Father brushed aside Grandmother's worry, to put her mind at ease, but Grandmother shook her head.

"Of course he'll take the circular road. But that's four miles longer. Four miles sounds pretty short, but think of walking four more miles in this rain. And his feet frostbitten, too!"

Paternal Aunt came the day before the appointed day. As soon as she arrived, she inspected the cupboards and shelves in the kitchen and complimented Mother and Paternal Grandmother for their thoroughness. She seemed quite satisfied with the preparations that had been made. Aunt had as complete a faith in the homecoming of my uncle as did Paternal Grandmother. It was she who had introduced Grandmother to the blind fortune-teller. As she was thus the one who induced my grandmother's complete faith in the fortune-teller, it was understandable that her belief in Uncle's homecoming was as firm as Grandmother's. But even her idea of a proper welcome for the returning uncle was so perfectly identical with Paternal Grandmother's that my mother, though she was chary of complaints against her in-laws, marvelled secretly to Maternal Grandmother and Maternal Aunt at the resemblance of taste between her mother- and sister-in-law. It was not as if Mother was not hoping for Uncle's return. Even Maternal Aunt, who hardly ever spoke in those days, and Maternal Grandmother, who had once invoked curses upon communist partisans, silently wished for the happy reunion of the relations as they watched the heated preparations. But wishing and believing are two different things. I also ardently wished for my uncle's return. But even in my childish judgment it did not seem very likely that an event like that could occur as easily as predicted. If Uncle were to come, in what status and by which road would he be coming?

I had chanced to overhear Father talking to Mother in the kitchen. Father said that such a thing was impossible. If one detached oneself even a little from Paternal Grandmother's touching faith—and it was a complete, unshakable faith—and examined the matter with any objectivity at all, the impossibility of the prediction being fulfilled was so clear that it made our hearts ache. As a last resort, Father even thought of the possibility of Uncle's having surrendered himself to the police somewhere. But he quickly dismissed the idea. Had that been the case, we would have had by now some notice of interrogation from the police. Father knew better than anybody else that our family was under surveillance. From time to time, a man could be seen sauntering up and down along our twig fence and casting suspicious glances into the house. Though outwardly we had freedom of movement, we were like fish securely cooped inside the net drawn by the man. I knew from long before that the man sometimes dropped in at our neighbor Chinku's to gather information about what was going on in my house, and once or twice he even called my father out to a tavern for a talk.

I shuddered most of all when the man came into view. His appearance had dreadful significance for me. It always awakened anew my guilty conscience, which I was trying to lull to sleep. The sight of him made me recall Paternal Grandmother's words that I was a butcher of men who had sold my uncle for a sweet. Father should have struck me dead that night with the wooden pillow. It gave me excruciating pain to behold Father's face as he returned from a talk with that man.

The only way I had of escaping from my paternal grandmother's censure that kept reviving in my memory was to imagine myself dying in the most pitiful fashion. That was the only way of evading, even temporarily, the tormenting consciousness of guilt. I imagined the scene in which the whole family, especially my paternal grandmother, shed tears without end in front of the dead youth. The greater Paternal Grandmother's sorrow and regret, the more consolation I felt. But, when I woke up from the daydream, I always found myself as impudently alive as ever, and I could not but dread meeting Paternal Uncle face to face. Because of this guilt, while I ardently wished for my uncle's return, I also secretly harbored the horrible wish that I might never have to face Uncle again—that Uncle had died long ago in some steep, deserted valley, and his body would never be found. The anticipated day, which was just one day away now, really filled me with mortal dread. I was so terrified that I prayed today would never end.

But I think my terror and anxiety were nothing compared with the pain my father endured. I had heard Father pleading in the kitchen with Mother, who was complaining about Paternal Grandmother's excessive vigilance.

"I feel the same as you do. It's a hundred to one that he won't come. And even if he does by some extraordinary chance, it won't be the kind of event Mother expects it to be. That I know better than you do. But what can I say to Mother? It's best simply to do everything she bids us. That's better than making her think we're trying to thwart her joy and giving her a grievance. Don't you think so?"

Father was appealing to Mother by telling her of his own agony at having to follow his old mother's lead, even feigning assiduity in doing so, while he knew the waited-for event would be an impossibility. Even though Paternal Grandmother's faith, nourished by her boundless motherly love, moved our hearts at first and made us pray for the fulfillment of her expectation, we were far from having the same faith ourselves. We were only hoping and waiting with her because we did not want on any account to disappoint the old lady. Father had already foreseen the despair that would follow if Grandmother's expectation is disappointed, and what would result from that despair. But there was nothing any of us could do except try our best not to cross the old lady. It was a pity that the blind fortune-teller, reputed to be divinely inspired, had not told Grandmother which road Uncle would be taking to return home.

It was already night. The rain, which thinned down from around dusk, was now a mere misty drizzle. Into the hazy halo of the lamp hung on the gatepost, the rain descended in sprinkles of powdery drops, as if it, too, was quite exhausted. Although there had been no express order, ever since the beginning of the war, the whole village was in the habit of extinguishing all lights after supper-time. However, we had hung out a lamp tonight, letting it keep vigil through the night like a lonely sentinel. It was, of course, at Paternal Grandmother's insistence. Who knows, she said, even though Uncle was slated to come between eight and ten o'clock in the morning, he might show up in the middle of the night due to some sudden change of plan. Grandmother did not want it to look as if the family was unprepared for his return.

"It was for an occasion like this that we have saved up the expensive kerosene."

She ordered one more lamp to be hung from the eaves and warned us not to let the lamps die out in any of the rooms. She explained very succinctly the reason we had to keep the house as bright as day.

"We have to keep the lamps burning bright so he can spot the house from far, far away and run all the way home, knowing his mother's waiting for him with wide-open eyes all through the night."

The night deepened. Even so, nobody seemed to be thinking of going to bed. No one in the family had the guts to spread our bedding when Paternal Grandmother was tensely surveying every corner of the house. The weather also seemed to be flattering my grandmother. The long, fierce rain had changed to a drizzle in the evening, and then by degrees withdrew out of sight and out of hearing, so that as the night deepened even the dripping from the eaves ceased. And the cool wind that carries away humidity began to blow. Well, the rainy spell had lasted long enough, and it was time for the rainy front to retreat. But Grandmother quickly related the change in the weather to the forth-coming happy event of the morrow, to her great satisfaction.

It must have been long past midnight. I had left the inner room to come to the guest room and lie down beside Maternal Grandmother. Neither my maternal aunt nor my maternal grandmother was asleep. I suppose they couldn't fall asleep, because of all the tense excitement in the inner quarters. Aunt was lying still on her back, facing the ceiling, and Grandmother was seated leaning on the wall, facing the door. My eyes were tracing the flickering shadow of the lamp's sooty flame on the ceiling. My ears were wide open, and were listening to the songs of the night in the distant grass beyond the darkness outside the door.

All around was quiet. The house couldn't be quieter, even had ev-eryone been asleep. It was so perfectly still that the stillness rather hampered my listening to the sound of darkness. It was as if my audi-tory organs were paralyzed under the pressure of the stillness that weighed all around. So much so that I sometimes suspected that the sounds that came to my ears were not sounds that actually existed in the world but rather some illusion created by my bewitched brain. But collecting myself and listening again, I seemed to be hearing some wakeful being besides myself patiently filing away with a sharp file in the darkness at the edge of the vast stillness. For a long time I had been concentrating on distinguishing the chirping of the crickets from that of the katydids amid the whisper of the wind, and was relishing the sweet and sour notes of those sounds. Suddenly, amidst the murmur of insects, an unfamiliar sound intruded, and its strangeness made me tense. But the sound ceased as unexpectedly as it began. It fled, just as I was about to grasp the tail end of it, and I felt again that I might have been bewitched by something. But the sound came again after a pause. It was very distinct this time. It was not loud, but it was distinctive among the many hushed sounds of the night. It was like the sound children made when they blow into the mouth of an empty bottle or like the siren of a ship on a distant sea. It was, at any rate, a faint but pregnant sound. It was also a very obscure sound, and I was completely at a loss as to the direction it was coming from. It seemed now to be coming from somewhere around the river's shore outside the village, or from the kitchen garden of our house, right outside the door. I lay bewitched by the strange, secretive sound that stole through the stillness of the night. Like a boy chasing fox-fire in the graveyard, my consciousness, drawn by the mysterious strain of the eerie sound, was already rushing to the river's shore.

"It's the king snake calling up the snakes."

Grandmother's words coiled around my body like a huge snake darting out its forked tongue, and I could hardly breathe. It was my beloved maternal aunt who chased away the chilly feel of the snake against my body. I had a protector. I was infinitely thankful that I was not the only one to have heard the sound. Aunt was already sitting up beside me and staring at the door. Grandmother twitched her lips, preparatory to saying something more. Aunt put her hand on my shoulder and gave Grandmother a sideways stare.

"Don't."

But Grandmother kept twitching her lips. Had Aunt not subdued her once more, Grandmother would surely have said something.

"Please don't!"

Aunt pulled me under her quilt. Buried snugly under Aunt's armpit, I heard the sound again. The sound, like a ship's siren from a distant sea, once more scattered chill all over the room. This time, too, it was hard to tell whether the sound was coming from the river's shore or from the kitchen garden of our house. Then there was a long interval. The snake's call sounded for the third time, and then came no more. But the aftertaste of the sound lingered in the room for a long time and kept our mouths shut. Maternal Grandmother was still sitting in an awkward posture, stooping forward toward the door. Waves of emotion crossed her face. Sometimes she would look vacantly into space, like a person hit hard on the head, but the next moment she would gaze beyond the door with narrowed eyes, like someone trying to work out a very complicated problem. At last she turned towards me and Aunt.

"Tongman," she called. "Tongman, my dear."

But when my eyes met hers she averted her face. After some hesitation, she slowly opened her mouth again.

"Do you think so, too?" she asked, apropos of nothing, and again hesitated for a long while.

"Do you also think that what happened to your uncle happened because of me?"

I decided to answer the question. There was such urgency in the voice asking the question that I thought I had to say something in response. But I realized the next moment that no answer was needed. She was not looking at me, nor was she paying any attention to me. She was completely absorbed in her own thoughts. She would not have heard me even if I had said anything in response.

"No! What happened that night was none of my willing. I'd no thought of spying on anybody. I'd been to the outhouse and saw the light in the inner room and heard whispering voices, so I just went nearer to see what was going on. Who'd have known it'd bring about such consequences? A team of horses couldn't have dragged me there if I'd known such a thing was going to happen. I'm not saying I did well to be so curious. I know I shouldn't have done it, but it wasn't because of me that things ended that way. Even if it hadn't been for me, your uncle would've returned to where he came from, as he was fated to do. That was his lot."

Aunt hugged me tightly. With my face buried snugly between Aunt's breasts, I heard Grandmother's murmurs in a dreamy coziness. Then, my whole body loosened up as after a heavy flogging and violent weeping, and drowsiness utterly overwhelmed me. Even in my dreamy exhaustion I vowed to myself that I would marry my aunt for sure when I grew up, and I stopped heeding Grandmother's muttering.

6

I was far from refreshed when I woke up from the sound of Paternal Grandmother's furious reproaches, uttered just inside the gate. Although the sky was brightening, it was still early dawn. Summer nights are short, and, as I had gone to sleep long past midnight, to wake up in early dawn meant I had as good as skipped sleeping that night. I felt a numbing pain inside my head, and my eyelids kept sliding down. But my condition was vigor itself compared with the rest of the family's. Because of many days of fatigue and tension, Father's face was swollen and yellow as if jaundiced, and Mother had become gaunt as a mummy. Maternal Grandmother and Maternal Aunt weren't doing any better. But Paternal Grandmother was energetically imperious, loudly scolding the weary family from early dawn. She was giving Mother and Father a horrendous reprimand.

The lamp hung on the gatepost had died out. The wind must have blown out the flame—the oil can was more than half full, and the glass shade was wet with drops of water. The extinguished lamp had infuriated Paternal Grandmother. She took it as a proof of Father and Mother's insufficient devotion. Grandmother's ire was not soothed even after she gave Father and Mother a severe reproof. She declared that this proved to her that Father and Mother were unfit to be trusted with Uncle's welfare, and announced her resolution to take charge of the keys to the barn and the safety cabinet until she saw signs of improvement in their behavior.

"I won't say anything more this morning, because a woman shouldn't raise her voice on the morning of festivity. I'll leave the rest up to you. I won't move a finger, but just entertain myself watching what you do." Then she clicked her tongue in self-pity, as she turned around to head for the inner quarters. "Lucky woman I am, to have such a thoughtful older son!" She strode across the yard toward the inner room. "What sins am I expiating, to be blessed with a son and a daughter-in-law like them?" she grumbled to herself as she passed in front of the guest room, loud enough to be heard by neighbors.

Paternal Grandmother was as good as her word. She really did not move a finger. After she went into her room, slamming the door shut, she did not utter a single comment on what was going on outside. Instead, she kept a keen watch over what was happening in the yard through the glass pane of the small window, and a disapproving, discontented look did not leave her face. All of us in the family came out with brooms, rags, or dusters and, with a keen consciousness of supervisory eyes upon us, swept the yard, scrubbed the floor, cleaned cobwebs, and tidied up the house. Both aunts also joined in, and the house regained the neat appearance it had had before the long rain. Maternal Aunt and Paternal Aunt went into the kitchen with Mother to prepare breakfast, and Father and I, sweating profusely, dug a deep ditch between the footpath leading from the gate to the yard and the kitchen garden, to drain the water from the yard.

The sky was still cloudy. We had hoped to see the sun for the first time in a long while, but the sky did not look cheerfully disposed. Nevertheless, a patch of the western sky was clear, and there was a cool wind that drove away the clouds. There was no sign anywhere of a renewal of rain. Even that much beneficence was a blessing to us. Not only my family but everybody felt the same. Village people who dropped in on us from early morning began their greetings by talking of the weather, and the women went in and out of the kitchen. My house overflowed with village people, as on a feast day, and the members of the family were kept busy responding to questions from inquisitive neighbors. What the neighbors were most curious about was to what extent the members of our family believed in the prophecy. Of course they did not use words like "superstition." Although they marvelled at the fact that one word from a fortune-teller led to such large-scale preparations, they were polite enough not to treat it as mere foolishness, at least in our hearing. They tended rather to be sympathetic, and commented encouragingly that the devotion of the family, if nothing else, would bring Uncle back. Father simply smiled. Father saw, in the attitude of some of the people who spoke thus, that they were amusing themselves with what was going on in our house. Some of them were taking exactly the tone of the doctor who tells his dying patient he'll recover in a few days. As the appointed hour drew near,* more and more people gathered, so that our yard was teeming with people as on a village festival day. It looked as if everyone in the village who could walk had come. I could see the stranger smoking a cigarette, sitting on the porch of Chinku's house. My house was bustling like a marketplace, and the family had still not had breakfast. Grandmother had forbidden us to eat, as all of us were to eat with Uncle when he came. It wasn't as if we were starving, so I resolved to be patient, but my stomach howled pitifully.

At last it was eight o'clock, the beginning of the period appointed by the fortune-teller. Time sped by amid the tense excitement of every-

---

* The fortune-teller had predicted that the uncle would return in *Chinsi*, the hour of the dragon, which in this story appears to be between eight and ten o'clock in the morning, but which in fact is between nine and eleven o'clock. The author seems to have been slightly mixed up about the period divisions. [Translator]

one. Soon it was nine o'clock, and then it was approaching ten o'clock. But the long-awaited Uncle did not show up.

After the villagers had all dispersed, we sat down to a late, late breakfast. Only the village head and Chinku's family remained, trying to console us. Paternal Grandmother remained in the inner room, and the rest of the family sat around the table set in the side room. The spoons moved slowly although the table was luxuriously laden with colorful dishes. Paternal Grandmother refused to eat breakfast, even though she told the family to go ahead and eat. Her spirit was not weakened, even though the time appointed by the blind seer was quite past and gone. Well, she still *looked* spirited, anyway. She said that from the first she had not thought the hour was all that important. What was important, according to her, was the day, not the hour. She said that there could be accidental errors even in events supervised by Heaven; and man cannot always move exactly according to schedule. She insisted one must make allowances for slight errors even in the prophecy of divine seers. For Grandmother, the day has only just begun. She said that, since Uncle would not fail to come that day, she would wait a little longer and have her first meal of the day with her son. She did not betray any tiredness.

Our dog Wŏlly, who had been peering in at the rooms, standing with his forefeet on the edge of the living-room floor and smacking his lips, suddenly stepped down to the dirt veranda. Then he barked, turning to the gate. The shouting of children followed hard upon. Father's spoon stopped in mid-air, and all our movements instantly ceased. Children's exclamations were rapidly approaching our house. Flinging the spoon away, I ran outside. The noise instantly surrounded our gate. I was hit by the shouts of the children in the middle of the yard. The first thing that came into my view was a pack of children with gaping mouths. All of them had rocks or sticks of wood in their hands. The children hesitated a little before the gate, not daring to rush into the house, and raised their weapons threateningly. One of the boys threw his rock forcibly. Where the rock fell I beheld the thing.

There was a long object sliding into the house. It was a huge snake, longer than a man's height. My whole body constricted the moment I saw its horrible bulk slithering with its yellowish scales glittering dazzlingly, reviving in my memory the eerie whisper of the night before. But I was a boy, and a snake meant an adventure. Horror had a momentary grip on me, but the next moment I was as excited as any of the

other boys who kept screaming and throwing rocks. I could not control
the aggressive, destructive urge that male children instinctively feel
towards all reptiles. I ran over to the barn and fetched the big wooden
staff that Father used when carrying heavy things on an A-frame. I
raised both hands high in the air, ready to strike the snake dead if it
moved an inch closer to me, but a hand grabbed my arm roughly. I
looked around to see that it was Maternal Grandmother. At the same
moment, there arose a piercing scream from behind me.

"Aaaack!"

With that, Paternal Grandmother fell on the floor, as limply as a
piece of worn-out clothing. Maternal Grandmother twisted the staff
from my grasp. Her eyes glared at me in silent reprimand.

The unexpected appearance of the huge snake threw the whole
house into utter confusion. The most urgent problem was Paternal
Grandmother, who had fainted. The family gathered in the inner room
to massage her limbs and spray cold water on her face in an effort to
revive her. The village people, who had dispersed, gathered in the
house once more, and talked and exclaimed so noisily that it was like
sitting in the middle of a whirlwind. Only Maternal Grandmother did
not lose her calm amidst the noise and confusion. As if she were
simply carrying out a pre-arranged procedure, she put things in order
one by one with a truly amazing composure. First of all, she drove
away the people. With the help of the village head and Chinku's father,
she drove out all the village people who came for the show and locked
the gate fast. The children and grownups who had been driven out of
the gate came round to the part of the twig fence next to a persimmon
tree. Taking advantage of the heated confusion, the snake had slid
down the kitchen garden through the brown mallows and lettuces and
had already coiled itself around the upper branches of the persimmon
tree. With its yellow body wound around the persimmon bough, it kept
darting its wiry tongue in and out. It must have suffered a deadly blow,
for its tail was more than half cut from the body and dangled precariously. The tireless children had followed it up to the persimmon tree
and were still throwing rocks and sticks.

"Who's that throwing rocks?"

Maternal Grandmother's reprimand was as sharp as a sword.*

---

* The giant, venomless snake was believed to have supernatural properties and
powers. It was believed that spirits of the dead could enter it to visit people in this

All the throwing ceased. Then Grandmother began to slowly walk up to the persimmon tree. Nothing happened even when she stood just below the tree with the coiled snake, and sighs of relief escaped from the people who had been watching her with breathless suspense. She did not waver a bit, even though the snake's fiery dots of eyes gleamed in all directions and it raised and lowered its head threateningly. She slowly lifted both her hands and clasped them palm-to-palm on her bosom.

"My poor boy, have you come all this way to see how things are going in the house?" Grandmother whispered quietly, in the tone of one singing a lullaby to a fretful baby. Somebody giggled. Instantly, Grandmother's eyes grew sharply triangular.

"Which mongrel is sniggering there? Come up here at once! I'll wring your neck!"

Everybody became still as death at Grandmother's fiery rebuke. Grandmother turned to the snake again.

"As you can see, your mother's still in good health and everybody's doing all right. So put your mind at ease and make haste on your way."

The snake did not stir a muscle. It only darted its wiry tongue in and out and raised its head a couple of times.

"You mustn't linger here crouching like this any more when you have such a long way to go. You shouldn't, you know, if you don't want to grieve your family over-much. I know how you feel, but you must consider others' feelings, too. How would your mother feel if she knew you were lingering here like this?"

Maternal Grandmother was earnestly entreating, as if the snake had been a real live human being. But, however ardently she pleaded, the snake did not show any inclination to move away. A neighborhood woman then told Grandmother the method for expelling snakes. The woman, whose body was hidden from view and whose voice only could be heard, said that you could chase away snakes with the smell of burning hair. At Maternal Grandmother's bidding, I hurried into the inner room to get some of Paternal Grandmother's hair.

Paternal Grandmother was lying under a quilt, stiff as a corpse. Although she was breathing, she was still unconscious. I urgently demanded some of Paternal Grandmother's hair from the family members sitting around the unconscious form with ashen-grey faces,

---

world. It behooved people, therefore, not to hurt it but to conciliate it by all means. [Translator]

waiting for the arrival of the doctor. My demand must have sounded preposterous. It took quite a long time to explain for what purpose Grandmother's hair was needed. It took a while longer for Paternal Aunt to collect a handful of hair from the unconscious old lady with a fine-toothed bamboo comb. The hair collected from repeated combing was given to me at last. When I came out to the yard, Maternal Grandmother had in the meanwhile prepared a small tray laden with a few dishes. On the round tray were Uncle's favorite dishes of fried squash slices and seasoned fern, and there was also a large bowl of cold water. After taking the knot of hair from me and putting it on the ground, Maternal Grandmother slowly raised her head and looked up at the persimmon tree.

"These are what your mother has prepared for many days for you. Even though you can't taste them, take a good look at them at least. They're all proofs of your mother's devotion. It's not that I'm trying to get rid of you. You must understand that. Please don't blame me too much for the bad smell. It's just to hurry you along on the long way you have to go. Put your worries at rest about your family and just take good care of yourself on the long way ahead of you."

As she finished talking, she turned up the live coal in the tinder bowl. When she placed the knot of hair on it, it burned with a sizzling sound. The smell of burning protein quickly spread all around. What happened next drew an exclamation of astonishment from everyone. The huge snake, which had till then been immobile as a rock despite all Grandmother's entreaties, slowly began to move. Its body, which had been coiled around the persimmon tree, smoothly unwound itself, and it slithered down to the ground. After hesitating a little, it slowly and waveringly crept towards Grandmother. Grandmother stepped aside to make way. She followed its tail as it slid away and kept chasing it, making a swishing sound with her lips. Like one chasing away sparrows from the fields, Grandmother swished and even clapped her hands. The snake crawled over the ground noiselessly, twitching its gleaming scales. All the members of the family also spilled out to the living-room floor and fearfully watched it sliding across the yard. Wŏlly, whose tail clung to his inner thighs, dutifully barked with a fear-strained voice from beneath the living-room floor. The snake slowly coursed its way through the empty space between the barn and kitchen, its half-detached tail shakily trailing behind.

"Swish! Swish!"

Spurred on from behind by Grandmother's hoarse voice, the snake had already slid past the well and crossed the backyard. Before it now was the densely overgrown bamboo grove.

"Thank you, dear. Just trust your brother to take care of all the household, and think only of keeping your body whole for your long, long journey. Don't worry at all about what you're leaving behind here, and take good care of yourself. That's a good boy. Thank you, dear."

Standing beside the well, Maternal Grandmother saw the snake off with earnest entreaties until it completely disappeared through the bamboo trees and the bamboo shoots which had sprouted thickly during the long rain.

Chinku's father arrived with a doctor from a neighboring village. Paternal Grandmother regained consciousness several hours after she had fainted. On waking up from her stupor of a few hours, she looked around the room like one who had been on a few months' trip to a faraway place.

"Is it gone?" were her first words after regaining consciousness. Paternal Aunt quickly understood and nodded. Paternal Grandmother lowered her eyelids, as if to say that was all that mattered. Paternal Aunt quickly recounted all that had happened after Paternal Grandmother had fainted away. She told how Maternal Grandmother chased away the neighbors, reasoned with the snake under the persimmon tree, made it come down from the tree by burning Paternal Grandmother's hair, and saw it off every step of the way until it disappeared through the bamboo grove. Mother occasionally added details to Paternal Aunt's account. Paternal Grandmother was weeping quietly. Tears gushed endlessly from her eyes, flowed down her sunken cheeks, and wetted the pillow case. After she had heard all, she told Father to go and ask Maternal Grandmother to come to the inner room. Maternal Grandmother, who had been resting in the guest room, followed Father into the inner room. It was the first time Maternal Grandmother had stepped into the inner room since the day of the unhappy clash between the two in-laws.

"Thank you," Paternal Grandmother said huskily, raising her sunken and lusterless eyes to Maternal Grandmother.

"You're welcome." Maternal Grandmother's voice was also tearfully husky.

"I heard it all from my daughter. You did for me what I should've done. What a difficult and fearsome thing you have done for me."

"It's all past now. Don't exert yourself any more with talking, but try to regain your strength."

"Thank you. Thank you so very much." Paternal Grandmother held out her hand. Maternal Grandmother took it. The two grandmothers just held hands for a while, unable to speak. Then Paternal Grandmother expressed her remaining worry.

"I wonder if it went on its way all right."

"Don't worry. It must have found a comfortable place by now, and is keeping a protective eye on this house."

Even that brief conversation drained Paternal Grandmother's strength, and she fainted. Everyone sat around her until she fell asleep with difficulty and then, leaving only Paternal Aunt to watch over her, we all came out of the room to breathe a little.

Paternal Grandmother fainted again that night. She vomited the few spoonfuls of broth and herb medicine we had spooned into her mouth. From the next day, it was as if her consciousness was playing hide-and-seek in and out of her body like a playful urchin, and there was not a moment's rest for anyone in the house.

Grandmother struggled on for a week, though she had lost control of her body. On the night of the seventh day, the old lady who always thought more of the son away from the house than the son at home closed her eyes softly, like a spent candle flame quietly going out. It may be that in Grandmother's long life the happiest and proudest times were the few days she commanded and scolded the family with amazing vigor, without sleeping and eating, in rapturous expectation of her younger son's return—like the last radiant soaring of the candle flame before going out. On her deathbed, Grandmother held my hand and forgave me all my misdeeds. I also in my heart forgave her everything.

It was a long, weary rainy spell indeed.

A Pasque-Flower* on That Bleak Day

Park Wan-so

Born in 1931, Park Wan-so made her literary debut as late as 1970, after her fifth and last child began school and left her time for writing. Her mastery of the medium of fiction surprised readers from the first, and she has been a prolific writer since her late beginning.

She has a sharp, unerring penetration into her characters' mentality that lets escape no hypocrisy, attitudinizing, or self-deception. The subject of most of her stories is the everyday life of everyday people in the modern world. With surgical precision, she exposes the vacuity of prosperous middle-class existence, the enormous cost of maintaining mistaken values, and the unintentional cruelty of people toward themselves and one another. In her stories, the delight of the critic in exposure coexists with the humanitarian's pity and horror at the discovery. She has treated a wide variety of themes in her stories, important among them the meaning of the Korean War experience. "A Pasque-Flower on That Bleak Day" (1973) cannot be called a characteristic story of hers, but the bold succinctness of the conclusion bears the stamp of her directness and force.

---

*A Pasque-flower is called in Korean an "old woman flower," because it has very little attraction of any kind. The name of the flower, therefore, is often used as a simile for old women who have lost all attraction as women. [Translator]

Dallae was a village of innocent farmers.

I say "innocent" because they always earned their living by diligently tilling the land, and abided by those laws that all who call themselves human beings must abide by, regardless of whether anyone notices or not.

But the roaring of canon came even to this innocent village, which nests cozily in the lap of mountains. Considering that there was a violent clash in the adjacent town, the damage to this village was very small. The village itself had never become a battleground, and it had escaped bombing. The village people only knew by hearsay how houses collapsed into dust within the blink of an eye and frolicking children instantly turned to pieces of torn flesh.

The village people firmly believed that such a fortunate escape from injury was due to the grace of the mountain spirits of Dallaebong Mountain, to whom they offered sacrifices every year on the first of the tenth month by the lunar calendar.

But the number of war victims in the village was not much smaller than that of the neighboring village which had been a battleground and which had suffered bombing. There was a massacre each time the occupying government changed according to the fluctuation of the battle front.

Besides, early in the war young men joined the Republic's army as volunteers or were conscripted by the communist army; there were people who fled south as refugees, and some people were kidnapped to the North by the communists. The village population had shrunk by more than half. Well, those who left the village, for whatever reason, were all men, and in the village now remained only women. There were widows and there were grass widows; there were maidens and there were old women. Except for suckling babies there was not a single male in the village. All males who could walk had been sent away with fathers, uncles, or any distant relatives fleeing south for refuge.

Men were sacred beings who were entrusted with continuing the family line, and it was the women's duty to safeguard such sacred beings. Even though all duty and morality came to be disregarded and despised, this duty of women had become even more urgent and inviolable.

From the time there remained only women in this village the informing ceased, and consequently the killing ceased also. The command for slaughter had come from the elementary school building at the entrance of the village. According to whether the Republic's army or the communist army occupied the elementary school building, accusations were made against neighbors as communists or as reactionaries, and slaughter ensued.

But the women were not interested in who occupied the elementary school building. Whichever side occupied the building now, there were no more men to be killed off or conscripted, and no more property to be requisitioned. And of course they knew there were no benefits to be derived, whichever side the occupying army might represent.

Their only concern was how to remain alive until peace came and the men returned.

Spring was still far away, and barns were empty in every house. Administration was in a vacuum in this village, even though the elementary school building was still occupied by some army.

One day, there spread a rumor in the village that the occupying army at the elementary school was now neither the Republic's nor the communists', but that of the "big-nosed Americans."

Soon, big-nosed Americans began to saunter around the village, noisily chewing gum and peering into houses.

"Saxi have yes?* Saxi have yes?"

Whenever they spotted women they accosted them with such words, making lurid gestures. The horrified women hid deep in their houses. They trembled. The naked carnality that glowed on the faces of these big-nosed foreigners made them shudder. The big-nosed men seemed to be looking for professional prostitutes who catered to foreigners, but there could be no such prostitutes in this rustic village.

---

*"Saxi," in Korean, is a young or relatively young woman—in her twenties or thirties, or even early forties. The term is applied to any young or youngish woman who is or looks married. (In the old days, married and unmarried women were told apart by their hairstyle.) However, the word is sometimes used to designate "prostitute," really short for "tavern saxi." "Saxi have yes?" is the translation in the same word order of the Korean for "Do you have a saxi?" or "Is there a saxi?" [Translator]

Terror engulfed the village. After dark, the women were too scared to remain alone in their houses, and so they gathered one after another in the biggest house in the village.

That house was not only the biggest in the village but was also the village matriarch's. Although in troubled times the villagers might make accusations that led to the deaths of their neighbors, still this, like many other country villages, was a clan community.

As night deepened, the big-nosed men's cry of "Saxi have yes? Saxi have yes?" took on an urgent and threatening tone, like the wailing of beasts in heat.

The young wives and maids, sitting in a circle around the matriarch, stayed awake all night trembling. Even the next day the big-nosed men showed no sign of moving away.

It was night again. The big-nosed Americans went around, knocking on the gates, urgently wailing "Saxi have yes? Saxi have yes?"

"I'm afraid we won't be able to spend tonight in peace," the matriarch said in a parched voice.

"I'd bite my tongue and die first, rather than suffer defilement." A young bride who saw the outbreak of the war a few days after her marriage and lost her husband to the volunteer army a few days later spoke decisively, putting strength into her lean shoulder-blades.

"I'd die, too, by hanging myself from the beam."

"I would, too, even if I had to jump into the well."

All the women declared they'd die. They declared it heatedly, lest they be suspected of harboring secret wishes for rape by the big-nosed Americans.

The matriarch smiled weakly. "That's enough talk of dying, for young women who've got many decades ahead."

The wailing of "Hello, saxi have yes? saxi have yes?" approached nearer.

"I suppose I'll have to play saxi to the big-nosed men tonight," the matriarch said slowly and drily.

"You?"

The maidens and young wives who had vowed to preserve their chastity even at the cost of their lives, with faces solemn as stone monuments, instantly writhed, giggling.

"Come, Okhi, fetch your cosmetics." The matriarch did not giggle but commanded sternly. Okhi was her granddaughter, a bride-to-be, whose fiancé was at the front now.

"Are you growing senile?" Okhi was embarrassed, and gave her grandmother a jabbing and sideway stare.

"I'm not senile yet. Go and fetch your cosmetics." There was an irrefutable authority in her voice.

In peaceful times, the biggest festival in this village was the day of sacrificial offering to the mountain gods. On that day the men killed a sow and the women baked rice cakes. The women's work was always supervised by this matriarch, who always spotted at one glance the women who were menstruating or who had had intercourse the night before and excluded them from the preparations. At those times her entire body gave off indisputable authority, as if the safety and welfare of the whole village for the year ahead depended on her.

The young women now sitting around her saw the matriarch giving off the same authority as on the days of the village festival. That threw the room into solemn silence.

An elderly woman, however, dared object. "Ma'am, that's very generous of you to try to protect these young girls. But take a moment to think. The big-nosed Americans aren't blind. Cosmetics can't hide all your wrinkles."

The woman broke into giggles halfway through her words, and the other women also stifled their giggles.

"Don't waste any more words, but bring the cosmetics case quickly," the old woman's parched voice calmly commanded again, silencing the murmurs.

Okhi at last brought her cosmetics case, and the women's eyes by degrees lit up with curiosity.

As the cosmetics had been purchased for use on Okhi's wedding day, there was a complete set, although not of the most expensive brand.

"Now put make-up on my face," the matriarch commanded, pushing the cosmetics case toward a young woman who used to be well-to-do and wear very elaborate make-up on her pretty face before the war.

"Oh, what an absurd idea!" The young woman hesitated embarrassedly.

"Are you interested yourself?" the old woman interrogated maliciously.

"You *are* getting senile, aren't you?" the young woman protested hastily, and began to put make-up on the old woman's face with experienced hands.

The wailing of "Saxi have yes?" became more insistent. The lamp-light grew dimmer as the oil can was depleted. The old woman, leaving her face at the young woman's disposal, murmured as if to herself, "We can't tell the big-nosed people's age by looking at them, can we? It must be the same with them regarding us. Different races age differently. And that thing is bound to be done in the dark, anywhere or any time. Oh, yes, it's done in the dark." The old woman spoke more to assure herself than for anybody to hear.

The make-up job was completed. The old woman looked at herself in the mirror and smiled contentedly. Well, it was not so much a smile as a forced coquettish twitching of the mouth, and it cast a horror on all the women gathered there.

The scream of "Saxi have yes?" now reached the gate of this big house. The big-nosed men seemed to have perceived stirring of people inside, and they shook the gate like mad.

"Okhi, lend me your clothes, too."

The old woman changed into Okhi's flowing red skirt and yellow blouse. Then she wrapped her head with a colorful striped muffler.

The "Saxi have yes?" was by now a violent scream, and their kicking almost knocked the gates down.

"I'm ready now, so open the gate and give me away," the old woman said sharply and dryly.

Someone slid aside the crossbar of the gates. The gates opened wide. The other women shook with mingled thrill and shame, as when releasing water they could hold no more, and hid away in dark corners.

There stood the only saxi in the lamplight. A huge big-nosed soldier stepped in and lifted the saxi in his arms. But perhaps perceiving human presence in every dark corner of the house, he did not lay her down on the spot but strode out of the gates with her in his arms.

"Come on."

The other big-nosed soldiers who came in after him also went out of the gates. A jeep was parked not far from there. All through the trip the saxi sat submissively on the big-nosed soldier's lap, as light and yielding as a baby.

It was a short ride to the elementary school. The building was completely dark. But as the soldiers opened the glass door and the plank door, an incredibly strong light fell on the old woman. Simultaneously, there arose a shout of glee. The old woman crouched herself like a shrimp in the big-nosed soldier's arms and covered her face with both hands.

She was soon thrown on the bed. She collected herself by force of will and looked around the room through the fingers hiding her face. She wanted to see how many big-nosed soldiers she would have to entertain that night. Fortunately, there didn't seem to be more than five or six.

The huge soldier who had brought her in his arms began to undress her. The old woman was in despair. She knew that the Westerners were barbarians who did not observe the Confucian and Mencian rules of decorum, but she had never imagined that any human being could do that thing under a light brighter than day. She and her late husband had been a fond couple till they were in their sixties and had had no less than seven children, but they had never done that thing even under lamplight. The most light they had had was moonlight shining through the paper-paneled window.

The old woman desperately held on to her blouse ribbons and skirt strings. She thought no more of what her face looked like.

But she was as powerless as a fretting baby to stay the huge soldier's fingers. The big-nosed soldier stripped off her garments one by one as easily as he would corn husks. The old woman had thought that surely these men would turn off the light when taking off her undergarments. But alas! Her shriveled body was revealed under the light stronger than daylight.

Her breasts, which had nursed seven children, were pasted to the ribs, and her belly, cracked and wrinkled through repeated pregnancies and deliveries, was like a dried-up canal. These now were exposed under a light brighter than the midday sun's.

She gave up struggling and, hiding her face behind both hands, began to cry weakly.

Well, even though she had stopped struggling, the gray flannel knickers, the last item of her undergarments, clung to her hipbones, which were as lean as barren hills, and did not go down any further.

The woman thought, crying, that she had no choice but to bite her tongue and take her own life if that also came off and her private parts were revealed under the bright light, and thought how difficult a thing it is to take one's own life.

She hoped that the big-nosed soldiers would kill her with a bullet, without bothering to strip off that last item, as they must have discovered by now that they had been duped.

Suddenly, there arose a noise of merry laughter. In her miserable and desperate state, the old woman thought she had never in her life heard such heartily merry laughter.

Before the war, there had been many unfortunate events in the village, but also many happy events. The young people of the village often got angry, but they also often laughed. But however pleasant the occasion, in her compatriots' laughter there seemed to be some sediment of stale sorrow at the bottom of it, and the aftertaste of the laughter was very much like the aftertaste of sighs. To her knowledge, only babies could laugh such hearty, merry laughter as these foreign soldiers were laughing now.

Even in her miserable state, the woman began to steal glances at the big-nosed soldiers through the fingers of her hands covering her face. The big-nosed soldiers had all rolled off their chairs and were roaring with laughter, rolling on the floor and squeezing their sides.

Well, in the room there were only herself flung on the bed and the soldiers; the room was bleak and there was no amusing sight whatever. But the laughter was so merry that the old woman raised her crying voice, so as not to laugh along with the soldiers.

The laughter ceased at long last, and one of the soldiers pulled her up from the bed and put her clothes back on her one by one.

When the old woman had all her clothes on, the soldiers led her out into the dark. Her heart contracted, as she thought that they were leading her outdoors to shoot her.

But the soldiers put her in the jeep. And they loaded some heavy boxes in the jeep, too. They brought her to the big house they had taken her from, put her down in front of it, and unloaded all the boxes as well.

To the old woman, who stared in bewilderment, the big-nosed soldiers smacked their lips, repeatedly carrying their hands to their mouths in simulation of eating, and pointed to the boxes.

"Mama chow chow, okay? Mama chow chow, okay?"

The big-nosed soldiers got back in the jeep and drove off toward the elementary school.

On hearing the departure of the car, all the women in the house rushed out at once. The old woman quickly summoned her dignity and ordered the women to carry the boxes the big-nosed soldiers had left there into the house.

There was food in every box. There were canned fruits, canned meat, sweet preserves, fruits, milk, sweet and sour and fragrant powders, chocolates wrapped in silver foil, sweets, jelly, and crisp biscuits inside colorful boxes. The old and young women looked at them ecstatically, and hardly dared to breathe.

It was the old woman who, befitting her age, first recovered composure. She calmly recounted her adventure of that night and concluded thus:

"It was thanks to their being Yankees that I returned alive and even received presents. If they had been Japanese, they'd have shot me dead the moment they found out they were deceived. Oh, yes, they'd have killed me a hundred times over. And if they had been Russians they'd have raped me nonetheless, regardless of my age. Oh, yes, I'd have died crushed under their weight, and there'd have been no need for them to shoot me with a gun."

All the women gathered there completely agreed with her and shuddered.

Of course, neither the old woman nor any other woman in the village had ever set foot outside this country, and none of them had ever seen or become acquainted with any foreigners, whether Yankees or Russians. This was their first contact with any foreigner at all.

Nevertheless, the old woman pronounced such a confident dictum with a hundred percent certainty, and all the other women were unanimously of the same opinion. That much intuition into national characters is simply basic knowledge to anyone born in this land.

That Winter of My Youth

Yi Mun-yol

Yi Mun-yol, though still in his late forties, has been a reigning figure in Korean literature for almost two decades now. He has won both high critical acclaim and a huge popular following. But he has not always been so fortunate. In fact, he was extremely unhappy throughout his childhood and youth, his family having been put on the police surveillance list as the family of a communist defector to North Korea. So, he had to struggle against poverty and social prejudice, and he repeatedly dropped out of school for financial and psychological reasons. However, throughout his boyhood and youth he read voraciously, and his vast store of reading as well as his early sufferings became his great assets when he became a writer. And his vigor matched his creative fervor as well, as he has produced a dozen novels, several collections of short stories and two collections of essays, besides two ten-volume translations of classical Chinese epic novels and other writings. Like most serious Korean writers, he is concerned with the economic inequality and political oppression in Korean society and what they do to the human character and psyche. But his deeper concern is with the national heritage and how modern Koreans might cope with it. So, he is "must" reading for those who want to understand Korean culture and the mental apparatus of the contemporary Korean.

"That Winter of My Youth" is one of Yi's most poignant and personal stories. It is the first story in the trilogy A Portrait of My Youth, *which helped make him an idol of the younger generation in the early*

1980s. The narrator of this story may be regarded as an incarnation of the romantic nihilism that infected most educated Korean youths until recently. Having to struggle with doubts about himself, his distrust of the world, and his inability to change the world or make anything of himself all contribute to the despair, but the greatest cause is youth itself.

⁓

I can talk about that winter now. I am now the head of a family and an established member of my community, with a steady job at which I work in a respectable and serious manner. I am also over thirty and know how to control my emotions. And I have begun to feel ashamed of exaggerations and embellishments in writing.

That winter, exactly ten years ago, I was a "pang-u" at a tavern in a remote hillside town in Kyŏngsang Pukto. "Pang-u" really is a commonplace name in such remote places, but in those days it also served as a common appellation for a factotum.

Of course, it was not to work as a houseboy in an out-of-the-way rural tavern that I quit college and left Seoul.

At first, I went to Kangwŏn-do, with the idea of becoming a miner. In those destitute times, however, even mines weren't short of hands, and owners weren't eager to hire inexperienced strangers. After a while I was given a trial run in a private mine. The first day cured me once and for all of any wish to become a miner. Accidents in private mines are not rare even today, so you can imagine what they were like ten years ago. On my first day in the mine the tunnel collapsed and fell on two workers. I quickly gave up the thought of exiling myself in a mine. In those days I always carried, at the bottom of my small travel bag, a packet of chemicals powerful enough to extinguish my life within a few minutes, so my thoughts never strayed very far from death. However, the prospect of being buried alive in a mine had no attraction whatever for me.

Straying south from Kangwŏn-do, I first stopped briefly in a small fishing village on the east coast. I toyed with the idea of becoming a fisherman, but that wasn't easy, either. I hung around the pier of the fishing village, most of whose inhabitants used small wooden boats to fish in the nearby sea, but nobody so much as threw a glance at me. At last I summoned up the courage to ask a small steamboat owner to take me along. The man, who looked like a pirate, noted my white complexion and smooth hands and quipped, "Well, young master, I suggest you go back home to your books. That'd be better than retching up last New Year's casserole before sailing out a mile."

I had to give up. I started walking inland, without any set destination in mind. I remember the beautiful maple leaves and indigo-blue sky as I stubbornly trudged over a hill. After walking for five days through a totally unfamiliar part of the country, I arrived at that remote inn.

On the first night I paid for a room and supper with my last penny, and went to sleep pleasantly drunk, like one who had no worry in the world. But the next morning reality stared me in the face. I was penniless and stuck in a totally strange place. Out of desperation, I asked the proprietor of the inn if he knew of anyone in the neighborhood who needed a houseboy. He kindly hired me in his own establishment. The terms were that I would have my room and board in the inn, and get some pocket money now and then. I was in no position to negotiate, so I accepted without demur. Considering the rather easy nature of the work, the terms were not bad at all.

Before talking about what happened that winter, I guess I'd better say something about the state of my mind from the time I left Seoul until I reached the inn. I admit it was preposterous of me to think of becoming a miner or a fisherman. But there are psychological explanations behind even such outrageous behavior.

As I said earlier, it was not a rational decision that prompted my wanderings. It was a result of the fatigue and confusion I felt after two years of college life, and the emptiness and despair I experienced after the death of a close friend. The confusion, fatigue and despair became more and more oppressive, until I felt as if life itself was urging me to some decisive action. I felt I had either to throw away my life in order to be freed of the burden of life, or swallow the rest of the bitter cup in one gulp. My desperation may well have been excessive, but then, I was only twenty-one.

On the other hand, deep down in my consciousness I also had the optimistic hope that my desperation was something most people experience in their youth in varying degrees, and that my confusion and fatigue would some day be overcome and turned into valuable assets for my future. Perhaps it was to realize that optimistic hope that I thought of becoming a miner or a fisherman. I must have reasoned that my fatigue was owing to a long abuse of my brain with abstract ideas and vague speculations, and that the best way to give the brain a rest was to exploit the muscles. I must have hoped that I'd be able to come up with a way of sorting out my life once I gave my brains a rest with physical exertion.

At the same time, what drove me to such a rough mode of existence and mental desperation was an element of calculated self-flagellation that was akin to asceticism but not identical to it. In other words, I inflicted self-torture as a kind of penance that would cancel out my past mistakes and also mobilize my latent powers by creating a sense of crisis. I admit it was not really intended to bring me to a face-to-face encounter with life.

But these are all rational explanations that I came up with after the fact. At the time, I was conscious only of apathy and absentminded-ness. I strenuously avoided all mental and sensual stimuli and often sank into a silence and lassitude akin to idiocy. I think it was more my self-abandon than economic destitution that made me a factotum. If you like, it was also a very sophisticated strategy for coping with my then state of mind.

The inn and tavern I worked for was uncommonly large for the small hillside town. It accommodated travelers during ordinary times but at the special season turned into a high-class restaurant/salon with a host-ess in each of its nine rooms.

In those days remote hillside towns had neither electricity nor oil nor gas boilers, so my work at the inn consisted mainly of taking care of the oil lamps in each of the nine rooms, to make sure that they'd burn brightly and evenly throughout the night, and keeping the ondol floors warm all night.

My duties also included sweeping the large yard clean and carrying the liquor and food trays from the kitchen to the rooms, as well as fetching liquor from the brewery. But the diligent proprietor always swept the yard himself; the hostesses carried the food and liquor trays themselves; and the brewery had a delivery man who was a good friend of the inn people, which obviated the need for me to fetch and carry liquor barrels.

Still, even the simple work was difficult and time-consuming at first. It was hard work to make the nine lamp flasks sparkling clean and free of soot that had collected overnight. It took some practice to trim the wick so that it would be long enough to provide adequate light throughout the room and at the same time produce no smoke or soot. Splitting the logs brought over from a nearby forest to make enough firewood for the nine rooms was not light work, either. Moreover, on the days wet logs were brought, I had to dry the wood first with dried pine needles before feeding them into the ondol* stove. Often I had to work until midnight.

But one gets the hang of most any work soon enough. I mastered my tasks in less than a month. In fact, I rather enjoyed and took pride in my work.

I always felt purified after I cleaned the lamp flask of the soot that had accumulated during the night of intoxication and futile passion. When I dried the flask with a towel, after soaping and rinsing it, even my head felt clearer. And when I lighted the wick that I had trimmed with exquisite skill, I felt as if the translucent, neat flame was a work of art, a creation of my own ingenuity and devotion.

I felt the same way about heating the rooms. I was never greedy or fastidious about preparing firewood. I chose about six logs—three knotty and three smooth—from the lot carelessly deposited on the edge of the yard. Then I sawed them into one-and-half-foot chunks, and then, removing my jacket, split them with an ax in the afternoon sun.

It was a pleasure when the smooth trunk of a red pine was neatly split with one swing of the axe. And it was a rare delight when knotty and gnarled pines split neatly along the grain by my precise aim at the correct angle. What thrilled me most of all, however, was lighting the fire with the wood. I don't know how I looked to the people of the inn when I lighted the fire. I wonder if they knew I was performing a solemn ritual of fire worship.

Each evening, as the sun was about to go down, I lighted the lamps in all nine rooms and ate an early supper. Afterward, I carried an armful of firewood to each of the nine ondol stoves. Then, with some newspaper and a bottle under each armpit, I made my pilgrimage to my shrines. The bottles contained wine and kerosene. The wine came

---

*Rooms in traditional Korean houses have stone or cement floors, which sit on top of heating flues running the entire length of the room underneath. These are called ondol floors, and are covered with special flooring paper. [Translator]

from the jars in the kitchen. The proprietors didn't mind my drinking their wine. The kerosene, on the other hand, I purchased out of the pocket money they occasionally gave me in lieu of salary. It was to make my life easier by eliminating the headache of flintstones.

By the time I completed the tour of all nine shrines, the two bottles were empty, as were the pockets of my jumper which earlier had bulged with snacks to go with the wine. Drunk with the wine and also with the ritual, I went to the corner room that was allotted to me and stretched out on the bedding. Sometimes I returned to the kitchen to drink more wine, but most of the time I went straight to my room and either fell asleep immediately or gazed raptly at the flames that still danced before my eyes.

I am determined to study the theology of Zoroastrianism some day. It was the figures of the two gods of good and evil that I gazed at in pious silence each night before the nine stoves. I also beheld a solemn ritual of purification and sacrifice and glimpsed at something soaring up with new life in the midst of the combustion and annihilation. My peace and satisfaction, which made me feel I'd be content to go on like that forever, was no doubt owing to the mysterious magnetism of fire.

Now I must talk about that "season"—the season when the quiet country inn turned suddenly into a high-class restaurant/salon with nine clandestine chambers and half a dozen hostesses, and teemed with scores of customers every day. During the spring and the summer, the inn was patronized by stray travelers or legal clerks doing business with lumbermen or new teachers taking temporary lodging. When the autumn wind started to blow, however, that same inn suddenly came to life.

The flowerbed which had been neglected all summer was trimmed; the walls were newly plastered; and the gate and the posts received new coats of paint. The tattered and yellowed doorpaper was torn off to be replaced with crisp and translucent new paper, and even the wallpaper and floor paper were replaced. To top it all off, curtains were hung over the windows papered with Korean paper.

When the house was completely redone, the proprietor went as far as the provincial capital to fetch hostesses, and his wife went to the nearby A city to buy food. While the season lasted, no other customers except the special government employees called "inspectors" were admitted.

It must sound odd that so many hostesses and cartsful of foodstuff were needed to entertain a few government officials. It certainly seemed very odd to me at first. But I understood as soon as the season began. The inspectors were in charge of grading and weighing tobacco leaves, the main product of that region. At the time the inhabitants of the whole district numbered about ten thousand, and the income from the tobacco was as high as seven hundred million won. It was truly a colossal amount ten years ago, an indication that tobacco leaves were the lifeblood of the district's whole population.

Tobacco leaves were graded entirely by the judgment of the inspectors. Of course they must have had standards of their own for grading tobacco, but mechanical exactitude could not be expected. It was possible that the same tobacco leaves could be rated a grade or two higher or lower according to the subjective perception of different inspectors. And the difference could not be objectively proved or made to be accounted for.

That difference of one or two grades was what made the inspectors so important to the tobacco growers. Their entire year's toil could turn out to be profitless or amply rewarding, depending on the inspectors' evaluation. And there was a slight leeway in weighing and packing as well. Of course, each pack had to be of certain dimensions, but tobacco leaves could not be packed with uniform density. The same size packs could contain different amounts of tobacco. I heard that an inspector could make the difference of one hundred thousand won or more to an average farmer. As one semester's college tuition was fifty thousand won at the time, it was only natural that farmers would do anything to get into the good graces of the inspectors.

I suppose such practices have disappeared by now, but at the time there were two ways in which the farmers could bribe the inspectors. One route was through the tobacco growers' association representative. This was generally a less safe and less effective route, since the association had many members, and the practice might become known to others. The second route was through the proprietor of my inn; this was the surer and safer route and the reason the inn thrived each year.

I can still vividly recall the excited drinking parties where the inspectors were surrounded by giggling hostesses and fawning farmers. Two of the inspectors stand out in my memory as carrying on like emperors. I was astonished to learn at a later date how far down in the hierarchy they were as government officials.

Please do not misunderstand me. Even though they were arrogant and rude to me, and I felt considerable hostility toward them at the time, I am not writing this story to accuse them of corruption.

The hostesses naturally occupy the most prominent place in my memory. Some of them were beautiful and lovely, but they were all sad and pitiful. They came from all over. The proprietor fetched them from an employment agency in *D* city, but they came from all different places and had varying backgrounds. One of them came from an island in the south; another from the mountains of Kangwŏn-do; another had already had a career at an American military base; still another was a junior college dropout. Twelve hostesses in all passed through the inn while I was there.

On the surface their lives looked like gaiety itself. But the reality of their lives often brought tears to my eyes. In the early evening, after they had carefully made up and got dressed in colorful Korean costumes, they looked as beautiful as fairies. When they got pleasantly drunk and sang popular tunes excitedly or giggled merrily, they seemed born for pleasure. When I saw the girl who was the favorite of the two most dreaded inspectors taking out from the folds of her sock or out of her bosom the five-hundred-won notes the anxious farmers had tucked in there, I thought their job was not so bad.

But there was another side to their lives. Sometimes I caught sight of them being completely stripped and molested by the patrons. They had to drink as much liquor as their patrons offered them, in whatever mixture, so that after the parties they often threw up everything in their stomachs and were limp with exhaustion. And it made me wince to see their faces after they had washed off the makeup in the morning. Because of alcohol and cheap cosmetics, many of them had blue-green skin, and some of their faces were red with irritation.

None of them ate breakfast, and for lunch they ate hot and salty noodles or rice mixed with spiced vegetables. And then again none of them ate dinner because they had to consume as much wine and food as they could cram into their stomachs. That was almost a code of ethics with them—a code the bawds in the city had drilled into them. Many of them retched habitually from the constant abuse of their stomachs and livers.

Let me tell you a small incident. One day, we were about to begin our late lunch when one of the tobacco inspectors suddenly came in and asked for a young hostess named Kim. She was just about to eat her first spoonful of the rice mixed with spiced vegetables but stuck her spoon in the rice bowl and followed the inspector into a room. Returning about a quarter of an hour later, she took the spoon out of the bowl and slammed it down on the table. She muttered "Son of a bitch!" and her eyes were tearful. A few five-hundred-won notes peeped out from her sweater pocket, as if to mock her. I also put down my spoon, because my throat tightened.

One of the hostesses, a new mother who had left her infant behind to earn its keep, couldn't sleep on account of her swollen breasts; another hostess went to the penitentiary in *A* city every Sunday to visit her husband; another cried every night because she had left her younger brother with their stepmother. There was also a stupid woman who had burns and bruises all over her body but who cried with longing for the man who had abused her so whenever she got dead drunk. Such idiocy annoyed me at the time, but now I can only feel sorry for her.

Also engraved in my memory are the spending sprees of the farmers who suddenly became rich from tobacco farming. Before becoming tobacco planters they grew only millet or corn on the slopes, and were barely able to keep body and soul together. There were also lumber barons, who were formerly nothing more than tree robbers. They often got together in the back room of the inn to play mahjong for days at a stretch. Some of them had handled the mahjong pieces so much that their fingerprints were all but rubbed off. And then there were the reporters who swarmed in like flies smelling corruption—they were unpaid "branch managers" of local newspapers who made their living by blackmailing. But I won't talk about them any more. I am not yet in a position to judge or to commiserate with any of them, and this story is not about them.

At any rate, for a time my life at the inn was rather pleasant. What pleased me most was that I was living by using my muscles. I had been self-supporting before, but this was the first time that I supported myself through bodily exertion. It gave me an entirely new and interesting sensation.

What made life there the more satisfying was that there was nothing to excite complicated thoughts. I know I spoke about tobacco growers and inspectors and entertaining hostesses somewhat like a city desk reporter, but I was far from observing them in the manner of a social scientist. At the time they were nothing more to me than specters hovering outside my wall of apathy and indifference.

But the satisfaction could not last long. Before two months were over, I heard two conflicting voices from deep within my slumbering consciousness. One voice whispered in sinister tones: "You left your city and your school like one searching for enlightenment. You wandered here and there like a solemn ascetic. So, have you divined the true face of the emptiness and despair that drove you out? Have you gotten any nearer to that "resolution" that you so ardently sought to reach? Are you not rather covering up for your cowardice and irresolution by mistreating your body? Isn't the peace you have reached only a respite or evasion?"

And the other voice whispered gloomily: "Your search was brave and meaningful. You have refused to bow to worldly values and have sought your own. But it would be a waste of your youth and talent if you keep this up any longer. The smart kids are marching ahead at full speed, leaving you behind."

The two voices, which first came to me early one morning as I awoke from my drunken slumber with a keen thirst, became more and more insistent. And then, two local people also pressured me into putting an end to that aberrational mode of life. One of them was a new arrival there, a hostess named Yun. She seemed rather absentminded, and she was often seen scribbling in a notebook verses that looked like popular song lyrics. This girl somehow made me the subject of her literary imagination.

"You know, mister, I think you're a poet. I could see that at once. And you are from Seoul aren't you? And you went to college, too, right? I know. I was once in love with a man like you. We parted because we didn't want to hurt each other."

There was simply no curbing her literary imagination. She searched my knapsack while I was lighting the ondol stoves, and she sneaked out of parties to talk to me. She would get angry if I was unresponsive, and if I talked to her she would ask wilder and wilder questions. "Your father's the president of a big company, isn't he? And your sweetheart died of leukemia, right?" She positively drove me mad.

The other was an anvil-jawed and frog-eyed vice superintendent of the district police office. After seeing me once, he conceived an extraordinary interest in me. For my part it was a most unwelcome interest. He seemed to think that I was some sort of an important fugitive, whose capture would make his career once and for all. After answering his summons a few times I showed him my student ID, to set his suspicions to rest. But it had quite the opposite effect. He began grill-ing me with questions: How many times did I take part in demonstra-tions?; Did I ever engage in any anti-government activities?; What was my relationship with the ideological organization now on trial? It was quite unbearable.

So, I decided to leave. On the morning of my departure, frost shone on the boughs of the persimmon tree in the next house. I said good-bye only to the proprietor and left the town hastily. But I was to endure another farewell. When I had walked about a mile out of the village, someone called me from behind. Miss Yun was running up to me breathlessly. If I hadn't looked at her so coldly, she might have jumped into my arms. As it was, she only proffered me a small packet.

"Here. It's a handkerchief. I had it ready from the first. I knew you'd be leaving." Then, when she got her breath back, she added, in a desolate voice: "As a matter of fact, he wasn't a poet. He just used me and abused me, and ran away with all I had. But I said he was a poet because I wanted to love a poet. Will you remember me long?" Her eyes were wet as she said this. At that moment her eyes didn't look vague. Now that I think of it, she herself could have been a true poet at heart.

It was deep in winter. I walked on steadily until I came to the road running east-west, west inland and east to the sea. Strangely enough, it was the road to the sea I took. It was strange I chose the sea, as I was not born near the sea, nor did I have any meaningful connection with the sea. I wasn't thinking of becoming a fisherman any longer, either. And I was moving even farther away from home, too.

In my journal of those days, which I have saved till now, I had written that the sea beckoned me. It states, as a matter of simple fact, that the sea had been beckoning and alluring me for a long time. That makes me think that the voice I listened to was a voice urging me to desperate action.

I must have chosen the sea as the locale of my fatal decision—whether to smash or to swallow the bitter cup. Well, I was only twenty-one. One might say that at twenty-one no course seems too preposterous to take.

At any rate I walked toward the sea. The sea was only thirty miles distant on the map, but because the road ran along the steep Taebaek mountain range, it was nearly sixty miles to the sea by road. For me, who was flat-footed, it was a good three days' walk, but I stubbornly trudged along, dismissing the possibility of vehicular transportation.

At first my tread was heavy. Nobody heading toward such a momentous decision can be lighthearted. I recall that I even felt a tragic solemnity and a sinister foreboding that I might never walk the road again.

But my somber mood dispersed quickly enough. I drank a few glasses of wine with a late breakfast at the first roadside inn. Pleasantly drunk, I was soon excited like a boy setting out for an adventure in a strange place. I noted with pleasure how the road continually curved along nameless mountain slopes, the winter sky visible through the bare poplar branches, and the pungent smell of gasoline that accompanied the dust raised by passing vehicles. I even recited from memory the passage in Virgil praising traveling. "If I could decide my own fate, I'd choose a life spent in the saddle . . . "

I was a merry wayfarer that day. Whenever the cold wind made me sober, I drank some more at the next inn or store, and whenever I came to an especially beautiful spot, I sat down and enjoyed the sight until my sweat dried and I felt chilly.

I made all the fellow wayfarers, who walked by hurriedly on account of the cold, my traveling companions. I made myself into whatever kind of companion their attire and facial expression seemed to ask for, and delighted, surprised, and moved them. When I met a member of a rural branch of the opposition party, I presented myself as a student dissident fleeing the police. I moved him by telling him as my own the tales of students' struggle and suffering that I overheard, and delighted him with snippets from a radical essay I once read denouncing the paucity and stupidity of the government's agricultural policies. When he introduced himself formally and unfolded before me his grand political aspirations, I gave him as mine the name of a famous student dissident. He was so impressed with me that he pressed me to stay the night at his house, and I had a hard time begging off.

When I met a country bum, I impersonated a gangster from the backstreets of Myŏngdong. I intoned the names of famous mobster bosses and recounted anecdotes I remembered from a gangster novel as events I had taken part in. He was overawed. Luckily he didn't challenge me to a fistfight.

The deacon of a country church, a solemn farmer in his fifties, stopped my palaver by sternly denouncing alcohol as the great source of evil. I also walked a couple of miles with a factory girl coming home for the Lunar New Year holidays. She let on that she was a clerk at a company in Seoul, but I divined at one glance her fatigue and low wages. I also knew that if she couldn't find a marriage partner during the holidays, she would probably drift to a red-light district soon enough.

I shared a bottle of sake with a middle school teacher returning to his school to be on duty during the holidays. There was also an ox and cow dealer who bragged about the army lighter his son had brought back from Vietnam. . . . In short, it was a pleasant trip. I forgot why I was on that road and what awaited me at its end.

I didn't feel the least bit anxious to see the sun going down when I reached a small chapel at the bend of a low hill. I didn't expect to find an old castle and a feudal lord to give me a troubadour's welcome. Nor did I require a princess to extend her soft hand to me. After a few months of the wandering life my body had become accustomed to rough food and exhaustion, and I had become insensitive to the beauty of evening glows and the pain of solitude.

As I had expected, there was no inn in the mountain village. But that didn't scare me. In such a village, there was bound to be a house or two which provided a lighted room for youths of the village to make straw ropes together or play cards. It was not hard to beg a night's lodging at such a house. Village heads, whose salary amounted to no more than a few sacks of grain a year, were also generally hospitable to passing strangers. When such lodgings were not to be had, one could always go to the village cooperative building or the 4–H association building. They were usually unheated, but at least they shielded one from the wind and precipitation. At the time there were also military guard posts scattered all over the country in whose warm booths you could spend a night if you had a proper ID. So, it was not necessary to knock on a strange house for a paid accommodation. That night, I had had a leisurely dinner at a small eatery and was wandering around when I was stopped by a military police patrolman. That took care of my lodging problem. The young military policeman and the two village youths on patrol duty that night became friendly as soon as they learned my identity. They offered me liquor and gave up the warmest part of the floor to me. Even the lice crawling over my body the next day did not entirely obliterate my feeling of gratitude.

My good mood continued into the next day, even though my head ached and my stomach churned from having drunk several kinds of spirits. I set out early, after breakfast with a cup of warm rice wine at the boarding house of the young combat policeman. Although I had walked only about thirty miles the previous day, the soles of my feet were swollen. The pain wasn't unbearable, but I took off my jungle boots and covered the bottom with whittled shreds of laundry soap, which I had heard helped in such cases. Then I resumed walking, casting indifferent glances at the buses passing by raising whirlwinds of dust. If I hadn't run into a pale consumptive on the road, the journey would have been a pleasant one all the way, however solemn the objective.

As soon as I saw him I didn't like his pale face and his long unkempt hair. I didn't quite believe him when he said he had been loafing in his hometown for several years on account of his illness. I should have noticed his smooth white hands and the big bump on his middle finger, a telltale sign of a pen wielder. I must have missed such unmistakable clues owing to my hangover.

After casually sizing him up, I resumed my game of the previous day. As he gave off an intellectual and philosophical scent, I turned myself into a seeker after the truth. I began an oration on God and man, morality and value, and the world and being. Admiration showed on the face of my listener, as it did on all my road companions of the day before. Noting that, I went on with greater fervor.

Then, the admiration vanished from his face by degrees as my tirade went on. He kept listening attentively, but it was clearly mockery and contempt that were written on his face in the last few minutes before we parted. Sensing the change in his attitude, I became more and more fervent. At last, with mounting desperation, I began to talk about the books I didn't understand, and quoted passages from their introductions as my own interpretations.

I parted from him with a dismal feeling that admiration hadn't returned to his face. But it was a couple of minutes after we parted that I experienced the worst disgrace of my life. Hearing what sounded like a shriek I ran in the direction he had gone. But it was not a shriek. It was his suppressed laughter exploding in violent coughs. He was leaning against a rock, and his body was convulsing with laughter and coughing. His lips and palms were smeared with blood.

Finally sensing my presence, he muttered between spasmodic coughs: "I'm . . . sorry. I can't . . . help . . . laughing. Your philosophy lecture . . . was int . . . interesting. Although you misunderstood . . .

Heidegger . . . and you obviously haven't read . . . the Daily Language School."

I could have killed him. No words can express my misery of that moment. A tightrope walker who fell from his rope could not have felt such dire misery and shame. My face still burns when I think of that morning. And then and there I conceived an immitigable grudge against Heidegger and the Oxford school of daily language. I still can't bring myself to read them.

My journey for the rest of the day was gloomy. The wind grew mercilessly cold, and the sky brooded low. I was beginning to feel the futility and pitifulness of my wandering, and the sea became a real option for me. The sickly young man had shown me up for what I was.

I admired and longed for the legendary bravery of my senior school-mates who were student protest leaders, but I had neither their courage nor their convictions. Their attraction lay not in their ideology and will-power but in their glory and fame. When they were trampled and broken by merciless power, I gave up their way without any regret, carrying away only the husks of a few abstract ideas and exaggerated indignation.

My literary passion, too, was not altogether genuine. It was not the reality of beauty that I was in quest of. It was more the cheap applause and easy fame that the recitation of a verse on an evening of poetry reading, an essay published in a coterie magazine, brought me. I was no better than a phony.

It was true that I had read a thousand books by then. But can I really say it was in search of truth? It wasn't the fire of the pure idea that was burning in my bosom. No. In all honesty, I must say it wasn't. It was a mere boyish vanity, done for the sake of showing off before a crowd in a pub or in front of credulous ladies in a coffee house.

But I dared to claim that ideology had betrayed me, that beauty had refused my approach, and that learning gave me nothing. With my immature judgment I repudiated values, and I exaggerated my despair and emptiness. And at last I ruined everything by indulging myself in pleasures of the senses.

Tormenting myself with self-contempt, I walked on, oblivious to hunger and liquor. I was no longer conscious of the scenery, and didn't notice the passersby. It was no doubt because of my self-absorption that my first encounter with that man left so little impression on me.

Late in the afternoon of the second day I was walking on a small road running along a brook when my eye caught a thin stream of smoke rising from the side of the brook. Someone was absorbed in whetting something beside a fire. As I casually approached, I saw an old man sharpening a knife on a whetstone. A box with shoulder straps lay beside him. I could see knives of different sizes neatly arranged in the open box. Several whetstones and a small grinder lay on the ground beside the fire.

When I came within a few yards of him, the old man raised his head and examined the blade of the knife he was whetting. His face looked younger than I'd expected from his posture and grizzly hair. The knife emitted a blue sheen. It looked like a kitchen knife, only narrower and sharply pointed at the tip. He looked up from the knife at me. It was only a passing glance, but it was so piercing that it made me wince. The sharpened edge of the knife he was holding emitted an eery sheen, and his deeply furrowed face revealed murderous hatred.

Coming out of my self-absorption, I observed him more carefully. But he had already returned to being an ordinary knife-sharpener. The knife he had begun to sharpen next was an ordinary kitchen knife, a bit rusted. I left him sheepishly.

It was after walking about a mile farther that I realized why the knife-sharpener had struck me as being so odd. Most country houses have whetstones, so professional knife sharpeners rarely frequent such remote places. Moreover, there can hardly be a need to sharpen knives on a freezing cold day with melted ice beside a brook. But I was too preoccupied with my own problems to give the matter much thought. The sun was already setting, and Y town, enveloped in evening smoke, was awaiting my tired body.

It was a lonely evening. It was as desolate as my wedding night a couple of years later which I spent in a cheap inn comforting my sobbing wife. Y town looked as forlorn as my worn body and tired mind. Even though it was the county seat, it didn't have any street lights. From early evening the streets were quite deserted. The only sound was of the wind hitting the electric pole; not even a dog barked.

Although I had only little money left, I had no choice but to look for an inn. But there wasn't one to be found in the whole town. Giving up, I spotted a small Chinese restaurant and headed toward it. I was going to eat a simple supper there and ask for directions to an inn. Just as I was about to lift the dusty bamboo screen in the doorway of the Chinese restaurant, I heard someone calling me from behind.

"Yŏnghun? Could it possibly be Yŏnghun?"

I looked back in astonishment. A young woman was approaching in the semidarkness of the evening and peering at me in disbelief. I didn't think there'd be anyone I knew in that remote country town, but I couldn't help peering back at the woman.

"Oh, it really is you. I'm glad I called you, even though I didn't think it could be you," she said.

I recognized her, too.

"Whatever brought you here?" I asked.

"Oh, what else but the Board of Education? But what on earth brings *you* here?"

"Oh, I . . . I just . . . "

"Anyway, come to my place. Oh, it's starting to snow."

It really had begun to snow. So it was not just my gloom that made the sky look so threatening.

Walking together to her place, I recalled my memories of her. She was a member of my clan, and a few years older. My first and strongest impression of her came from an autumn day. I was a primary school student in my hometown, and she was a middle school student in nearby *B* city. It was a Saturday, and I was returning home late after playing at school till nearly sundown. On the road I met her returning home from *B* city.

I don't know whether she had been very fond of me before that day. Anyway, we walked hand in hand, and she plucked cosmos flowers from the roadside and tied them into a small bouquet. Then she gave me the bouquet with an affectionate smile. I stood there a moment dumbstruck and then ran away from her as fast as my feet would carry me. It was many years later that I realized that what dazed me so was her beauty.

Then, while staying home for a year after finishing middle school, from time to time I went to borrow books from her. She was a college student then. She had many books that were of interest to me.

Later, in my senior year in high school, I heard the rumor about her unfortunate love affair. The rumor was that she had fallen in love with a married man and ruined herself. My clansmen were furious because she was a college graduate and a rare beauty. But as a lad of nineteen I was having a difficult time in Kangjin and had too many problems of my own to give much thought to a distant relative.

"This is really unbelievable. How could they have put you in a place like this?" I asked, at the gate of the old traditional house she was rooming in.

"Well, a place like this needs schoolteachers, too," she responded lightly, but there was a trace of sadness in her voice.

"Well, go in and rest a bit. I'll fix dinner quickly. My roommate hasn't returned from her holidays yet."

Her room was more spacious and cleaner than I'd expected. And it was obviously divided into two parts, with an invisible line running down the middle. On one side was a steel cabinet and a low table, and on the other side was a formica chest of drawers and full desk. The books were different, too. On the low table was a three-tiered shelf containing sets of literary works and books and essays, and only a few hardbound books lay scattered on the desk.

"Which side is yours?" I asked, not wanting to trespass on her roommate's side of the room, even though I could guess.

"The side with the drawers. But the other side is warmer," she replied from the kitchen. Through the wall I could hear twigs breaking. She was obviously making the fire for the stove.

I leaned against the chest of drawers. It was warm on that side, too. My body, which had been frozen solid all day, thawed, and fatigue and drowsiness overwhelmed me.

"Hey, Hun! Wake up and eat your supper."

I must have fallen asleep. The room was lighted up and there was a meal tray in front of me.

"I think you'd better wash up before you go to sleep. You stink all over, you know," she said after we finished eating supper. "There aren't any public bathhouses nearby. I boiled some water, so you'll just have to manage with that in my kitchen."

Now that my hunger was appeased I just wanted to lie down and sleep, but I went into the kitchen. After I washed myself as best I could in the small kitchen, she stuck through the door a set of men's underwear. They were clean but not new. I took them but didn't feel like putting them on. Perhaps sensing my mood, she said through the door, "He won't come any more. I don't need them now."

Once again, the voice carried a hint of sadness. Not to awaken her sad memories, I quickly put them on.

"I hung your jacket and trousers outdoors. They seem to have lice. Whatever is the matter, really?"

"I'm utilizing my vacation to tour the country."

"That's not true. I heard that everybody's worried about you."

She seemed to have heard rumors about me.

"So what makes you wander around like a bum? Oh, I heard you can beat the devil in drinking."

"Will you buy me some liquor, so I can beat the devil?"

"I'll give you some. Anyway, aren't you going back home?"

She took a bottle of whiskey from her chest. In answer to my questioning glance, she said, "That's what he left behind."

"So you parted?"

"Yes. Probably forever."

After drinking silently for a while and beginning to feel drunk, I asked: "Was he a nice guy?"

"Yes. Very."

"Couldn't you have gotten married?"

"Strange you don't blame me like everybody else. We could have."

"Then why didn't you?"

"His wife died . . . "

"Then there was no hurdle. . . ?"

"It was a suicide."

I didn't know what to say.

"He emigrated with his two daughters. Last fall. Pour me a glass, won't you?"

She sipped the liquor slowly, like one carefully savoring its flavor. I asked, becoming vaguely sentimental.

"What're you going to do now?"

"I'm not going to wander aimlessly like you."

"Then why did you come to this place?"

"I chose this town because I wanted a quiet place to study. I'm going to graduate school next spring. And I know what I want to specialize in."

I looked at her in silence.

"Ethics."

"Are you really all right?"

"You'd like to tell me that studying is no answer to the problems of the heart?" she said, looking at me with her deep eyes. "Do you think it'll only be an escape?"

"I hope not."

"Don't worry. There's no purer or more violent passion than despair. People become unhappy because they try to evade genuine despair. You, too, I'll bet."

I had no defense for myself.

"Go back to school. Go back to the youth of twenty-one that you are."

"That's what I'm going to do."

"Go back, read more books, and do some more thinking. I think you'll be able to face despair without paying the price I paid."

We emptied the bottle as we talked intermittently. Her cold reasoning began to crumble little by little. Even though she was later able to control her emotions sufficiently to go on to complete graduate school and teach in college, that night she was still a young woman suffering from unhappy love.

When I came back with a new bottle from the store, there were traces of tears around her eyes. That aroused the sadistic impulse slumbering deep in my unconscious mind.

"You've been crying," I said roughly, gulping down the liquor.

"It's a woman's privilege," she said weakly. She looked much older than just a while ago. That incited me.

"Why don't you get married?"

"Maybe I will."

"I suggest you have five children."

"Not a bad idea."

"And grow old."

"Sounds fine."

"And then die."

"Okay."

I don't remember the rest. We might have sobbed together, or sang some sad songs together. Then we dropped off to sleep, without even bothering to spread the bedding. It's a sorry tale to tell.

It was almost noon when I woke up the next day.

"Come, look at this snow! There's at least eight inches of snow piled up in the yard!" She cried from outside.

The room was put back in order. Her voice and face were also calm. There was no trace of her emotion of the night before.

"I don't think you can leave now. This place is surrounded by peaks, so all traffic comes to a stop even with a little snow. There's no way a car can move through this snowfall," she said to me as I spooned into my bitter mouth the soothing soup she'd brought.

Through the open door I could see huge snowflakes whirling around. The room felt warm and cozy, and I felt tempted to accept her sisterly invitation to stay. But I was stubborn about leaving.

"I'm going to walk, so I guess I'll leave."

"What a strange kid you are. Why do you court hardship like that? Do you have an appointment with the sea or something?" She scolded my rashness as would a real sister. But I was obstinate.

"It's ten miles to the peak, and another ten miles to cross the peak. You're gambling with your life." She gave up trying to detain me and said good-bye at the entrance to the village.

The world seen from the mountain road was entirely snow-covered. The steep ridges and the sharp peaks, the meager fields and the villages along the road, the aged poplar trees and the electric poles painted with tar—all these looked diminutive and lonely, covered with snow. Snow kept falling. My swollen feet were killing me, but I hurried on. I wanted to cross Ch'angsuryŏng Peak that day.

The villages disappeared before long, and I was all alone in the snow-covered world. Snow kept falling. That night, I wrote in my diary, "Is mine the passion of an idiot? Or the madness of youth? I trudged through hills and fields in knee-deep snow. This village is Changp'ung, lying at the foot of Ch'angsuryŏng. I walked all afternoon, but it is only five miles away from *Y* village. I ate my supper with the kindly village head and am now lying in the village hall. The soles of my feet hurt, and my whole body aches.

"But will any of this be of any avail? There is no guarantee that my physical pain will nourish my soul, nor any indication that the sea I'm running toward like a madman is waiting to give me a revelation. I am just running as my heart commands. I wonder, how much longer is this winter of my soul going to last?"

The snow kept falling till the following morning. While eating breakfast at the village inn, I heard on the radio that that was the heaviest snow in thirty years.

Even though the breakfast was much too expensive, I felt a lot more up to braving the weather after the full meal. I had good appetite, since I hadn't drunk the night before. Before setting out again, I got some straw rope to make shoulder straps for my travel bag, and I bound my feet and my boots together with rubber straps.

Although there was already almost two feet of snow on the ground, snow kept falling. All vehicular traffic had completely ceased. The villagers strongly urged me to delay my departure. The landlady of the inn told me to my face to be careful not to freeze to death. But I didn't mind.

Fortunately, it stopped snowing shortly after I left that village. I forged ahead, pushing through snow that came up to my knees. Because I couldn't tell the road from the field on account of the drifting snow, I had to rely on the poplar trees to keep me on the right track. My boots and trousers got soaked quickly, and in time even my upper garments were wet. Because of the mild temperature following the snowfall, steam rose from my whole body.

I must have walked a mile or so. Suddenly, the snow-covered Ch'angsuryŏng blocked my way like an unvanquishable giant.

We tend to remember for a long time things that make a deep impression on us. I still remember vividly the Ch'angsuryŏng that I beheld that day. But memories are prone to distortion and exaggeration. Rather than trusting my fickle memory, I will rely on my journal entry for that day. The journal is written roughly and my conclusion is hasty. And it is filled with excitement throughout. But I think it gives a more truthful representation of my feelings than any account I can give from memory:

"Ch'angsuryŏng. Two thousand and three hundred feet above sea level.

"Oh, I have seen the true face of beauty. I will never be able to forget the three hours I spent crossing Ch'angsuryŏng. Other, world-famous peaks could not move me as did Ch'angsuryŏng. If such a thing as perfect beauty is conceivable, that conception is embodied in Ch'angsuryŏng. Oh, Ch'angsuryŏng is awesome because it is beautiful. It is sublime because it is beautiful. It is holy because it is beautiful.

"I will never forget the magnificence of the snow-covered peak. Nor the mystery of the valley which looked bluish from its shadow. Nor the tragic beauty of the red pines whose boughs break from the weight of the snow. Nor the commanding presence of the oak tree whose branches shone in the sun with melted snow. Nor the elegant form of the larch which stood like a bride, veiled by the snow. Even the arrogant and challenging juniper stood modest and small.

"The creeping vines that covered ash and hazel trees like dark veils, and the fragile beauty of the azalea and scouring rushes, only whose tops rose above the pile of snow . . . I was thrilled through and through when passing a grove of bush clovers. The dark stripes of their branches made a sharp contrast against the white snow! What artist could create such striking yet elegant, lofty yet not forbidding beauty only with white and black?

"The sky had cleared in the meantime, and the sunshine was more dazzling than usual. The winter sky looked the more clear and fathomless because it was such a light blue. Illuminated by the sun, the distant Taeback range shone sublime and mysterious.

"It seemed as if even the birds were avoiding that peak and that the wind too made a detour. In the absolute stillness, accompanied only by the music of the spheres, I moved silently, trying to suppress even the sound of my breathing. Because my feet were swollen and sore, I walked barefoot more than half the way, but I scarcely even felt pain, so awed was I by the magnificence of the peak.

"On reaching the foot of the hill, I almost burst into tears. The ecstasy I felt then! Nobody can understand the ecstasy I felt at the moment. It was the true nature of beauty. Aestheticians might be inclined to dispute it, but at the moment I not only perceived but understood the true nature of beauty.

"Beauty is the beginning and end of all values, and the sum total of all ideas. At the same time, it is an absolute void. Truth owes its being to beauty, and beauty to truth. Goodness owes its being to beauty, and beauty to goodness. Holiness owes its being to beauty, and beauty to holiness. While beauty itself has no property, it is open to all values and endows and permits all ideas. That is the reason for beauty's greatness.

"My wanderings were all for this one moment."

But my elation suddenly turned to dark despair before I got past the hill. In spite of all my irresolution, I had had a premonition from early on that I was going to have a literary career—that my life would be devoted to the creation of beauty. Despite much theorizing about beauty and some practice in its pursuit, I had been hesitant to name beauty as the object of my life.

What turned my elation to despair was the realization that the other face of beauty is divinity, a perfection no human being can ever attain. I reasoned that Man is a puny castaway on this earth, and whatever he creates can be no more than a very imperfect imitation. Therefore the life I was likely to lead was no more than a step toward imperfection. It seemed stupid and rash to live a life destined to end up in imperfection.

Suddenly, mental and physical exhaustion overwhelmed me. Physically, too, I was exhausted. Even though I had walked only a couple of miles that day, I had been overexerting myself for the past few days, and that morning I had crossed a steep hill through more than two feet of snow. As I had walked barefoot for more than half the way, my feet were frozen numb. The small travel bag hanging on my back felt ten times heavier than its actual weight.

At last I was forced to give up going any farther and knocked at the first inn I came upon. I meant to thaw my feet and have a bite of lunch. Luckily, the warm room of the inn was devoid of customers.

As I was finishing up the instant noodles I ordered for lunch, someone stepped in. It was the knife-sharpener I had seen two days ago beside the brook. His wet trousers and soggy feet indicated that he, too, had crossed the peak through the snow.

With an inexplicable feeling of gladness, I welcomed him. But without so much as a glance at me, he ordered a bowl of instant noodles and a bottle of soju, after which he stretched out on the floor, putting his feet on the doorsill. I felt rather snubbed, but it didn't make me angry. I thought of trying again to draw him into conversation but decided to observe him closely instead.

I was wrong to take him for an old man. In spite of his bushy beard and deeply lined face, he could be no more than fifty. It was on account of his gray hair that I took him for an old man.

He never once looked at me. He kept staring at the ceiling with desolate eyes, and when the food came ate it in silence, squatting on the doorsill. After buying a few packets of instant noodles from the innkeeper, he put them and the half-emptied soju bottle in his box and set out on his way without a word.

His appearance distracted me for awhile but I soon forgot about him. The true face of beauty that I beheld on Ch'angsuryŏng Peak and my despair about ever reaching that perfection soon oppressed me again. I felt like a gambler who had been deprived of his last card. *Now what can fill the empty cup of my life?* It was from such gloomy thoughts that I turned to liquor again. I called to the discontented innkeeper who had been hovering in the yard and asked for a bottle of soju. The liquor had an instant effect on an empty stomach. When I had drunk about half the bottle, the pain in my feet disappeared completely, and by the time the bottle was emptied I was quite drunk. My gloom had almost disappeared, too. I asked for one more bottle. Even now I dread getting sober when I begin to feel drunk. That day, I had all the reason in the world for not wanting to sober up. I must have lost myself in drunken elation.

But a sudden thought pulled me out of that inebriation. When the second bottle was almost empty, it occurred to me that the knife-sharpener was also going to the sea. That thought eventually turned into a conviction, at which point I felt an urge to overtake him. Somehow, it seemed that I had to reach the sea before him, or my whole quest would have been in vain.

I hurriedly emptied the bottle and set out on my way. The fatigue and the pain in my feet were completely gone by now. The winter sun was already on the horizon. The icicles hanging from the thatched roofs of the houses on the roadside looked like crystal ornaments.

But I was not to go far that day. In the second village from the inn I met a group of merry young men, all of my age, who were on their way back from a rabbit chase. One of the two wild rabbits, which couldn't elude the chasers because of the deeply drifting snow, was still alive. Whether from drunkenness or because of the setting sun, I joined them. I think I offered to buy them the drinks to go with their wild rabbit barbecue. And they accepted without hesitation.

The drinking party was held at the 4–H club building of the village. But wild rabbit meat wasn't as tasty as I had expected and, as I was already drunk before the party started, I couldn't help them finish the two bottles of soju. After a couple of rounds and introductions all around, I fell asleep.

It was purely on account of the bitter cold that I woke up from that deep slumber at dawn. The room, which had been heated with several armloads of split logs the night before, had cooled to iciness. And the draft was merciless. A cutting wind was rushing in through the torn doorpaper.

The disorderly table was there, but the youths were all gone. It was a little after 4 A.M.

I looked around for something to shield me from the atrocious wind, but in the dim lamplight I could see nothing that would be of any help, not even a straw sack. I thought of going to any house in the village to ask for a few hours' shelter, but I could not see a light in any direction. It was too dark and too early to set out again, even though the snow provided faint visibility. To appease my burning thirst I packed and ate some snow, but that made me freeze from the inside as well, so I came back into the room to wage a desperate battle against death by freezing.

It was the terror of death that I felt even more urgently than the cold. Feeling a very real need, I wrote my will, blowing on my frozen hands. I don't have that ridiculous document with me, but I clearly remember some of the passages I wrote with tragic intensity.

Written to my childhood best friend, it began with "If." I wrote that death had been with me for many months past, but that death had always been an idea and an alternative, not something as wretched and concrete as this. I wrote that though it was true I engaged in a sinful game of ideas, it was always in the darkness before dawn, not on the threshold of dawn as I then was. And I reminded him how I had loved life and the world in the past.

I suppose I was trying to make it clear in the letter that I was not committing suicide. People have a strong prejudice against that unhappy mode of death. Even when someone has chosen death for an understandable reason, people always believe their own preposterous speculations or scandalous fictions over the more laborious explanations of the deceased. As the dead cannot talk back, these wild surmises go unchecked. I cannot hope to be an exception to that rule. And I won't be the least bit responsible if they attach momentous significance to my death. Such must have been my feelings at the time.

I went on to ask my friend to get rid of my prolific literary scribbling of the past year. I also asked him to compensate my friends for the financial losses I caused them because of my drunkenness and bravura. I enumerated all the damages I deemed myself responsible for. Then I asked him to join his pious sweetheart in praying for me.

Dawn broke as I completed writing that long-winded and hollow document with my frozen hand. I pushed it deep into my travel bag and set off down the road.

It was still not bright enough for a safe journey, but I could discern shapes. As if to make it harder for me, it began to snow again. And it was not feathery flakes as on the day before, but mixture of snow and sleet borne on a merciless wind. The only luck I had was that the wind was blowing against my back instead of in my face.

At first I thought I'd find an inn, warm myself a little and eat something, and then set out in earnest. But the village didn't wake up from its deep slumber until I had walked quite a way past it. I had no choice but to hope to find an inn in the next village.

The world was strange that morning. Except for the trees moaning in the wind, there was no sign of life anywhere. The fields, buried deep in a fresh quilt of snow, were literally a sea of snow. The road was a white river, distinguishable only by the trees lining it on both sides. Strangely enough, there were footprints on the river of snow. But they drew my attention just momentarily. I was almost beside myself from the unbearable cold.

Once out of the village, I began to run. First of all to shake off that horrible cold. On an ordinary day I could have built a fire with dried twigs, but in that world where everything was buried under more than two feet of snow, running was all I could do to try to make myself warm.

The snow had frozen and hardened during the night, so I didn't have to wade through knee-deep snow as I did the day before. After I ran awhile, my frozen body thawed a little and my breath came out in white mist.

But when the cold abated a little I felt excruciatingly hungry. Not only did my stomach churn, but my whole body became constricted with hunger. I regreted having neglected food in favor of liquor during the past three days. On the previous day I had only one proper meal in the morning, and for the rest of the day I ate very little and drank too much. Unable to stand it any longer, I stopped to pack and eat some snow, panting wildly. It stung my stomach, and only made me colder.

I began to run again. I raced on, with all the speed that my body, driven to the brink of death by cold and hunger, could muster. The trees lining the road flew past me as if I were looking at them from a speeding vehicle. I had the illusion that I was flying. But in reality my steps were growing heavier and my feet were dragging along the ground. It was only much later that I realized that I had traversed less than half a mile while running for what to me seemed like an eternity that morning.

My hunger and cold disappeared. My consciousness grew intermittently dim, and drowsiness began to attack me. The thick layer of snow lured me like a fluffy warm quilt. Repeatedly I had the urge to just sink into the bed of snow and drop off to eternal slumber. I could barely make out the road. All I could see was one big sea of snow. I trusted my instincts to carry me forward.

I don't know how long I went on in this way. Suddenly I heard in my dim consciousness someone shouting at me.

"Hey, you. There's no road on that side. Come this way."

I woke up and looked around. I had wandered off the road and veered into a rice paddy.

"This way." The voice said again. With my dim eyes, I scanned the direction it came from. I saw a bonfire first, and then a covering on stilts that looked like an orchard shed. Lastly I saw the figure of a man. My senses returned gradually. I ran toward the fire with my last ounce of strength. The figure turned out to be that of the knife-sharpener.

"You shouldn't have set out in this weather," he said with a dry voice, as he prepared a cushion of millet stalks for me to sit on. I flopped down and almost threw myself on the bonfire.

"Be careful. Your hair will catch fire," he said a little less dryly, pulling me back to save my hair. But the meaning of his words didn't register in my brain. The unbearable cold renewed its attack on me, and I could do nothing except to drink in the warmth of the fire with my whole body, like a thirsty man gulping down water.

"Pull in your legs. Your clothes are on fire." He said, rubbing out the fire on my trouser leg, his voice quite warm now.

"You've got to eat something," he said when I had collected myself somewhat, and he took a soot-stained pan out of his box. Building a makeshift stove beside the bonfire, he put packed snow in the pan and made a fire under it. He put snow in a few more times until water filled half the pan, and then took out a packet of instant noodles from his box.

I recovered my senses fully only after cleaning the pan of every bit of noodle and every drop of soup. All the while he just watched me in silence.

"Thank you so much," I said rather sheepishly.

"You have to pay me for the noddles," he said, his voice dry again. I hastily took out all the money I had left and proffered it to him.

"Not so much," he said, picking up one 500-won note and giving me four 100-won coins in return. There was such authority in his gestures that I didn't dare offer him more.

"Well, what made you set out so early in this weather?"

He spoke rather casually, as I nursed my burned palate. I felt flustered. I wondered if the man could understand my reasons if I explained them to him. But I felt I could not tell him a lie. So I told him

as truthfully and simply as possible where I was going and with what
end in mind.

"That was my guess. There are always absurd reasons behind absurd acts. A fishmonger would never have set out for the port at such
an hour on a day like this," he said, and added, with a smile that might
have been a self-mockery, "We'll do opposite things when we get
there."

He seemed to have intuited my true purpose. I didn't quite like the
implications of his words.

"Are you going to Taejin as well?"

"That's the nearest sea from here."

"Well, what do you mean we'll do opposite things?"

"I mean I'm going there to kill, and you're going there to die," he
said quite matter-of-factly. I, on the other hand, felt a shiver run
through my body.

"Kill who?" I asked, stupidly.

He looked at me, with the sharp look of a detective. His lips twisted
into a sarcastic grin.

"The temptation to trust is the risk of betrayal. Anyway, you owe
your life to me."

"What do you mean?"

"I mean I feel like trusting you. I feel like telling you my story."

Then he asked, before I could get over my bewilderment, "How old
do I look to you?"

"Well, about fifty?"

"So I look exactly ten years older than my real age. It's on account
of those accursed nineteen years."

"What nineteen years?"

"I'll tell you about those nineteen years." He said but hesitated a
little before he began. He made up his mind pretty quickly, however,
and began his story in the absorbed tone of one delivering a soliloquy.

"We had dreams then. Magnificent and dangerous dreams for the
cause of liberty and equality. So did many of our generation, but ours
were more extreme. We bought nitric acid and glycerin, mimeo-
graphed handbills, and sharpened knives. Except for our leader, we
were all youths of about twenty."

I could only listen in silence.

"Then a clever one among us awoke from the rash dream. He informed the police. The one who killed himself just before the arrest

was lucky. The rest of us were soon arrested, tortured, and tried. Our leader was sentenced to death, I and another received life sentences, and the rest got ten and fifteen years each. That was just before the outbreak of the Korean War. The only reason we were not killed when the war broke out was that we had no connection with the communists."

I was listening intently.

"What sustained us in prison was our hatred toward the traitor. What tormented us more than the shattered dream and the frustrated ideal was the sense of betrayal. We vowed revenge. And the symbol of our revenge is this knife. It was made by one of us, who learned ironwork in prison."

He took a knife out of his box. It was the knife I saw him sharpening beside the brook on the day I first saw him.

"The one who got the lightest sentence of ten years had it commuted to seven. He left the prison with this knife. The traitor was not easy to find. At first he looked for him earnestly. But by and by he made his way back into the world. It was relatively easy for him, as he had been shut out of it for only seven years. He soon got a job, earned money, and became the head of a family.

"When the second one left the prison after eleven years, the first one was already living a comfortable life. He turned the knife over to the second one with many apologies."

I grew more and more involved as the story went on.

"The second one was no better. Before the end of two years he came to see us at the prison and told us he would like to turn the knife over to the next one.

"He couldn't turn the knife over to the third one. The third one was serving a life sentence like me, but he became terminally ill. He died soon after his release.

"The knife was finally turned over to me, freed after nineteen years. That was last March. I'm not like my former cronies. For me, a man of forty who had spent nineteen years in prison as a political prisoner, returning to society isn't easy. I followed the traitor's trail thoroughly. Posing as a knife-sharpener, I was able to carry this knife legitimately, and I was also able to earn my keep. And I am now at the end of my chase."

"Then he's in Taejin?"

"Yes. He didn't thrive, either. He was hired as a policeman as a reward for betraying us, but he was soon kicked out on bribery charges. His life has been a series of disasters, and he's now a fisherman in Taejin operating a small boat."

He stopped his narration and looked me over once more. Then he said, "Well, don't you feel like informing on me to the police?"

His lips twitched into a mocking smile again. Then he clamped his mouth shut, as if regretting having told his innermost secret to a passing stranger. He didn't say a word again until we parted. It was after it had stopped snowing and the day had completely brightened that we left the shed. After walking about two miles together in silence, we parted at the junction of the road near the entrance to the town.

"You'd better put some distance between me and yourself; otherwise you could be letting yourself in for some unwelcome interrogations," he said dryly, and strode ahead. I gazed at his back like one struck dumb, forgetting even to say good-bye.

That winter was now drawing toward its last chapter. It was nearly two o'clock in the afternoon when I arrived in Taejin. I had tarried about an hour in *I* town to dry my clothes and to rest a little, as snow and sleet had begun falling again.

Taejin was no more than a squalid little fishing village at the time, even though it is now a thriving swimming beach, one of the few in Kyŏngsang Pukdo. The small deserted fishing port in the depth of winter felt eery.

I don't think the last half mile to the sea was easy, either. I find the following words written in my sleet-stained diary of that day:

"Oh, sea! I have come to you at last. There was no disobeying your sudden call.

"For the past few days you beckoned me in many guises and called to me in many voices. I saw you even in the face of the lowering sky and through the scudding snow, and heard your voice in the whistling north wind and the wailing trees. Your call rang in my ears even in sleep, dreams, and drunkenness.

"So I came. Not even the heaviest snow in thirty years, nor the roadless peak, could stop me. The sixty miles through freezing cold, snow and sleet did not deter me. My feet are swollen with frostbite and sores, and my face burns as if on fire.

"The last half-mile to your presence was torture itself. The great void all around. The sea wind mixed with snow and sleet mercilessly lashed at my body. Snow falling on my face and neck ran down my body, and my jungle boots were frozen on the outside and soggy inside. My hair stood stiffly on end. Its frozen roots stung my scalp. But I am here, like a faithful dog answering its master's whistle at whatever cost.

"Now tell me. Say why you called me. I am listening with my whole being."

I stood there on the shore silently for a long time. The ferocious sea wind kept whipping the rocks and clawing the sands. The mist rising from the breaking waves and the white snow scudding out of the darkened sky enveloped me like a haze. Oh, I can still see it all too vividly: the mad sea, the dark horizon, the lonely gulls and their doleful songs, and my puny, squalid self.

My silence that afternoon may have been a trance. It may have been a trance in which I expected to have a mysterious communion with the sea. I was praying to hear the answer to my question, which had been formed a long time ago, and which, although it seems preposterous now, was most urgent at the time and couldn't be resolved without some mysterious revelation or intuition. I was waiting for the sea to decide for me whether to throw away the bitter cup of life or to gulp it down.

But the sea was intent only on roaring, and I could make no sense of its thunder. Oh, tell me. Answer me. I approached the water, like one beseeching an answer. The surf washed over my feet and thawed them. Soon, waves lapped up to my knees and staggered me.

I stopped to recover my balance and listened, watching the darkening sky and the wild writhing of the sea. On the seething water not far away from me, a few gray seagulls were resting their tired wings.

I closed my eyes. I felt a faint gleam radiating from the depth of my consciousness and spreading through my whole body. I felt as if the mysterious counsel of the sea was about to reach me, with the long-sought answer to my question.

I waited for that counsel to become more clear and distinct.

It went on like that for quite awhile. But it was a hard blow on my thigh and the dreadful sound of the waves hitting against the rocks that woke me up from my reverie. Then a small incident caught my eye. Did I see wrong? I thought I saw a small gray gull which had been resting on the water not far away being swallowed up by a mountainous wave that broke over it suddenly. The gull fluttered its wings once but did not rise again. Even in my dreamy state I prayed ardently that the small bird would rise again. But it didn't. Instead, the rough waters that had swallowed it pounded my waist and knocked me down.

I think I left myself purely up to my instinct then. Despite the lure of the sea which felt oddly warm, I pulled myself up to the beach with all the strength I could muster. My survival instinct, stimulated by that momentary crisis, suddenly flared up with a fierce flame.

That flame of my libido was fierce but at the same time tragic and gloomy. It illuminated my figure, which was as puny and exhausted as the small gull just swallowed up by the waters. My pitiful being was afloat on the vast sea of annihilation and despair!

Then the sea's roar suddenly seemed meaningless, and its undulations looked like the senseless movements of inorganic matter.

"I'll go back. It's about time I put an end to this desperate game. The sea, too, is an imposter, like all the others that seduced us till now. How can anything save us, we whom even the Gods have given up for lost?

"But gulls should keep on flying and life should go on. When the gull gives up flying, it isn't a gull any more. When a human gives up breathing, he is not a being any more. We must drain our portion of the bitter cup of our being.

"Despair is not the end of being but its true beginning."

That was the conclusion I recorded in my sleet-stained diary that day. But, in spite of the decisive tone of my conclusion, I don't think I overcame my emptiness and sorrow that day. Despair cannot be overcome by a rational decision alone. I remember crying for a long time that day, while leaning against a rock.

To be honest, I have never yet so thoroughly steeped myself in despair as to make it the springboard of my life. But I can say that the despair I recognized on the shore that day liberated me.

If an objective and absolute value cannot guide us, then our redemption is left for each of us to work out. If we are not to dedicate our lives to an external object or being, then each of us must find his or her own mode of inner fulfillment.

My cousin was right. Despair is the purest and the most violent passion, and the starting point of redemption. The recognition of that enabled me to make the decision about my life. I chose beauty as my value. It was owing to the experience I had on Ch'angsuryŏng Peak.

I believe that a truly artistic soul must make the despair of ever attaining perfect beauty the starting point of his pilgrimage. He is a great artist not because he had created beauty, but because he dared to pursue, fight for, and shed blood for it, knowing all the while the impossibility of its realization. That goes for this story as well. If this story has any value, it is not because of its imperfect representation of the truth and beauty of that winter, but because of the nights of agony and exhaustion I spent striving toward that imperfection.

It was after my sorrows and emptiness had subsided to some extent that the knife sharpener appeared before me again. Sensing a human presence even amid the fierce roar of the sea and the wind, I looked around. He was standing on the other side of the rock I was leaning on.

He looked tired and shabby. His box lay beside his wet feet, like a weapon abandoned by a defeated soldier. He was gazing intently at the sea, absorbed in his own thoughts.

He didn't seem to sense my presence. I approached him with a tender feeling. I came within a few yards of him, but he was still unaware of my approach. Not wanting to disturb him, I stopped there. After a few more minutes of self-absorbed immobility he turned toward me. It was not to look at me but to take something out of his box. What he took out was the knife he had shown me that morning. He gazed at it for a moment. Then, making up his mind, he threw it far into the sea. The knife cut a long arc through the raging wind and sank beneath the waves.

"What are you doing?" I asked, feeling an inexplicable disappointment and a strange thrill running through me. He seemed to recognize me for the first time. After looking at me gloomily for a while, he muttered, "I threw away my long delusion."

I understood why he looked so tired and shabby. He had thrown away what had sustained him for so long—that tenacious hatred.

"The bastard was living in a crumbling hut with his sick wife and sore-infested children. The children were crying for food, and the wife was dying. To let him live on—was the better revenge."

He smiled bleakly. I could tell from his smile that his last sentence did not express his true feelings.

"He begged me to kill him. I refused," he added, as if in self-justification. I wanted to ask him the real reason for his forgiveness. But a stronger urge compelled me to rush to my small travel bag. I took out the letter I had written the night before and the bottle of drugs that had been lying there for the past six months. I gazed at them for awhile, as he had at his knife.

This time, he walked up to me slowly and watched me in silence. Had the time really come? I wrapped the bottle in the letter and threw them far out to sea. After inscribing a white arc, they were instantly swallowed up by the waves.

"What did you throw away?" He asked in a puzzled tone. I felt a little sad but answered, trying to smile. "My sentimentality. And my rationality that became morbid before reaching maturity."

I met him a few years later in *B* city. He was running a small store selling burnt wood pictures.* He must have learned the skill of making burnt wood pictures in prison. It was a small shop, but it looked as if it were thriving. He also had a pretty young wife and a one-year-old son.

Strangely enough, I can't recall how we parted that day on the beach.

The next day I was on the train going to Seoul. It was a bright sunny afternoon in late winter. As the train ran past a peach orchard, I saw at the tip of every twig pink shoots promising a radiant spring.

---

* Pictures drawn with hot iron on a wooden board. [Translator]

His Father's Keeper

Ch'oe Yun

Ch'oe Yun, born in 1953, is a writer of formidable intellect and stylistic versatility. In real life professor of French Literature Ch'oe Hyŏnmu of Sogang University, she utilizes many of the modern fictional techniques in her writing, such as mixing fantasy with reality, disjointed time sequence, multiple versions of an episode, and so forth. Her novella "Yonder a Flower Is Fading Quietly" is rated as one of the finest stories depicting the devastation wrought by the Kwangju massacre, which was carried out by the military strongman Chun Doo Whan in 1980 to tighten his grip on power. Ch'oe utilized her memory of her college days spent in the oppressive shadow of military rule to write another much-acclaimed story, "The Soiled Snowman," which takes an ironic look at the "heroes" produced by the resistance movement under the military dictatorship. Another theme Ch'oe frequently explores is the national legacy, most often the legacy of the ideological split that devastated the country and resulted in the Korean War, but also the ethical, intellectual, and artistic heritage left by Korean ancestors. Ch'oe shows that though modern Koreans seem to have traveled far from their past, there is really no escaping from their national heritage and that they have to find meaningful and constructive ways of embracing their past.

"His Father's Keeper" holds out a possibility for the healing of the wounds inflicted by traumatic ideological warfare by showing the difficult reconciliation between a father and son who had been separated for nearly four decades by the country's division.

Father was sitting with his eyes still glued to the television screen, in the same stooping posture on the wooden stool, exactly as I had left him in the morning. With his head bent slightly forward, like someone trying to come up with an answer to a tough question the interviewer on television posed, he sat there immobile, showing no sign of having heard me come in. I felt as if he were pretending to be absorbed in the news to avoid facing me, even though the news, in French, could only be a stream of gibberish to him. The long weekend was just beginning.

I stared at the back of Father's gray head, feeling a tide of resentment rising in my throat. On the TV a political commentator was analyzing the various factors that might influence the future of post-revolution Romania. Having been exposed to his views for several weeks now, I could feel no conviction in his high-strung voice, and thought he sounded rather melodramatic. Father inflamed my irritation by continuing to sit on the narrow stool, despite my repeated urging to sit more comfortably on the sofa.

I was tired of playing host to Father, even though it was barely a week since he had arrived from China. Each night, I spent many sleepless hours trying to remember Father before he had defected to the North during the Korean War, but of course it was useless. Not even a genius can remember things that happened two months before his birth. From earliest childhood I acquired the habit of committing to memory those anecdotes and descriptions of Father that Mother related to me, as well as the bitter trials my family had endured as the relations of a defector. Those vague stories took such strong root in my consciousness that from the time I was old enough to understand the emotional consequences of those events, I had to carry their weight with me all the time. And I became prematurely old from those vicarious experiences. Whether Father disappeared before my birth or after didn't make any difference to me. Those who have been placed in a situation similar to mine will understand at once when I say that the more one tries to keep one's father hidden from the world and out of one's consciousness, the more insistently he pops up at every turn. I tried to imitate him when I was in a pessimistic mood, and rejected and denied him when I felt optimistic.

Ever since Father's arrival, I lay awake at night pushing farther and farther up the tunnel of the past, trying to uncover the least bit of information that might warm my chilled heart. But memory after bitter memory only made me more awake. Mother, who used to tell us about Father in the most glowing terms of admiration, began to avoid mentioning him when we became teenagers; the only remaining family photo was taken down from the wall and concealed in Mother's scruffy dressing table. Thereafter, we gradually succeeded in getting rid of Father's ghost, and for more than a decade we had been able to devote ourselves to the business of living. Until, that is, Father's letter inquiring about his family came from Communist China to his parents' former home, like a bolt out of the blue.

The letter, which had no definite addressee, passed through many hands before it finally reached Mother, who was staying with me in Paris, five months later. At that time I was just beginning to feel that I had finally settled down to a life and a career, having at long last earned my doctorate after struggling at it twice as long as the others and having brought Mother over to live with me.

When she finished reading the letter, Mother stared into space for a long time and then at length said, stammeringly, that she would go along with any decision her sons made. So I flew to Seoul at once to consult my two older brothers. To my brothers and me, who were together for the first time in a long while, the letter signed with the name Yi Ha-un evoked not so much joyful surprise as a certain misgiving, as if criminal evidence which we had long been carefully concealing had suddenly been exposed. It was a natural reaction from three sons who had paid dearly for their Father's defection to the North. My brothers and I had many opinions about what we ought to do with this father who had thus suddenly come back from the dead, so to speak. One of us felt that to invite Father would only open old wounds and create new heartbreaks and inconveniences, as he was sure to have remarried and have a new family by now, even though he was quite vague about his present circumstances in his letter. Another of us expressed the view that we should invite Father to visit us, since that would be what Mother would want. We did agree that we should reply in any event. Even though none of us said so in so many words, all of us were wondering whether Father's reappearance might not cause us inconveniences and disadvantages, even though the situation surrounding defector's families had altered greatly since the post-War days.

Anyway, we three brothers, each busy with his own life, and with no compelling desire to see Father, came to the conclusion that we would leave the matter entirely in Mother's hands. That was the message I carried to Mother.

"You're not worthy to be called his sons! This has nothing to do with you any more, so just forget about it," Mother said with cold finality, putting the letter in her pocket, when I conveyed the "consensus" of her three sons. She never referred to either the letter or to Father after that. Then suddenly she took ill, though until then she had enjoyed such good health and vigor that few would have believed she was almost seventy. Well, it could be that her strength just gave out after leading a life which consisted almost entirely of hardships and heartbreaks. I wrote a letter on her behalf, using the strange word, "Father." I also enclosed a photograph of my mother and us three brothers. Father's succinct reply came in his bold handwriting. It was exactly two years and five months ago.

Mother seemed to regain strength when the correspondence began. Seemingly recovering her zest for life, she began to make plans for Father's visit. She even made grandiose plans for visiting her and Father's old hometown to see his long-lost relatives and becoming reconciled with them before she passed away. The photograph, now so badly faded as to be almost a blank piece of paper, reemerged from its place of concealment and was placed on Mother's night table.

But the authorization for Father's journey was constantly postponed, and at the end of seven months Mother became critically ill. In compliance with her last wish, I took her to my oldest brother's home. Mother died not long afterward.

Not taking into consideration her advanced age, my brothers and I blamed Mother's death on the reemergence of our father. That vague resentful feeling came out from one of us at a moment of our blinding sorrow, and we did not hesitate to brand Father as a messenger of death who had brought disaster not only to Mother but to us as well. Then we forgot about Father in our sorrow at losing our mother. It was well over three months later when I, being the channel of correspondence with Father by reason of my residing in Europe, wrote to Father again. There was no reply for a long time. Then, a long, eloquent, moving letter addressed to our dead mother, full of sorrow and hope for reunion with her in the next world, was delivered simultaneously to my oldest brother in Seoul and to me. It was the first long letter we had from Father. Strangely enough, after that I wrote to Father with more enthusiasm than before Mother's death. But Father's replies did not grow any longer or more prompt.

As if to underscore the desolate and cramped atmosphere of his son's bachelor apartment, Father spent his days glued to the narrow stool, without moving or speaking. The first week I spent with Father, I was in the uncomfortable grip of an odd dread, and avoided any serious topic. The first couple of days went by without too much trouble, as I was at the institute during the day and made telephone calls to my brothers in Seoul in the evening. In fact, the first three days passed rather smoothly. My brothers and I asked after Father's health as would people talking to a distant relative at a reunion. I asked questions about Father's past. Questions such as what kind of jobs he had held at what periods and when he remarried, how many "children" he had, and how he escaped from North Korea to China, what he did in China and what his present circumstances were. . . . The kind of questions an employment agency asks a client to fill in the blanks in his application form. . . . Business-like questions one asks when one doesn't know what else to ask; embarrassing questions to ask a father whom one has just met for the first time. But Father answered them without evasion, as if they were just the kind of questions a father expects his son to ask in such a situation. Like one reporting events in someone else's life, he said that he had remarried to avoid being suspected of planning to return to the South. And he rather emphatically informed me that I had two younger brothers and sisters. He also said that in North Korea he used to be in charge of cultural administration, and that he had decided to flee to China only after long deliberations. And then, after an interval of silence, he added that he had been forced to leave "one of my younger brothers" in North Korea due to the difficulty of fleeing, and that he had been living with my two younger sisters and a younger brother. Besides that he had nothing more to say about his life in China except for repeatedly asserting, "I am a private person. I am content with my life as a private person." An odd dread prevented me from questioning him further, though nothing he said really gave me any clear idea of the kind of life he had been leading.

I briefly told him about the present circumstances of my brothers and myself without mentioning the long and manifold hardships we had endured on account of his defection. Concerning my oldest brother, who suffered the most as the son of a defector and was still without a stable job or solid financial footing, I just said that he was preparing to start a private business. I rather exaggerated the success and prosperity of my other brother, who was the executive director of a modest company. Then, thinking that my own status as a Ph.D. and a researcher in a French national research institute might be the most impressive, I explained to him that I had decided early on to live abroad because I wanted to escape the hateful stigma of being a defector's son, a statement that must have sounded like an accusation to Father.

After that momentary outburst, I recovered my composure. Then I was at my wit's end as to what subject to bring up next. Father never asked any specific questions, never inquired after any of the relatives; I even felt he was refraining from asking questions about Mother. So I was the one who had to come up with subjects for conversation. Father never started a topic; nor did he change the subject in the middle of a conversation.

On the third day after his arrival, I felt an acute longing for Mother. What would they have talked about if Mother were alive? Feeling the void left by Mother's death widening the distance between Father and me, I kept talking for the sake of talking, about how Seoul has grown to be an international metropolis, how Korea has developed, how Korean goods are conquering world markets, and so on and so forth. Once I started, I couldn't stop. Father, instead of trying to bring the conversation to matters nearer to heart, responded in kind, briefly describing the manners and mores of Yanbian, the Koreans' autonomous region in China, and Beijing. I couldn't stand the superficial conversation in which each party was trying to avoid touching the other's sensitive spot.

From the fourth day I gave up all efforts at conversation and took Father to a roadside cafe, as if he had been a friend who came to Paris as a sightseer. Father also apparently gave up efforts at conversation, so the two of us came back home after sitting silently for an hour in the cafe with beer mugs between us. I could only look forward to my brothers' arrival to rescue me from this oppressive situation. But that was still ten days off. Father had arrived a fortnight earlier than I had expected.

As the days wore on, my old regrets about the father who had defected to the North abandoning us all were replaced by a certain disappointment and resentment toward the man who had suddenly appeared and declared himself our father. The resentment developed in a peculiar direction, and made me keep a stern watchful eye over his every movement and gesture.

While standing alone in the airport welcoming area holding a slate with Father's name on it, my excitement amounted almost to hysteria. In spite of our repeated requests, Father had not sent us a recent photograph of himself; and, try as I might, I could not recall the features of the tiny face in the almost completely faded family photo. Neither could I draw even a rough likeness of Father from the detailed and impressive descriptions that Mother never tired of giving us in our childhood. For the first time in my life I took to studying my face in the mirror with the eye of a detective, trying to figure out if there were features in it that bore any resemblance to my father. It was because I recalled my maternal grandmother's repeated assertion that I resembled Father like a coin minted from the same mold—something she exclaimed with an oddly sour expression.

When I spotted the sharp-chinned old man with close-cropped hair wearing an old-fashioned woolen suit under a faded dark blue padded coat, I recognized him instantly from memory—from prenatal memory. Oblivious of the crowd, I rushed to him, held him fast, and cried in his arms with loud sobs. To be sure the tears rose from a deep well of resentment and bitterness. At that moment, however, I was weeping more for Mother who passed away before her long dream of reunion with her husband could be realized, rather than from the exaltation of having a parent come back from the dead.

I called out "Mother!" between sobs, thinking of the woman who had always regarded me as a special object of pity for being born fatherless and later for being an old bachelor, and who had spent her last year in a strange country without any friends to talk to, trying to look after her last-born. Thinking of her, I writhed in Father's arms, sobbing convulsively. But however hard I rubbed my cheek against Father's, his cheek remained bristly and hard. Tears also flowed out of Father's eyes, which were beginning to be covered with white and whose wrinkled lids were limp. His tears at once canceled out the mythical image of the young Yi Ha-un so vividly implanted in our minds by Mother. For a moment I had the illusion that Mother had deliberately ended her life early, for fear of finding her husband in this disappointing state.

I gave up trying to make Father more comfortable and began to leaf through the papers I had brought from the institute. But, hard as I tried, my dissatisfaction with Father threatened to erupt every few minutes. My emotions were looking for the least excuse to explode. If it had been during the week, I could say I had to go back to the institute for some unfinished work, but it being Friday afternoon I felt trapped, like when I used to babysit during my student days. On TV, the news had ended and an interview program between a woman anchor and the new Romanian prime minister, Petro Roman, was on.

"Mr. Prime Minister, last month you said you would postpone answering a reporter's question about whether you were still a Marxist after the revolution that overthrew the communist dictatorship. How would you answer the same question now that a month has elapsed?"

The young Romanian prime minister was just about to answer the intelligent, ambitious and good-looking woman anchor's question, creasing his whole face into a good-natured smile, when Father took out a handkerchief from his pocket and blew his nose loudly, so loud that the room seemed to reverberate with the noise. Then he folded the handkerchief again and sneezed into it, so hard that his torso shook perceptibly. Then he rubbed the corners of his eyes with a corner of his folded handkerchief. From where I sat I could not see his face, but I decided that he was thus sitting immobile because he was absorbed in thinking about his family back in China and that indeed he might even be shedding tears of yearning for them.

All right, I thought, you lived with this other family of yours for four decades, no less; and you risked your lives together when you fled from North Korea to China. It's only natural that they are more precious to you than us, whom you supposedly lived with for seven or eight years, but it was really only a fraction of that period. Well, it might have been a little different if the wife who had waited for you all her life had met you and covered you with her tears. But the only one who received you was a son whom you'd never met before, in a distant alien country far from old familiar faces. So, what affection could spring up in you for a son who's as good as a total stranger?

Handing over a box of tissues, I stole a glance at Father's eyes. But, even though a part of his left eye was whitened, there was no trace of tears or melancholy around his eyes. On the contrary, Father had his alert eyes fixed on the television screen, like an eager student. It occurred to me that Father, who was known as a versatile genius in his youth, might be proficient enough in French to be able to understand everything that was going on on the screen. So I asked him—more, however, to corner him than to ascertain his knowledge of French— "Do you understand what they're saying?"

Without turning his body, he twisted his neck uncomfortably, smiled at me until his wrinkles grew twice as numerous, and turned his eyes toward the screen again.

"Would you like me to explain?"

This time, Father pulled out a tissue from the box on his lap, sneezed loudly into it, and said in a husky voice, "Why put yourself to such trouble? I'm just looking at the pictures."

"But you seem so interested . . ."

"Oh, they're all very interesting. The woman announcer staring up at her subject from every angle, the young revolutionary who keeps smiling, and the French language which sounds like corn popping in a hot kettle," Father said in an affectionate tone, turning his broadly smiling face fully toward me, like one really amused. But his rare tone of affection only provoked my resentment. I couldn't understand myself. I struggled mightily to control my temper and be reasonable, thinking to myself, "after all he came all this way to have a reunion with us his sons," but at certain moments that very effort stung me to fury. In my anger, I saw in Father's affectionate tone only a trick to avoid a possibly embarrassing topic.

Glaring at the television screen which seemed to arouse such great interest in Father, I soliloquized, in a melodramatic tone:

"Well, who could have imagined that the Romanian dictatorship would crumble like that? And it's the same story pretty much throughout Eastern Europe. None of them even shook the earth as they fell— they just crumbled, like a rotten wall."

I studied Father's face carefully while I spoke. He just kept gazing at the TV attentively, with the same amused smile. I couldn't resist adding, "You seem to find the collapse of Communism extremely amusing?"

What I really wanted to say was, "So, was that crumbling dust heap what you gave your life for?" Or maybe, "So, where do you stand now? You don't mean to tell me you're still on that side?" Of course I couldn't be so openly sarcastic.

Father's profile seemed to harden for a moment, but the smile came back and he said slowly, "Amusing? Well, I guess such an unprecedented spectacle is a matter of interest. Of course nations have to change their clothes when their bodies put on flesh."

I detested such answers of Father's which made the questioner look silly. My anger seethed in the face of Father's attitude, whereby the collapse of Communism seemed to be a matter of no concern to himself. If he knew it was something that could fall apart without even a bang, why did he sacrifice his whole family for the sake of it? And why, if he once made his choice for life, didn't he stay rooted in the fatherland of his choice and get new outfits made for himself at appropriate moments, instead of risking his and his new family's lives to flee from it? Wasn't it an excessive sacrifice, for something whose collapse seemed to give him only amusement? These were the thoughts that buzzed in my head, ready to explode at the least provocation.

I criticized the Communist regimes of China and North Korea vociferously whenever the television news made mention of them as exceptions to the phenomenon of the collapse of Communism the world over. It was to elicit comments from Father. But his only response was a tender gaze. I couldn't help thinking that he was deliberately refusing to clarify his position. The calmer Father was, the more agitated I became. I asked him in elaborately devious ways what he did during the day, even though I could have asked him straightforwardly. It was as if I suspected him of conducting clandestine meetings in a corner of Paris in my absence. I refused to believe his answers, even though there was no reason to doubt his reply that he had walked around the block or that he had watched TV all day long, or that he read the Korean books on my shelf. The minute I stepped in the door, I ran my eyes over Father's shoes and the overcoat which hung on the clothestree, trying to detect the least sign of recent usage. Two days before, I called up Father from the office no less than three times, gripped by a sudden misgiving. But Father disappointed me, answering the phone in his circumspect voice every time. Father seemed moved, thinking that I was worried about his comfort, and told me not to worry about him but give my undivided attention to my work.

When the program ended, Father turned to me with a face innocent of any inkling of the storm brewing in my heart, and took out something from his pocket. Holding it out to me, he said, "Would you mail this for me?"

Judging from the address of the recipient, it was obviously a letter to his family in China. Aha, I thought, so you can't go for more than a week without writing to that family, even though you never wrote more than once in a couple of months to us, even after you renewed contact after all those years. Perhaps sensing something from my face, he murmured in a low voice, half in the tone of one speaking to himself: "They don't know I'm here. I just told them I was going to Beijing for a few days. It was really thoughtless of me."

I felt like a child severely rebuked by his parent for an unworthy thought. But even at that moment I didn't believe his explanation, and was tempted to open the letter and ascertain Father's honesty. Like one escaping from a mischievous temptation, I rushed out and headed straight for the post office.

I breathed a bit more easily outside. That afternoon suburban Paris was warm, even though it was winter. Walking in the sun, I swayed from side to side, shaken by a storm of nostalgia in my heart for the happy days that were gone forever. The memory of Mother's smile when we did something to make her proud of us. Or the memory of the day I waited for Mother in the sunny courtyard of a police station while she registered our change of domicile. On my college commencement day, Mother smiled like a shy girl, wearing the tasseled scholar's cap we placed on her head. Letting myself be swayed by the flood of those at once sweet and bitter memories that often held me captive since Mother's death, I glared at the familiar but always alien street with my eyes. Oh, if only Mother had been alive! Then reunion with Father would not have been such a bumpy affair. I recalled once more the rough feeling of Father's face against my skin when I writhed in his arms at the airport, and blotted out the memories of former days floating in my head. I entered the post office like someone being sucked back into the dark prison of Fate.

To postpone going home, I ordered a whiskey at a cafe in the neighborhood and read the local paper lying on the table. But, although I read everything in the paper from the news to the Want Ads pages, as soon as I put down the paper I could recall nothing of what I had read. I had been thinking of something else all the time. I was trying to fix in my mind an image that kept becoming blurred. It was the face of a man in his early thirties, making a fervent speech before a crowd of people. And the faces of a small woman and a boy of six or seven at the end of the front row, regarding the speaker with intense absorption. It was the face of Father I had put together from repeated descriptions provided by Mother and my eldest brother. It was a face idealized and embellished in every possible way, and at one time it had made me triumphantly proud. It was the face of Father as he looked to Mother and my eldest brother before I even began my existence, a little more than a year prior to his disappearance. The young man in my "memory" had a moustache and was wearing a black cape as he fixed the audience's eyes with his soft but riveting eyes while he poured out his fervent words. This young man sometimes appeared in my imagination wearing armor and riding a steed, galloping at full speed over the mountain behind our village in the country.

As years went by, this same young man disturbed my sleep by appearing in my imagination as a North Korean spy, tapping lightly on the window pane of my house in which my family was asleep. His image, as I grew older, lost its magic quality and became more of a practical handicap and inconvenience. But the surrealistic image of Father had never bothered me so excruciatingly as it did that day on that alien street. The prosaic image of my wrinkled and tired father was in a way reassuring but also provoked a fierce fury and feeling of betrayal. It was always like that. My feelings toward father were as unstable as a boiling casserole. After I emptied my fifth glass of whiskey straight, I felt a dense red-hot emotion firing my cheeks. Then, I felt my eyeballs stinging and two hot streams running down my cheeks. Damn it, I thought, what sentimentality at my age! But the hot tears, instead of relieving my feelings, only heightened them, and I rose from the chair, feeling eager to pick a quarrel with anyone with little or no provocation.

The explosion came as soon as I stepped into the apartment.

"For God's sake, why don't you sit in a more comfortable chair! You make me so nervous!" I almost yelled the minute I saw Father sitting in his stooping posture on the same stool, bent over the plant encyclopedia that had been lying on the tea table. Father slowly turned his upper body and looked at me with a surprised glance. It was me who was more taken aback by my vehemence than Father. I added hastily, "I feel so uncomfortable when I see you sitting all day on that stool fit only for setting out flower pots."

"I'm sorry you feel that way. It's because this one is more comfortable for my back than the soft armchair or sofa," Father said in a tone of sincere apology and going back to his plant book. Then it struck me that neither I nor my brothers had seriously inquired after Father's health since his arrival. As if the violence of the feeling aroused by him were a gauge of his health. As if the fact that he was evoking memories in us of past calamities were proof that he was strong enough to withstand any kind of disaster. I don't think that either I or my brothers would have been at all surprised if Father had appeared before us as a young man in the height of vigor, in spite of his seventy-odd years. I gazed at father, who looked even older than when he arrived a week ago, as at an unnatural being.

Then I recalled that the last news we had of him after his disappearance, the only news Mother could get after questioning everyone and inquiring everywhere, was that he was severely wounded. Mother went through agony when she had to repeat the news of his injury at every regular check-up visit of policemen, after my family had been put on the police list of Communist defectors' families. Even so, Mother became anxious when the monthly visit by the police was delayed for some reason, which seemed to indicate to Mother that Father's death had been ascertained. Up to the very last minute of her life, Mother was indifferent to her own health but was worried that Father's injury all those years ago might still be having lingering effects. I seemed to hear clearly in my mind Mother's voice anxiously asking Father about his wounds. But my voice, as I posed the question, was gruff.

"When did you get wounded in the back?"

"Wounded?" Father retorted, studying my face which was still red with emotion.

"I recall Mother saying that the last news she had of you was of your severe injury shortly after you left."

Father was silent for a while and then his face grew rather somber. But before long the shadow lifted, and the same smile, which looked to my impatient mind sometimes blank and sometimes treacherous, was restored.

"When you say wounded, it sounds as if I received some glorious injury in battle. But my back has nothing to do with anything of that nature."

"Then, was it a false report that Mother got?"

"Well, I don't know what exactly she heard, but isn't one bound to get hurt once or twice in times of war?"

That was the kind of infuriating answer Father always gave. I resolved to get to the bottom of it.

"I heard that a friend of my aunt in Susaek saw you in a field hospital just before the January 4 Retreat of 1951 began."

"Now who was this aunt in Susaek?"

It was clear that he was trying to avoid giving a direct answer. I felt mortified, as if it were I and not Mother who spent whole nights awake after hearing the news and made several journeys to Susaek to talk directly with the person who saw Father. She had to walk many miles to Susaek, carrying my older brother on her back and with my oldest brother walking alongside. What mortal on earth could compensate for so much pain and heartbreak, spent to so little purpose? Well, the only one who could make the least amends was Father and no one else, and as to how, he would have to come up with a way himself. But Father seemed to be far from thinking of such questions.

I could not understand what had made Father undertake such a big trip, when Mother was no more. If he had wanted, I could have arranged for him to go to Seoul, to stay at my oldest brother's. But Father insisted on coming to where I was, even after Mother died. Well, how little importance he placed on this trip could be surmised from the fact that he did not tell his "family" in China that he was coming to France to be reunited with his original family. And he had been consistently vague about what he was doing and how he was faring in China. His presence was nothing to be excited about, and nothing was to be expected from him. Everything would go back to normal in a month, when he went back to his family in China. I felt the helplessness that often threatened to paralyze me throughout my adolescence and youth beginning to spread in me. It would be a veritable disaster if the plague of helplessness, which I managed to subdue after such strenuous struggles, was to engulf me again. I decided to give the whole thing up, and stood up. Just then, Father called my name in an affectionate voice. His eyes were still fixed on the plant encyclopedia spread on his lap. I half turned around, feeling a hot sensation in my nose, like a child who had been affectionately addressed by a parent after long neglect. But Father's question was as remote as it could be from addressing the turmoil in my heart. In the tone of one who had just spotted a long-lost friend, he said, pointing to a weed in the encyclopedia. "Isn't this one here a farm wife's tissue paper?"

The question, which under normal circumstances would have elicited only the briefest affirmative or negative, served as a detonator of my temper, with the aid of the alcohol in me. I cast off my somewhat exaggerated pose of courteous deference that I kept up since Father's arrival and yelled at him.

"Come off it, Father! Have you got so little to say to me? Why do you turn the conversation every time I ask a question?"

"Oh, I didn't know it was such an offence to ask a doctor of plant science the name of a common weed. I just asked because I thought you knew everything," Father said, disregarding my protest and thrusting out his chest, like one really proud of his son's achievement. I shot back, with unconcealed sarcasm.

"I know. One like me, who does nothing but study weeds all his life, must look like a pitiful clod to someone like you who devoted his life to a lofty ideal."

The relief was heavenly. Moreover, it instantly transformed my vague discontentment into a just indignation, making the contents of my accusation seem plain facts. At nearly forty years of age, I was sick and tired of my bachelor state, tired of my long wandering, and tired of my prospect as a lifelong researcher in a foreign institute. I had picked plant science as my major from some affinity I felt for the lot of weeds, and the decision to live my life in a foreign country was a desperate escape. The plain fact was that Father was responsible for my blind-alley existence. This perception, which struck me with the force of a revelation, released a torrent of emotion. I grew more and more aggressive. In order to hurt him more, I not only recounted all my own misfortunes but the tribulations of my mother and elder brothers caused by his defection. But I must have had a last bit of restraint working somewhere inside me—I refrained from calling into question the validity of his ideology itself. The restraint, however, must have owed more to my fear of having my suspicions confirmed than to some feeling of minimum filial deference.

Father was listening to my tirade with closed eyes, without being visibly shaken. That calm infuriated me beyond endurance and drove me to overstep the boundary.

"If it hadn't been for your reappearance, Mother would have lived at least ten more years. Do you know how your ghost haunted us all and left us all mentally crippled?"

But before I could finish the sentence, Father called my name and turned to squarely face me. Father's tone had completely changed.

"Ch'angyŏn, listen to me. You've said enough for one evening. The rest you can tell me later. I also have things to say to you. Haven't I come here to drive out that ghost in you? I've been thinking for a long time that I ought to expel my ghost from the three of you before it's too late. It's true I had hoped that the ghost was only a creation of my aging brain. That hope enabled me to live a relatively comfortable life as a private citizen."

Father was silent for a moment. I fixed my eyes on Father with a sarcastic expression, breathing roughly. I felt the urge to rush out of the apartment and deprive Father once and for all of the opportunity to explain himself. But before I could decide on my next move, Father spoke again, in the tone of one who read my mind through and through.

"Of course you have the right to refuse to listen to me. But even if you were to leave this room, I'd keep on talking, just as if you were here. But, if you're willing to listen to what I have to say, look me straight in the eye and see me for what I am."

It would have been a cowardly thing to rush out of the room. I raised my head and looked at him challengingly. Oddly enough, unlike his resolute voice, his face was almost devoid of expression. His blank face, bearing no mark of his past, ageless, and free of any trace of love or hatred, was demanding that I distance myself from him, as if I were looking at a black-and-white photograph of a stranger. Our glances met for a long time. Finally that peculiar smile of his was back on Father's face.

"I don't know what would be the best place to start my story, so let me just begin from any point that comes first to mind. A long time has passed since I left the four of you, but I feel neither disappointment nor satisfaction with what I did. It's only natural that you, who have never seen this father of yours but only encountered me as a ghost, should feel bitter about me on every count. I imagine you wanted to see me become either a total failure, wailing self-reproach and asking for your Mother's forgiveness on bent knees, or a big shot in the other world, to give some meaning to all the tribulations you and your mother and brothers had to endure all these years."

Father's words were interrupted here by violent coughs accompanied by sneezing. Father coughed so violently that his whole body shook. Needless to say, Father had misunderstood my attitude in no small degree. But I felt rather glad of his misunderstanding. And there was something in Father's voice that soothed my anger. Father's cough continued for a long time. It was only then that I recalled Mother saying that Father's asthma, which recurred every winter, erupted on their wedding night, much to his embarrassment, and that he could lay it to rest for that winter only after eating a whole barrelful of pears. It was strange that I never thought of that reminiscence of Mother's till then, even though he had been coughing a lot since his arrival.

"Well, as you see, I don't tearfully repent my past. Neither do I have any medals to adorn my long struggles. I must look to you like a . . . wasted life clinging pitifully to a meaningless existence.

"This may sound like impudence to you, but it is my belief that I have not done any wrong that would require me to beg anybody's forgiveness on bent knees. It is not that I cannot imagine the trials and hardships your mother and you three brothers must have endured after my defection. I have no way of justifying myself for that. But I am sure you are now old enough to know better than to hold me personally responsible for your pain. Your late mother understood. I defected to the north with her consent, fully intending to come back and take all of you with me. How could I have done it without misgivings and sorrow, especially as your brothers were young and your mother was near the end of her pregnancy with you? I believed then as I do now that the worst dishonor is to live only for one's personal welfare. So, how could I blame myself for my past? But I know all too well how difficult it is to forgive someone who insists that he has done no wrong."

Father's words were taking a direction I had not anticipated in the least. My suspicions, momentarily subdued by Father's earnest tone, reasserted themselves. For three years I had pictured every possible attitude Father could take with me, but his present words were so far removed from any of the myriad attitudes I had anticipated that I became confused and couldn't figure out how to react. Looked at one way, his words were insults heaped on us helpless victims of actions he had taken for his convictions, regardless of the suffering they might cause others. But, in some obscure way they were an indirect apology. In any case, what was all too clear—and to me totally unjustifiable—was Father's conviction that he could not have acted in any other way. His old and wrinkled face even seemed to shine with the glow I often imagined on his face in my childhood.

"Once again, I tell you clearly that it was not to ask your forgiveness that I came here. Whatever you may have thought, I'm sure you half forgave me when you answered the letter from a father you'd never laid eyes on. I think the remaining half of forgiveness will have to come in time, through our mutual efforts. My aim was something else. I don't know in what form I live in you, but if, as you say, I have been a ghost that has been haunting you, it must have had a very different face from my real one. But don't think that I dragged my old body all this way just to implant my real image in you. It is neither a very attractive nor a very admirable image that I can present to you, I know. Your father is now simply a private person who has been tending a farm for the last two decades and more, and one satisfied with the place he reached at the end of many turbulent years. And I wanted to show myself to you exactly as I am."

Father left his stool at last and walked over to the window. With hands clasped behind him, he looked at the darkening winter sky.

"I thought it was unusually warm for winter. I suppose we're going to have snow."

Of course I wasn't heeding Father's prognostication about the weather. In a way it seemed that the suspicions that had been dogging me for the past few days were confirmed. But then, I couldn't be sure of that either. For a minute I thought of posing the question point-blank, taking advantage of his confessional, or at least explanatory, mood. But I asked myself why I was harboring such an insidious suspicion. As if to reassure myself, I repeated to myself the "evidence" that had helped to set my mind relatively at ease. Like the fact that he had dared to escape from North Korea with his new family, risking all their lives. That could only mean that he was "converted." But, as always, this thought reassured me only momentarily, as I could not but remind myself that, unlike other people who fled from North Korea, Father never really criticized North Korea in any clear and unequivocal terms. Then I recalled that we never really talked about North Korea, and that I had not asked him any direct questions about North Korea. Of course it is true that I knew what North Korea was like without asking: every Korean knows what North Korea is like. That knowledge is engraved especially deep in the minds of people like me, whose whole lives are shaped by the existence of North Korea. During dinner on the day after Father's arrival, I unfolded before him my detailed knowledge of North Korea. I suppose nobody would have dared to contradict, or even modify, my conviction.

My head buzzing with confusion, I studied Father's back, bent from long farm labor. I recovered a measure of calm. Granted there is a possibility of his being a North Korean agent, how much espionage work could a seventy-four-year-old man do?

While I was busy with such hefty calculations, Father suddenly turned toward me. He looked at me with such intensity that it sent electric waves through my body. It was the first expressive glance that I had had from Father. His eyes were red but there was no trace of tears. Is that a glance of love? I, who had never experienced Father's love, asked myself.

"I think I'd better stretch out on the bed. Wake me up in half an hour, won't you?" he said and walked toward the room that used to be occupied by Mother. I felt a hot emotion pushing up my throat.

"Father!" I shouted impulsively, but I didn't know what to say. Father's tired faced looked down at me. I made haste to hide my heightened emotion and said, in the tone of one finding fault:

"Father, why did you escape to China, where life is so harsh? Why didn't you try to find a way to escape to Japan or the United States?"

Father stood there for a moment with a confused look, his head tilted to one side, as if trying to catch the drift of my meaning. Then he nodded, as much as to say he understood me, and said slowly: "People keep walking up an ascent believing that sooner or later they will come to a descent where there will be a place for rest and a fountain to slake their thirst. But sometimes there is only an endless ascent. Some people keep climbing even though they know it is forever an uphill road. Some vainly look for a descent not knowing that there's none. Some people just give up and come back down. Some make an impossible attempt to carve out a descent. Some get angry and blame others for the hardship. There are so many sorts. Which kind do you think I am?"

"There must be other roads besides that ascent. Why choose pain?"

"Because . . . no road stretches forever on level ground. And, even if there was one, I don't think even you would want to take it."

Father disappeared into his room before I had time to think of a rejoinder. And I was too tired to figure out the meaning of such a conundrum.

I don't know how many hours elapsed. My sleepy eyes glimpsed Father's shabby travel bag lying in a corner of the living room. I sprang up from my reclining position on the sofa and tiptoed to the door of my Father's room. At first I could hear nothing except my pounding heart. When I got my breath back a little I could discern weak snoring from beyond the door. I picked up the bag, went to my room, and after locking the door, began to go through the contents. My hands were perceptibly shaking.

Without knowing what exactly I was looking for, I groped among the folds of the garments, trying not to leave traces of my inspection. An old faded overcoat thickly padded with cottonwool occupied almost half the bag. There was also a shabby suit, so worn that the lapels shone. There were two rough woolen sweaters, and four well-ironed white shirts. For the rest, there was some underwear and several pairs of socks. But at last my hand touched a plastic bag containing some solid object. My heart beat violently, as if I was about to commit some heinous robbery.

But there was only a bottle of spirits, probably red sorghum, and a small booklet. I hastened to open the booklet, which had a black cover. Even with my limited knowledge of Chinese characters it was obvious to me that it was not a philosophical or revolutionary treatise but a simple travel guidebook. I groped through the folds of garments once again. But there was no trace of any paper. When I took up the book again, something fell out of it and made me jump with fright. The piece of paper that fell on the floor was a photograph. The same photograph that Mother had treasured more than all her other possessions put together. Father's and Mother's faces were seen in the second row, with my second brother in Mother's arms and my eldest brother a toddler of about three years. Of course I was not in it. I poured over each face in the picture, as if I was seeing them for the first time. But there was no way that I could detect anything new from a picture I had scrutinized hundreds of times.

Without trying to replace everything to eliminate the evidence of my snooping, I sat there gazing at Father's belongings, which somehow reminded me of my agonizing childhood. Then, the strange effect of Father's last glance shot through my body one more time. I woke up from my stupor and shuddered at what I'd just done. The faces of the police detectives, who combed the rooms with their suspicious eyes whenever we moved, passed through my mind. They seemed to regard me with triumphant sarcasm. At the end of that procession stood the sad face of a ghost who was at last unmasked. That miserable spy was no one but me. I gazed at my culpable hands as if they were monsters. I dared not touch the bag any more.

I woke up hungery and cold. The clock said it was past nine, but as it was light outside, I couldn't tell whether it was morning or night. I leaped up from the bed and looked around. Father's bag was nowhere to be seen, and the door was ajar. I had no recollection of replacing the bag, or of getting into bed. My head ached as if it would split, but I felt light of limb and heart. Afraid of Father disappearing with the bag, I stepped out of the room.

Father was sitting as usual on the stool and reading the guidebook to France. It looked as if he had cooked and eaten last night's dinner and this morning's breakfast by himself. Noting my complexion, he said, "So you liked the liquor? I brewed it myself and brought it over to give you and your brothers a taste. If I'd known you liked it so much, I'd have brought another bottle."

"I'm sorry, Father," I said, thinking more about the suitcase than the liquor. But without any sign of having taken offense, Father said, even with a conspiratorial wink, "Forget it. You must be a real drinker if you can smell a bottle hidden inside a suitcase. Won't you drink some of the soothing soup I made for you?"

As a matter of fact I was on my way to the kitchen to drink some liquid, any liquid. I had no choice but to sit sheepishly before the table set by Father.

"Won't you be my tour guide for today? I mean, since you won't have time during the week."

"Where do you want to go?"

Father spread on the table the page that had been folded for easy reference. Even though I couldn't understand all the Chinese characters, I could tell that it was about the Père-Lachaise Cemetery.

"Why a cemetery, of all places?" I began to say, but clamped my mouth shut. I vaguely divined why Father wanted to see it. During my student days I had done my sightseeing of the cemetery famous for its scenic park and all the gorgeous and fantastic sculpture adorning the tombs of the numerous celebrities buried there. In fact, after covering the more than forty hectares of the cemetery my feet were very sore, so that after that day I always avoided taking friends and acquaintances there when showing them the sights of Paris. Of course, Father wasn't interested in seeing the tombs of artists like Chopin, Apollinaire and Delacroix.

"Well, since I'm in Paris, shouldn't I at least see that?"

I went out with Father. Even though it was a popular tourist haunt, the Père-Lachaise was practically deserted that winter morning, which was chilly and overcast. When we entered the cemetery, a gust of wind met us at the entrance. To avoid roaming the huge labyrinth and shivering from the cold, I spread out the map bought at the entrance and asked Father, "It will take three or four hours to make a complete tour. Do you want to see everything, or . . . ?"

Father, who seemed a little overwhelmed, not so much by the fantastic sculptures as by the size of the cemetery, looked around at the endless rows of tombs for a minute and then said, with a face already half numb with cold, "Oh, no. Let's go straight over there."

"Where?" I asked, not liking his matter-of-fact reference to the particular place, even though I knew well enough what he meant.

"Don't pretend you don't know. What else could one like me have in mind?" Father said, with perfect nonchalance.

The expression "one like me" knocked around in my brain, creating shock waves. Without another word I began to walk toward the eastern end of the cemetery, to where the "Wall of the Communards" was. It had become a place of pilgrimage for Communist travelers to Paris. Father followed with brisk steps, with the lapels of his cottonwool-padded overcoat turned up, busily casting admiring glances at all the gorgeous sculptures arrayed alongside the path. I forgot to give Father some travel guide's explanation about the place and was busy pondering his expression "one like me." It was an expression vague as everything else he said, clarifying nothing. But I didn't interrogate him about its exact meaning; nor did I make sarcastic comments about it. The humid wind of the Parisian winter chilled us to the bone.

"How could these people have adorned all these innumerable tombs with such fantastic decorations? Is it still far?" Father broke the silence, perhaps to turn his thoughts from the cold, or perhaps to draw me into conversation.

"We're almost there," I answered briefly. I recalled vividly a certain summer's day more than a dozen years ago when I had visited the cemetery with other Korean students. We also had wanted to see the famous tomb containing the bodies of the Communists mowed down on the spot while fleeing from the army. My companions might remember the tomb merely as a bare wall with only a small wreath at the bottom, but I remember something more depressing that happened there.

We had just taken our photographs in front of the wall and were resting on the lawn beside it when three Asians, all wearing black trousers and white shirts and with heads close-cropped, approached the wall. One among them who looked slightly older than the other two said, "Take a good look at this place. It is where one hundred and forty-seven of our heroic people's champions were butchered after putting up a brave fight during the days of the Paris Commune."

Instead of feeling glad at hearing our mother tongue spoken in a foreign land, my companions and I instinctively pulled in our stretched legs. Then we studied the three men who spoke our mother tongue with such strange and strong accents, as if they had been some rare species of animals. They were the first North Koreans we, who were just beginning our studies in France, had ever seen. I don't know what went through the minds of my companions, but none of them dared utter a word in their presence. We just glanced at each other with defensive but also interested expressions.

The reason that the scene was so clearly imprinted in my memory was because I thought about my father at the time. Like my companions, I dared neither speak a word to them nor go near them. I watched them with bated breath, with my heart pounding. Two conflicting wishes, that they would go away quickly and that they would linger there for a long time and speak their thoughts without noticing our presence, clashed in my mind. And I was seeing, on their strangely alien-looking faces, the image of my father as a young man.

I could not take my eyes off the slightly stooping back of Father, who was walking briskly in spite of his age and the heavy gusts of wind. I ran after him, like one who had been living every day since that uncomfortable summer day in the hope that I might be able to meet Father some day and was now anxious to make sure he was really at my side.

"What unmerciful wind! Is it still far to go?" Father said.

I answered, draping my arm across Father's shoulders to screen him from the wind rushing toward us from the end of the path, "We're practically there, Father."

The Image of Mija

Shin Kyoung-suuk

Shin Kyoung-suuk, born in 1963, inaugurated a new era in Korean fiction. Her coming to prominence coincided with the beginning of the "civilian government era," which meant that writers no longer felt obliged to take up political and social injustice as their principal topic for writing. In other words, the inauguration of the civilian government gave rise to a rapid diversification of literary themes and styles. Shin Kyoung-suuk benefited from this trend immensely, and she also gave it an enormous boost. The haunting lyricism and the romantic anguish of her stories fulfilled a long-suppressed yearning in the Korean psyche. She is an ultra-feminine author obsessed with unfulfilled or unreciprocated love. In her stories love is almost always accompanied by pain, whether because the object of love is in love with someone else, or because such love is ethically impermissible. Shin makes this stale subject fresh and poignant by suffusing her stories with the acuteness of her characters' pain and the intimate details of their daily lives.

With her seemingly artless artistry, Shin makes the couple in "The Image of Mija,"—a semiliterate bum and an illiterate country woman—attractive to sophisticated modern readers. His deceitfulness and swaggering and her lying to him about her husband and stillborn child do not detract at all from the tragedy when the woman dies and the man takes a trip to her hometown to scatter her cremated ashes.

Mija. That was the name of my wife of the past five and a half years.
I'm stopping at this busy intersection on my way to her village. I
expect yellow earth and gravel will be there, and at this time of the
year dazzlingly white plantain flowers. "I was carrying a basket filled
with snacks on my head to my neighbor's paddy and saw those white
plantain flowers when I came to the railroad. They were so white I put
the basket down on the ground, covered it with the pad of towel on my
head, and just walked along the railroad," Mija had said. She came to
me from the plantain flowers like that. I suppose I'm going there to
return her to her hometown.

1

"Have you found the missing child?" the manageress of the coffee
shop asks her customer, a middle-aged man who looks like a town hall
clerk. The woman is wearing a diaphanous summer silk Korean dress
and unloading her charms on him. The square-jawed man shakes his
head vigorously.

"I don't think the child could have gone far with his tiny feet. Hey,
Yunhi, bring us two cups of ginseng tea!"

I hear low voices from the kitchen. Soon a young girl emerges with
a tray, her slipper heels clicking against the floor. She winks at the
male customer as she puts the teacup down on the table. Your waist
was thin like hers, Mija. The waitress then sprinkles water on the floor
with a water can and begins to sweep it with a broom.

"You're a new customer, aren't you?" the waitress asks me.

I smile at her. She becomes less guarded.

"Are you going somewhere?"

"Yes. To Gŏmdaeng-i."

"Oh, then you'll have to wait quite a while for the bus. What takes
you to that way-off place? Even the bus goes there only once a day."

The door of the coffee shop is pushed open, and a few young people
troop in noisily. They must be regular customers.

"Why, hello!" The waitress exclaims, throwing down the broom and
hurrying up to them. Through the open door, I see red meat displayed

in the windows of the butcher shop across the street. The redness seems to spread over to the faces of passersby. I pick up the rumpled newspaper and open it. Mija. You had no figure to speak of. And not much in the way of breasts. You were hardly tall enough to be visible over the bush clover gate. And . . . what else do I remember about you?

2

You said you didn't bid anybody goodbye before you left your hometown. You said you just put down the basket and walked on along the railroad, because the plantain flowers were too white. Why were they so white, even though nobody'd watered them with rice wine to make them bloom? Was it your fate to meet me by the railroad? You hadn't even brought a toothbrush with you.

"I lived with my father. He passed away a few years ago," you said. What else did you say? Perhaps you said you were frightened of going back to your empty house. When I first saw you, you were sitting on the winding embankment with your legs stretched out. When you saw my bicycle, you held up your arm, like one flagging down a bus.

"Where are you going?" you asked.

"Wherever you're going," I replied.

You were a young woman then. Even though you were small and thin, my bicycle tottered under the added weight of you. Did I look back at you then? Your face was tanned, like a fieldhand's. Well, I must have looked back at you. Or maybe I didn't. Why does it seem as if I only had a glimpse of you once in a long-ago dream, though I lived with you for five-and-a-half years? But I do remember that day, Mija. I had a fountain pen in the upper front pocket of my jacket. A Parker fountain pen. I never actually used it to write with—I stuck it in my pocket to show that I'm not a bum. It had the letters P.A.R.K.E.R. inscribed clearly on the lid. Mija, when you got on, the bicycle tottered along on the uneven road. My P.A.R.K.E.R. pen also tossed up and down in my front pocket. Fearing it might pop out, I handed it to you, saying, "Here. Hold this." And we rode six miles. The road weaved in and out of the mountains all the way. We rode like people on an urgent mission. When I stopped the bicycle beside a poplar tree by the stream, your dark face was livid with fear. Having to hold on to the fountain pen for six miles on the bicycle, how your arms must have ached! But you only handed the lid back to me. You held on to the lid, not realizing that the pen itself had fallen out on some slope. Taking the sweat-smeared fountain pen lid, I smiled, but my heart ached, like the time when I skinned my knee against the sand.

How that ache spread through my whole body, as if I'd been a scabbard fish stuck in a salt jar! My maternal uncle's wife kept her string of scabbard fish buried in a salt jar. The scabbard fish, which were salted to begin with, turned yellow in the salt jar. When is she going to cook the next one? I wondered each time I scooped up salt to brush my teeth. I tasted that fishy smell, which made my heart ache, as I rinsed my mouth with water. Only on days when we had important guests did she grill one scabbard fish. Then she'd give me a small piece. It was so salty that after the meal I had to run to the well several times to haul up bucketsful of water. When I saw your face as you held out your cramped arm to hand the fountain pen lid back to me, I smiled but my heart ached like the time I'd eaten salted scabbard fish.

3

The slopes of the bare mountain are red. Maybe there are nothing but dry, bumpy hills in this part of Cholla-do. The deserted oxcart road stretches in a lonely curve. My bus is running on that lonely road like an intruder. I can see through the windshield of the bus leaning roofs of the thatched houses, which look abandoned, and untended tombs scattered here and there. Mija, the front windshield of the bus is the size of the door of your hospital room.

"Where are you going?" The driver asks roughly. He had been glancing back at me frequently, as if he didn't like my taking the seat right behind his even though the whole bus was empty. I pretend not to hear him and just fix my eyes on the acacia trees and the swaying grasses by the roadside. The driver suddenly steps on the gas pedal to frighten me. The jolt caused you to bounce off my knees and roll the width of the bus, and me to flatten my nose against the back of the driver's seat. I quickly pick you up again and put you back on my knees.

"Are you deaf?" the driver yells furiously. His wrinkled neck is greasy with sweat, from the heat of late spring.

"I'm going to Gŏmdaeng-i. So there!" I snap back at him gruffly.

That very moment, the bus jerks to a sudden stop. An old couple, who had been climbing the slope with a jar on an A-frame rack, fall forward, frightened by the jumping bus, and the jar rolls down the slope. As the jar rolls down the slope, azalea flowers are scattered every-where. The old couple must have picked azaleas to carry home after spreading manure on their field. The driver honks furiously, and the old couple try to run, but only manage to totter forward, blocking the bus. Then one of the old woman's shoes falls off, and they almost bump into the bus as they run back to retrieve it. All this happened in a flash.

"Damn! Oldsters shouldn't live so long to bother everyone!" the driver swears.

It all happened in an instant. Life and death came face to face for a moment but the crisis passed quickly. The bus speeds along the yellow road as if nothing had happened. I look back. The old couple is sitting on grass, covered with red dust. They are still holding hands.

4

"Stop! Let me off!"

"This is not Gŏmdaeng-i," the driver shouts back.

He must have heard my reply in spite of that crisis. I pound on the door as if to say that's none of his business. I'd just caught a glimpse of a temple hall through the soiled window of the bus door.

"All right, all right! Damn your impatience!" the driver yells and lets me off. Then, the bus backs up a few feet and shoots forward, raising a whirlwind of dust that forces me to squeeze my eyes shut. I'm sure he did it on purpose. For a while even the cottonwool clouds look red, and the sky disappears from my view. But I must have inhaled all the dust instantly. The cottonwool clouds billow again in the sky. The clouds will billow on endlessly. Seen through the clouds, the sky looks distant. Mija, did you think there's no place for you in this wide, wide world? I step on the shadows of the trees gingerly. The road to the temple is rougher than I expected. I have to pick my way through oak, hazel, and maple trees. The maple leaves will turn red in autumn. But now the new foliage is intensely green. I walk about half a mile or so, and my heart tumbles with a thud. A big, fat toad jumps out of the woods, parks its belly on the road right in front of me, and looks up.

"Get lost!" I mutter, stomping on the road, but the toad only looks at me more intently, bristling up all its bumps. Do toads have such short front legs so that they could look up at you like that? The webs of its rear feet are tense as well. There seem to be only me and silence and the toad on this mountain road.

"Brother!" I swear and look away from the toad. My eyes light on a broken tombstone. Behind the tombstone is an untended tomb mound overgrown with numerous nameless flowers. They say pasque flowers, forever bent as if they are bowing, are children of the buried. There are a few pasque flowers bending low in sorrowful bows. But Mija, oh, look at that pheasant.

The male pheasant is turning round and round with a loud squawk, showing off its beautiful tail to good advantage. Mija, do you know what their squawk means? It means, "this is my territory. This is my territory." Its resplendent tail shines like a rainbow as the pheasant turns round lightly and elegantly. That's his courtship dance. I wish you were here to watch this with me. I'd like to squawk, "This is my territory. This is my territory" to you like that pheasant.

While I was distracted by the pheasant, the toad had disappeared. I look around at the foliage, so green that it looks menacing. How rash of me to get off the bus like that! The image of the toad still lingers before my eyes. Its popping eyes. Its drum-like belly.

They say there ought to be a temple on every mountain, but I wouldn't mind if there wasn't one here. I see winter has been here at any rate. In the yard of the temple that I reach after walking through brushwood groves and up several flights of steps darkly discolored crepe myrtles, which must have died during the winter, are hanging limp. I break a stalk and see that it is black inside as well. Whose prayers have lighted so many candles? Even though the myrtle shoots are quite dead, candles stand here and there all over the temple. The candles look pitiful under the blazing sunlight of a late spring noon, and I don't feel like lighting incense sticks.

A white butterfly, after trying to alight on the tip of the faded eave, changes its mind and flies away. Through the bamboo curtain hung on the edge of the veranda, the sunlight flutters and dances, and bees are buzzing about, hovering over the earthen wall. But there is no hint of human presence. There isn't even a pair of rubber shoes to be seen on the stepping stones. Besides the tiny yellow flowers in bloom beneath the dead crepe myrtles, there's a notice board that reads, "This yard was clean before you came." I put away the cigarette I had just taken out.

"Why don't we forget all about the world and become monks?" Was that what the toad wanted to say to me? If it was, then I'd be willing to take its advice.

5

Is there anything more pitiful than being penniless and alone under strange skies? And we had no parents or elders to watch over and guide us. We both wanted to belong to someone, to be tied to something. I suppose that's why we decided to go to Seoul together. Because we were both alone and knew it. I tasted Heaven when I saw all the seasonings arrayed in glass jars in our small kitchen. The ready-to-use seasonings constituted an order that was new to me. An order that I wanted to guard at all costs. When we sat facing each other across our small meal table, I always felt rich, like one who had divined all the deep secrets of the world. The table was so small that our knees touched under it. It was at meal times that I could lay to rest my misgiving about you arising from the odd reason you gave me for leaving your hometown—because the plantain flowers were too white—and my anxiety that some day you'd leave me just like you'd left your hometown and that I'd be left all alone under this alien sky. When you patted my forehead with a handkerchief, to dry my perspiration as I scooped up rice in hot soup, I could forget my fear that you might not want to come back to our room after a hard day at the restaurant. When we had our meals together, I was grateful for my job that put food on our table, and felt like I'd gone back to the days when I'd never heard of such a thing as weariness. It was as if all my life I'd been longing for that moment before the meal table. But I suppose life has a way of casually throwing treasures your way and then taking them away when they become indispensable to you.

6

"They say the land of the dead is far, far away.

"But it's just over that stream."

I retrace my steps through the deep green foliage, and see a funeral procession on the oxcart road where the bus had dumped me. What else in this world is as sad as separation? And what separation could be sadder than that between the living and the dead? But the funeral chant says the land of the dead lies just across the stream. It is so near because the living soon forget the death even of their most beloved. The dead don't want to part from the living. The dead want to watch over our paddies during the droughts and guard us day and night. But

Mija, you're gone, and you didn't even leave me a strand of your hair. I'm telling you, all the same, that I'm hungry and tired. And I have no idea how I can get to Gŏmdaeng-i. I trudge behind the hearse. There is no mourner in this funeral procession. The hearse bearers even chat and laugh, as if they've forgotten that it is a hearse they're carrying. One of the bearers is even wearing blue jeans.

Maybe more people die in the spring. Even terminally ill patients persevere through long, cold winters but succumb in the spring when the earth feels soft under the soles of our feet.

A raindrop hits my nose. How come it's raining on a bright sunny day? Mija, there must be a tiger getting married somewhere. My maternal grandmother used to say that a sudden shower on a sunny day means a tiger's getting married somewhere. I never asked anybody why there's a sudden shower on a sunny day even if a tiger is getting married somewhere. There are such things in life. Things you cannot ask anybody for the answer. Things you just believe must be so. Like saying to yourself a tiger must be getting married somewhere when you are hit by a sudden rain on a bright day. Like my thinking that once you begin to live with someone you just live with her for forty or fifty years without asking why. I just thought that's the way things are. I feel strength draining out of my limbs. The cottonwool clouds billow out like puffs of smoke, and the raindrops are quite forceful. The raindrops patter on acacia leaves. I flop down beneath the acacia, and the funeral bier and the funeral chant go on their way, leaving me behind. If it weren't for that chant, you'd have thought that these people were going on a picnic with white flowers stuck in their hair.

7

"I lied to you. I said I never lived with anyone before, but I lived with a squint-eyed man in Gŏmdaeng-i. Squint-eye was his name. My father found him in a bazaar and brought him home a long time ago. I was two years older than he, but I didn't mind. We weren't an especially loving couple, but we weren't unloving, either. It wasn't that we decided to get married or anything. He just came over to my room some time after my father passed away. My mother had died right after I was born, and there was nobody else in the house, so it just happened. I told you about Gŏmdaeng-i, didn't I? My house stood on the other side of the reservoir from the village. From my house, the slate roofs of the houses in the village looked like a patchwork quilt. When water rose in the reservoir after a rain, it looked as if the whole village would come floating over the reservoir to us. But I liked living away from the village. The reservoir shielded us from people's eyes. I thought I'd live there forever. I did odd jobs here and there, like laying ties for the railroad, or cutting hay, or catching fish from the reservoir to make hot fish soup, or digging holes to plant pumpkins. I wanted to have many children. If I'd had them, I'd never have met you. You might have passed my house one day on your bicycle and just thought, oh, there's a house beside the reservoir. And that would've been all between you and me. And I'd have lived and died beside the reservoir. On those nights you didn't come home, I tried to figure out how far I was from my house on the reservoir, listening for your footsteps. And I got frightened. But it was true that I put down the basket and left my hometown because the plantain flowers were too white. I could never forget that day. Sometimes I can't remember what happened that day at all, and sometimes I wish I'd died that day. I cast one glance at my house beyond the reservoir, and walked away slowly in the hot sun. Yes, I remember everything now. The flowers I crushed under my feet. The dark gravel by the railroad. Flowers were falling like snow from the persimmon trees standing in the houses of the village. I may have been crying. I'd given birth to a baby. Squint-eye buried it beside my father. The baby was stillborn. It died without even crying once. They said it was a boy. Should I have stayed there all the same? Squint-eye always went to the reservoir and stood looking into the water. Maybe he's still standing there," you said.

The shower passes quickly enough. Two magpies, which might have been taking shelter from the rain, flutter up from a tree. Mija, do you know what funny creatures magpies are? Once I cut down a poplar tree that had a magpie nest. It was during that time I was away for two weeks working on an apartment construction. I burst out laughing when I saw the inside of the magpie nest. It looked just like the inside of our houses. It had a dirt-floored room and stepping stones and then the inner room. The inner room was spread with soft leaves, just like a quilt spread on our *ondol** floor. I don't know if other magpie nests are like that, too. They say that you come to resemble those you live with. They say that old couples have wrinkles on the foreheads and creases

---

* See footnote on page 217. [Translator]

around the eyes that look like each other's. I guess magpies build their nests just like our houses because they've lived with us for so long. And I suppose I got this heartache from you, from living with you all this time.

8

I walk for a couple of hours and at last see a few farmhouses. From the hill I see white laundry fluttering on the clotheslines in every house. Would the five-and-a-half years of our life together flutter and dry up like that, if I hung them out on an orange-colored clothesline? Would our time together give off the pungent smell that I smelled from your back which showed when you bent down to pick up the fallen laundry? A bicycle carrying fertilizer sacks passes by, and the sparrows float up from the bean field. We were simple people. Who would know all the heartaches of your short life? Even my heart, mourning for you so bitterly at this moment, might change. By and by, I might just light a cigarette when the thought of you returns. Later on, I might also light a cigarette when I can't remember you.

"Would you like to have a bowl of rice wine?" a farmer who'd been drinking alone beside a vinyl hothouse calls out to me as I flop down on the slope. I walk over, lured by the aluminum kettle which shines chrome yellow in the sunlight.

"You look tired. There's nothing like rice wine when you're sad and tired. I used to lift up a full sack of rice on the strength of a bowl of rice wine. Here. Drink this up."

I drain the rice wine in one gulp. It's been so long since I heard such kindly words. I must have been thirsty even though I hadn't realized it. The white liquid streams down my gullet, cooling it, and reaches my bowels.

"Here, have some of this, too," the farmer says.

I see pieces of red pepper in the juicy kimchi. I pick up one.

"Well, you must've been real thirsty. Here, have one more bowl."

"Thanks, but one bowl's enough."

"Oh, come on. I was feeling kind of lonely, drinking by myself. Why don't you gulp this down and take a nap on the slope? Then the road'll seem much shorter, too. You don't get drunk on two bowls of rice wine."

I take the second bowl from him, putting down the bundle which I had been holding tightly. I must have looked funny holding on to my bundle like that. The farmer, pouring rice wine into the bowl, asks, "What's that you've got in there?" He may have thought I was a dried fish vendor and wanted me to share a little of my goods with him.

"This is Mija."

"Mija?"

"There was someone who went by that name," I say, with a snort.

He looks at me quizzically for a moment, then stretches out on the ground.

"Is it at the mountain you're looking,
    "Or at your sweetheart between the trees?"

The farmer murmurs a chant, using his arms as a pillow for his head. Like a farmer who'd worked on burning paddies all his life, his muscles are hard as iron but his eyes are vague. He studies me with those eyes.

"It's my wife."

His chant stops in the middle. His eyes opening wide, he looks at my bundle.

"You mean, she's dead?"

"Yes."

"And that's her cremated ashes?"

"Yes."

"How did it happen?"

"She was awfully sick."

"With what?"

"At first it was an accident. The restaurant she worked for was on the third floor. She fell down the stairs as she was leaving one night to come home. She broke her head."

"I'm so sorry. So what happened?"

"She was in the hospital for a whole year, what with several operations and all. By the time she came back home she was like a child. She was just like a five-year old. She craved candies, and she even talked like a child, too."

"Did you have any children?"

"No."

"Then it must've been like having a child around."

"That's right. She was just like a daughter, instead of a wife. She never showed her affection much, but after her accident she followed me around everywhere, as if she thought I was the only thing in the world she could hold on to. She was short of breath, but she'd follow me into the kitchen to watch me cook, or sit beside the water tap to watch me do laundry, like she was afraid I'd fly up and away if she let me out of her sight. She even followed me to the outhouse. Just like a puppy. I still feel as if Mija's right by my side. So I keep looking back and holding out my hand. She was breathless all the time, following me around. They said that's because there was something wrong with her heart. I gave her a heart operation with the money I'd saved up for five-and-a-half years, hoping to make it easier for her to follow me around, but that only sent her on to the other world ahead of me."

"I see. That's why you looked so limp. You know, a widower can spot another one from miles away. My wife died two years ago, too. She used to sing so beautifully. Come to think of it, those might have been laments, rather than songs. I took her for granted while she was living, but, boy, did she leave a big hole. I just thought she'd be there all the time, but everything's different now that she's gone. Nothing tastes the same. Look at those red peppers in the kimchi. My wife didn't put in red peppers like that. She'd split them down the middle and shake out all the seeds before putting them in the kimchi. Isn't life cruel? All she ever had was hard work. And just when we were beginning to have it easy she passed away. My heart jumps up and down whenever I hear the mill. The thuds of the mill have the same beat as my wife's chants. She wasn't much to look at, but I guess looks don't have anything to do with how dear you are to someone. She was my home. I could take my rest in her whenever I was tired and feeling low. Oh, I shouldn't ramble on like this to a new widower. Here. Drink another bowl. We can't live our life the way we want. We live and toil our whole lives just to have all that we worked for taken away from us one day."

9

I feel cold. My forehead feels chilly. I hear a cuckoo chirp. Then I doze again and feel the chill on my forehead. I open my eyes. The floating clouds cover the sun from time to time and make me chilly now and then. I must have fallen asleep, drunk on the two bowls of rice wine. Mija, tears gather in my eyes as I look at the floating clouds. The cuckoo cries somewhere on my behalf. "How far is it to my hometown? Is it beyond the blue sky over there?" Children pass by singing. "Now, when the white acacia blossoms dance in the wind, cuckoos must be singing in my hometown, too," the children's song continues. Oh, I must go to Gŏmdaeng-i quickly. If I tarry any longer, the cuckoo's song would get there ahead of me. I don't know where my hometown is. I remember the backyard of my maternal grandmother's house with its rows of storage jars, but I don't remember if I heard cuckoos there, even though I lived there until I was old enough to shave. Oh, yes, I heard cuckoos. No, it was I who mimicked the cuckoo's song. I made a cuckoo sound as a signal to my gang. I always lectured my gang on the virtue of loyalty.

"We're not blood brothers, but our oath binds us closer than blood. So, I'm going to give each of you assignments. You, Chŏljin, you must steal your grandmother's silver hair barrette tomorrow night when I signal with a cuckoo song in front of your house. I'm going to kill you if you come out with the nickel one. You must bring the silver barrette, or you won't be able to see daylight again."

Mija, I never told you that part of my life. I made my gang members snitch barley from their barn, sold it to the corn dealer, and gambled with the money, ardently hoping I'd pick the lucky number. But luck always eluded me. It was odd that I never suspected that there simply was no lucky number in the draw, even though I knew from early on that few things in life worked in my favor. My speech that our oath was more binding than blood always had a powerful effect on my followers. I made them buy rice wine with their school fees and went up the hill with them to drink it on grassy tomb mounds. But when the sun went down they all returned to their homes. I carried the rest of the rice wine into the barley field and drank it up. Falling asleep on barley stalks with the cuckoos that came to lay eggs among the barley, I longed for someone to tell me "Eat your supper before you go to sleep!" Mija, you always shook me and said, "Eat your supper before you go to bed," even when you were tired and limp as a sponge after a full day's work at the restaurant.

10

"Is this Gŏmdaeng-i here?"
"That's right."
"Where's the reservoir?"

"There. Over there. On the other side of the railroad. But you won't be able to fish there for a few days. A man was drowned. If you'd like to wait it out, stay at my house. You can't stay at Squint-eye's place any more."

"Squint-eye's?" My heart gave a jump in my chest. "Why? Has he gone somewhere?"

"That's the one who drowned."

"What? When did it happen?"

"The day before yesterday."

"The day before yesterday?" How on earth, Mija!

"About what time? How did it happen?"

"He was sickly after his wife Mija left him. Then he became more and more like a child, and then the day before yesterday he came down to the village in the morning muttering raving nonsense."

"Like what?"

"Why, do you know him?"

"What did he say?"

"He said his wife came to him the night before. Why, his wife had left him many years ago. How could she have come in the night and gone like that? The bus runs only twice a day, and nobody's seen her. So we told him he must've seen a ghost, but he said she really came and asked him to come with her to someplace far away. He kept saying his wife had been here, and then he floated up a corpse in the after-noon. So, neighbors collected some money and buried him in the hill over on the other side. I never saw a funeral without a mourner before. He had no kin in the whole world. Do you know him?"

The afternoon of the day before yesterday? Then it must have been Squint-eye's hearse I met on the hilly path. Mija. He departed with you. Then, was it because you made the trip here that you were so breathless the night before last?

11

I wasn't happy with you all the time. Before I met you, I swaggered around and thought myself important. I played tennis with government officials in the morning, and drank morning coffee with them in the tearoom with the comely manageress. Then in the evening I drove my motorcycle to a beer salon and drank beer with a young hostess. If I hadn't met you, my nickname might have been "Mr. Rayban." I was going to become a gangster with powerful connections. Even though you didn't choose me for your eternal partner, you were the woman who enabled me to live true to my nature. Mija, is this where the true story of your life began? You reached the reservoir before me. I see what you mean by the lighted village looking as if it'd glide over to you. Mija, you're white as nothing ever was white. Now, spread yourself all over the lake of your childhood. I sometimes missed my past life even while living with you. Sometimes I even left you to go back to my past life. But I always returned to you after a short time, pretending I'd been away to earn money. It was just as if you had put in my hand the other end of a rope you were holding.

Suh Ji-moon is professor of English at Korea University in Seoul and a dedicated translator of Korean literature. She received her Ph.D. from the University of New York at Albany. Her translations have appeared in numerous magazines and anthologies in Korea, the United States and England, and Hwang Sun-wǒn's *The Descendants of Cain*, which she translated with Julie Pickering, was published by M.E. Sharpe in 1997. She is also noted for the insightful and incisive opinion columns she writes for Korean newspapers. Her essays in English have been collected in *Faces in the Well* (1988).